A PR
THE PHILOSOPHY OF JOHN PAUL II —IN HIS OWN WORDS

CLOSE-TO-THE-TEXT SUMMARY
INTERPRETATIONS OF HIS THOUGHT ON
PERSON, LOVE, AND SEXUALITY
WITH A TIMELINE, BACKGROUND,
AND INTRODUCTION

Michael J. Healy, Sr.

Franciscan University of Steubenville
Veritas Center

En Route Books and Media, LLC
St. Louis, MO

Dear John + Betsy,
With much love!
Hope you enjoy it!
Doc/Pops/ Bobo

En Route Books and Media, LLC
5705 Rhodes Avenue
St. Louis, MO 63109

Contact us at
contactus@enroutebooksandmedia.com

Cover credit: Sebastian Mahfood

ISBN-13: 978-1-956715-20-0
Library of Congress Control Number: 2022930331

DEDICATION

To my wife, Maria

ENDORSEMENTS

"Professor Michael Healy has prepared a very accessible and usable introduction to the thought of Pope John Paul II which students and teachers alike—and even the interested general reader—will find to be a very good beginning in trying to understand and appreciate the author of one of the most profound and prolific teaching pontificates in the history of the Church. One would have to plow through many volumes to acquire what careful reading and study of this volume alone provides. Not least, the "primer" provides a clearer idea of what the student of John Paul II's thought should go on to acquire and study."

— Dr. Kenneth D. Whitehead

"Karol Wojtyła was very gifted as a speaker but, alas, when he made philosophy, he was extremely technical and rigorous. So much so that a familiar story in the milieu of Cracow was that all priests who in life had neglected their intellectual formation, before entering in Heaven, should have to pass an examination on The Acting Person (the philosophical masterpiece of Wojtyła). For some of them it might take even one hundred years. Now their task has been enormously facilitated (and their penance correspondingly cut short) by this "primer" of Prof. Michael Healy Sr.. Prof Healy has assimilated the spirit of Wojtyła so much in depth that he succeeds in rendering it in a smooth, plain, and easy expression. He is really the St. John the Baptist of Wojtyła: he prepares the way leading to our author and makes the paths straight. The book is good for the students who try to find a path leading into the complex conceptual construction of Wojtyła but is useful also to advanced scholars who want to better appreciate the particular and inimitable flavor of Wojtyła's philosophy."

— Dr. Rocco Buttiglione

TABLE OF CONTENTS

***

***

***

Preface

The genesis of this book was a philosophy course I have been teaching multiple times over thirty years at Franciscan University of Steubenville on Texts of Wojtyla. Though the course included only graduate students and qualified senior philosophy majors, I expected—from my own experience—that they were going to be challenged by John Paul II's original philosophical texts, especially *The Acting Person* and *Love and Responsibility*. These works are highly original and rather complicated. *The Acting Person*, in particular, is very closely argued, and the Holy Father proceeds carefully, often extensively recapitulating his points before adding another step in his argumentation.

As an aid to the students in comprehending the Holy Father's thought, I decided to do close-to-the-text summary interpretations of his major philosophical works. This was the origin of the current volume in which I attempt to condense the essence of John Paul II's philosophical teachings on the person and act, love and sexuality, using the Holy Father's own words as far as possible. Granted that every condensation—like every translation—is to some extent an interpretation, nonetheless I believe that the present work genuinely conveys the heart of Wojtyla's philosophical genius as well as the style and atmosphere of his thought.

The first part of the book consists of providing some background on the life of Karol Wojtyla and on the intellectual and spiritual influences that helped to shape his mind. Accordingly, I put together a "timeline" on the significant events in the life of the Holy Father, adapted from George Weigel's inspiring and comprehensive biography *Witness to Hope*. Then, I adapted two chapters from ***The Thought of the Man Who Became John Paul II***, Rocco Buttiglione's excellent work. The first chapter discusses the impact on Wojtyla of his Polish background and situation, the literary and dramatic influences in his life, as well as the intellectual and spiritual influences on the development of his thought, values, and worldview. The second chapter goes into more detail on the main philosophical influences on Wojtyla's thought, discussing the contributions of St. John of the Cross, Max Scheler, Immanuel Kant, and St. Thomas Aquinas.

In between these sections from Buttiglione, I review the dramatic works of Wojtyla, produced during and after World War II, in the unique style known as the theater of the "living word," or the rhapsodic theater. This style, a virtual necessity under both the Nazi and the communist occupations, relies almost completely on the word with very little accompaniment in terms of staging, music, dance, chorus, etc., but it does allow theater to open up to more universal philosophical themes. Here I utilize especially Kenneth Schmitz' insightful work ***At the Center or the***

Human Drama: The Philosophy of Karol Wojtyla/John Paul II. It is fascinating to see, in the reflections and dialogues of the characters in these early plays, wonderful anticipations of Wojtyla's later, more mature philosophical themes in *The Acting Person, Love and Responsibility,* and *Original Unity of Man and Woman.*

However, the most deeply formative and comprehensive influence on the thought of John Paul II was certainly not his Polish or literary background, nor even the great philosophers mentioned above, but rather his Roman Catholic faith. Therefore, I also included a complete summary of the wonderfully honest and appealing answers which John Paul II gave to the pointed questions of Italian journalist Vittorio Messori in ***Crossing the Threshold of Hope,*** wherein the Holy Father so personally expresses and applies his faith to contemporary questions.

With that as background I then address Wojtyla's main philosophical works, elaborating his insights on person and act, love and sexuality. This involves close-to-the-text summary interpretations of ***The Acting Person, Love and Responsibility, Original Unity of Man and Woman*** (now published as the first part of the *Theology of the Body),* and of two key articles from the collection on ***Person and Community,*** **"Thomistic Personalism" and "Subjectivity and the Irreducible in the Human Being."** In these summaries, I follow carefully the structure which Wojtyla gives to the works in terms of chapter headings and sub-sections. I believe that by extracting the essence of each section, the main point of each is highlighted while the reader's ability to grasp the whole is enhanced. I hope that this will assist in understanding the full works in question.

Wojtyla's philosophy is a creative synthesis of classical philosophy together with a modern emphasis on the centrality of the person and his subjective experience.

From John of the Cross Wojtyla carries with him an abiding sense of the mystery of being and of the life of the person, providing a safeguard to any facile rationalism in interpreting human experience. From Scheler he takes a deep interest in the inner life and experience of the person, especially in response to the world of values involving the awakening of the inner emotional life of the person as he is touched by the concrete existential realities of the world around him. From Kant he incorporates the categorical imperative addressed to the mind and will as the core of ethics, especially in relation to persons understood as ends rather than means—this imperative, however, arising from the material situation of the response to values rather than given formally in isolation from experience. From St. Thomas, he takes his fundamental classical realism in metaphysics and epistemology while calling nonetheless for a rethinking and representation of traditional Thomism with its cosmological emphasis in light of a new personalism. He calls for a reinterpretation of Thomism in light of the centrality of the person and ethics, rather than incorporating the person and his acts under the generalities of metaphysics, philosophy of nature, epistemology, and logic. These chosen emphases are expressed in the two articles from *Person and Community*, as well as elsewhere. He believes that this turn to the inner life of the person is necessary to attract the attention of men and women in the modern age to the genuine pursuit of wisdom and that this inner turn does not have to lead one to a false subjectivism, nor to the solipsism and despair characteristic of much of modern philosophy. Rather as the person responds to truth and to values, he freely decides himself for the good and incorporates it into his being.

In *The Acting Person,* Wojtyla then offers a creative integration of the human being in action, involving the insight into truth, the decision of the will, and the incorporation of the spheres of sentiment, bodily feeling, and bodily activities into that decision in the fullness of the human action. In *Love and Responsibility,* he elaborates on the theme of interpersonal relationships and appropriate response to others which is hinted at in the closing chapter of *The Acting Person.* Once again, we find a creative synthesis of traditional points approached and explained in light of phenomenology and of the inner experience of the person, culminating in the dictum that the only adequate response to the person is love. Finally in *Original Unity of Man and Woman,* Wojtyla expresses his highly creative teachings on human sexuality and all that it means and represents in light of the full truth about man. The life of the person as *gift* meant to be given back to its creator and, as called by God, to be given mutually in the love of man and women in openness to the further gift of life is revealed as the deepest dimension of personal being and the key to fulfillment and happiness. Few philosophers have written so movingly and deeply about embodiment and the intimate sphere of sexuality as an avenue for the expression of a self-giving love (the nuptial meaning of the body). Few philosophers have concretized so well in their philosophical reflections on the person *in act* the traditional understanding of the unity of man as composed of soul and body.

However, I wish the reader to proceed expeditiously to the texts of Wojtyla himself on these topics, albeit condensed from the originals. Therefore, I refrain here in the introduction from any extensive representation of or commentary on his points.

One note on my sources: In my summary-interpretation of *The Acting Person*, I made primary use of the version in ANALECTA HUSSERIANA, The Yearbook of Phenomenological Research, Volume X, ed. Anna-Teresa Tymieniecka, *The World Institute for Advanced Phenomenological Research and Learning*. This version includes Wojtyla's corrections, which did not make it into the original translation. The corrected version is now published as *Person and Act and Related Essays* by CUA Press.

My fervent hope is that the reader will benefit greatly from this one-volume review of Wojtyla's intellectual and spiritual background and of his main philosophical works in the philosophy of the person and of love and sexuality. His thought is well worth the effort. Thus, I hope the current volume will inspire you, the reader, also to devote your time and concentration to the original works investigated here in concentrated fashion.

General Introduction

Timeline

Karol Jozef Wojtyla

May 18, 1920 Born in Wadowice, Poland.

April 13, 1929 Emilia Kaczorowska Wojtyla, Lolek's mother, dies.

Dec. 5, 1932 Edmund Wojtyla, his older brother, dies.

May 27, 1938 Graduates high school, class valedictorian.

August 1938 He and his father, Karol, move to Krakow. Begins studies at Jagellonian University.

Sept. 1, 1939 World War II begins as Germany invades Poland.

Nov. 6, 1939 University professors arrested and deported by Nazis. Wojtyla begins clandestine studies and underground cultural resistance activities.

Feb. 1940 Meets Jan Tyranowski, who introduces him to Carmelite spirituality.

Sept. 1940 Begins work as quarryman at the Zakrzowek mine.

Feb. 18, 1941 Lolek's father, the elder Karol Wojtyla, dies.

Oct. 1941 Begins work at Solvay chemical plant.

Fall, 1941 Active in Mieczylaw Kotlarczyk's "Rhapsodic Theater."

Fall, 1942 Accepted as clandestine seminarian be Archdiocese of Krakow and begins underground studies in philosophy.

Jan. 1945 Nazis abandon Krakow and the Red Army arrives.

Nov. 1, 1946 Karol Wojtyla is ordained a priest by Cardinal Adam Stefan Sapieha.

Nov. 15, 1946 Leaves for graduate theological studies in Rome.

June 1948 Completes his first doctorate. Dissertation: *The Doctrine of Faith According to St. John of the Cross.* Travels through France during his time at Rome.

1948-51 Parish work in Poland. Begins student chaplaincy, organizes courses for engaged couples, establishes choir, publishes essays, poems, and plays.

April 1952 Father Karol Wojtyla is dubbed "Wujek" (Uncle) by his young friends.

Oct. 1953 Begins lectures on social ethics at Jagellonian University.

Jan. 1954 Habilitation (second doctorate) awarded by Jagellonian University Faculty of Theology. Topic: *An Evaluation of the Possibility of Constructing a Christian Ethics on the Basis of the System of Max Scheler.*

1954-56 Lectures at Catholic University of Lublin on Scheler, Kant, Aquinas, Plato, Aristotle, Augustine. Topics: Act and Experience; Goodness and Value.

Dec. 1956 Appointed to Chair of Ethics at Catholic University of Lublin.

1957-58 Lectures on sexual ethics at Catholic University of Lublin.

July 4, 1958 Named auxiliary bishop of Krakow by Pope Pius XII.

1960 *Love and Responsibility* published.

Dec. 1960 *The Jeweler's Shop* published.

1962-65 Bishop Wojtyla addresses Vatican II on liturgical reform, revelation, the Church as the "People of God," religious freedom, lay vocation, dialogue with the modern world, and the problem of modern atheism. Works on subcommission re-drafting the Council document "The Church in the Modern World."

Dec. 1963 Visits the Holy Land.

Dec. 30, 1963 Named Archbishop of Krakow by Pope Paul VI.

1966 Poland celebrates the millennium of its Christianity.

June 28, 1967 Karol Wojtyla is created a cardinal by Pope Paul VI.

Aug. 31, 1967 Polish communist regime shuts down the Rhapsodic Theater.

Feb. 1968 Krakow theologians under Wojtyla's guidance submit memorandum to Pope Paul VI, "The Foundations of the Church's Doctrine on the Principles of Conjugal Life," influencing the forthcoming encyclical *Humanae Vitae* in personalist directions.

1969 *Person and Act ("The Acting Person")* published.

Dec. 16-17, 1970 *Person and Act ("The Acting Person")* debated at Catholic University of Lublin.

1969-79 Cardinal Wojtyla leads Church in Poland heroically, sometimes defying communist regime; writes and acts for renewal of Church according to Vatican II; continues to publish poetry; continues to publish philosophical essays and participate in philosophical congresses; is active in Synod of Bishops; travels twice to USA and Canada.

Oct. 16, 1979 Elected Pope and takes the name John Paul II.

1979-1980 Wednesday Papal audiences on *Original Unity of Man and Woman: Catechesis on the Book of Genesis.*

1993 Selected essays from the 1950's, 60's, and 70's on ethical and moral considerations, personalism, and marriage and family published under the title *Person and Community.*

1994 *Crossing the Threshold of Hope* published.

2000 Great Jubilee of two millennia of the Christian faith. Beginning of Third Millennium with same message with which he began his pontificate: "Be not afraid."

Apr. 2, 2005 Dies in Rome. An estimated 4 million mourners gather in and around Vatican City.

Apr. 27, 2014 Canonization as a saint of the Roman Catholic Church.

—timeline adapted from *WITNESS TO HOPE*
by George Weigel

Wojtyla

Background and Information

The Unique Situation of Poland out of which Wojtyla comes—Poland exists on the border of eastern and western Europe, having chosen the Roman Catholic Church and the Western liturgy, yet bordering the east and with a Slavic ethnic and linguistic heritage. Because of this position the people of Poland are able to speak the "language" of two spiritual worlds and to link them together. There is a particular way of considering world history which derives from the specific experience of the Polish nation and culture, and which is deeply inscribed in the mind and though of Karol Wojtyla. He proclaims that Christ is "the key to understanding that great and fundamental reality that is man" but also that Poland "has become nowadays the land of a particularly responsible witness."

"Without Christ, it is not possible to understand and to appreciate the contribution of the Polish nation *to the development of man and of his humanity in the past, and his contribution also in our days.*"

Consider the Polish experience compared to a philosophy of history of a thinker like Hegel. Hegel interprets history in terms of the principle of force and power: where these go truth and greatness follow. But *one cannot understand the history of the Polish nation in this way.* There we have to deal with a great spiritual culture, which almost entirely lacks material force. In the eyes of a Pole, the limitations of a Hegelian vision of history are immediately apparent: truth and force do not walk together at all. The political-military history of Poland is a history of heroic defeats, of rebellions nourished by the desire to witness to the truth and to its own rights rather than any concrete possibility of victory, e.g., the Warsaw uprising against the Nazis in 1944 or the witness of Maximilian Kolbe in Auschwitz.* Thousands of times defeated on the terrain of force, the nation is reborn each time thanks to the spiritual awareness of its own identity and of its own right, animated by Christian faith. Thus, the particular vision of man which animates the Polish consciousness is the following: *the cultural and existential certitude that Christ is the keystone for the understanding of man and of history.*

Such certitude is lost or considerable weakened in the West where power and statehood have been more dominant. The latter approach, with Hegel, seems to imply (1) that ethics is immanent to the state and that what the state

---

* *Editor's note*: This is not to deny that at limited times in history when Poles did have power over others, they too were susceptible to the dangers of the principle of force and power, e.g., the pogroms of the nineteenth and early twentieth centuries. But Buttiglione is emphasizing the inspirational side of Polish history as it touched Wojtyla and his ideals in relation to the sacrifice of Christ.

successfully does is right, and (2) that the individual is not as important as the grand purposes of the state rolling through history. The Polish spiritual experience considered in the light of Christian faith teaches rather the unity of the human person (to be considered as a spiritual whole, not as a cog in the machinery of the state) and the primacy in the formation of this person of the recognition of truth over the capacity to impose domination by force.

The concentration camp at Oswiecim, the Polish town that the Germans called Auschwitz, is both the most potent symbol of the horror of the war and, at the same time, the culmination of the immanentist culture and ethics. In a universe from which God has been expelled, any reason to respect man is forfeited. Yet in the place constructed for the annihilation of man, for the negation of spiritual culture (the rejection of truth, dignity, and value), St. Maximilian Kolbe shows the essence of human greatness. Wojtyla says that through Kolbe's witness "is accomplished a particular victory of man through the faith"—man through faith has arrived at the possession of his own humanity. Kolbe's message is one of integrally catholic balance: the oppressed can and must fight for justice with worldly arms but the true victory is the spiritual victory, that which regains and rebuilds the truth in oneself and in others. His life demonstrates that in this tormented epoch of the history of man (with the totalitarian systems of the Nazis and the Communists and the secularization of the West), the Christian faith is more than ever called to exercise all its capacity for humanization, so the human heart does not surrender to barbarity. *The conflict, which marks contemporary history, is a conflict for or against the Christian image of the human.* Poland has experienced the two most violent forms of modern totalitarianism and, in the face of them, has reaffirmed another vision of man by creating an essentially moral opposition.

First Literary Influences—From his high school days on, Wojtyla was greatly interested in literature, poetry and drama. He was influenced strongly by the Polish romantic writers of the nineteenth century: Mickiewicz, Slowacki, Krasinski, Norwid (Wojtyla's favorite poet), and Wyspianski. These five poets were the defenders of the national spirit during the hard years of partition, when revolt was often suppressed with bloodshed, and when the Germans and the Russians stubbornly tried to eradicate Polish culture and language altogether. The key word at the time was "organic work," signifying the defense of the language and of national culture and religion, against the invader. Thus, while the West came to understand revolution as a complete break with the past, in Poland it continued to be understood as the resurrection of a forgotten value underlying the principles of the country's history. Mickiewicz concluded that a new religious order was needed for such a purpose and eventually one was formed: the Order of the Resurrectionists. It is interesting to note that the first thing Wojtyla did upon his election to the papacy was to make a pilgrimage to the sanctuary of Mentorella, near Rome, which belonged to the Resurrectionist Fathers.

Kotlarczyk and the Rhapsodic Theater—While still in high school, Wojtyla also met Mieczyslaw Kotlarczyk, professor of history and eventually director of the Rhapsodic theater, later to play a great role in the cultural resistance to the Nazis in Krakow. This was a unique type of theater. Kotlarczyk spoke especially of the evocative power of words, which not only communicate a meaning but also elicit an emotion, at once both entirely subjective and entirely objective. The value is in the profound intimacy of the speaker with those who listen: it is the actor who, through a unique personal ascesis, introduces us to that intimacy. The import of the performance, the plot, etc., are drastically reduced in this type of theater. What happens to consciousness is more emphasized than the events per se; the key thing is *the way in which* the objective reality is revealed in consciousness. This part of Wojtyla's biography can perhaps help us to comprehend the unique and original way in which he lived and experienced many of the themes of phenomenology, especially the theme of consciousness. In a certain sense, his first initiation to phenomenology came about indirectly and outside of orthodox philosophy, through the theory of the theater and, above all, the existential experience of being an actor under Kotlarczyk's direction. The latter understood *the liturgical character of theatrical action,* the way in which it revives the presence of a universal value which renews mundane existence, judging its falsity but at the same time offering the possibility of entering a new dimension and an unexpected authenticity. After the Nazi invasion in 1939, when leading intellectuals and all custodians of Polish language and tradition were to be eradicated, Kotlarczyk (continuing the "organic work") organized clandestine meetings of the Rhapsodic Theater in Krakow, staging the classics of the national tradition. At the risk of death or deportation to the concentration camps, Wojtyla performed in and directed many of these plays.

The Influence of Tyranowski—Jan Tyranowski was a leading layman in a Salesian parish who was of special help to the lone remaining priest of the parish Fr. Jan Mazarski (seven other priests having been sent to concentration camps). Tyranowski led meetings for young people every Sunday encouraging them to live the faith together. He was the leader of the "living Rosary"—groups of fifteen young people (the same number as the stations of the Rosary) who committed themselves to a friendship directed toward Christian perfection and covenanted to help each other. Tyranowski was a man of great psychological acumen and a devotee of Carmelite spirituality (St. John of the Cross, St. Teresa of Avila, St. Teresa of Lisieux), though he had no regular theological instruction. He was a tailor from Debnicki, but lived a profound and personal mysticism. Wojtyla remembers that his language was rather conventional but that the striking thing about him was that the doctrinal truths, which he spoke about, were for him *the object of normal experience.*

And That of Sapieha—Cardinal Adam Stephan Sapieha became the leader of the moral resistance of the Polish nation to the Nazis. He committed diocesan and personal resources to the immediate struggle and continued the cultural resistance or "organic work." For this reason he founded and nurtured an underground seminary in which Wojtyla was a seminarian. This too was at the risk of his life. The seminarians participated in aiding those persecuted by the Nazis (especially the Jews) and by being seminarians were furthering a religion and a culture which the Nazis wanted to stamp out. Sapieha had to hide the seminarians in the archbishop's house to protect them from the Nazis.

The Post-War Intellectual Movement—After the war, Sapieha founded both a weekly and a monthly journal devoted to the themes of religious and cultural identity. The intellectual movement out of which these journals flowed was progressive, influenced by thinkers from the West (especially France: Maritain, Marcel, etc.), but with a religious existentialism at its core. In Poland, the confrontation of atheistic existentialism (Marxism, allied with such thinkers as Jean-Paul Sartre in the West) and religious existentialism was won by religious existentialism and this intellectual movement, thus, retained its connection to Polish Catholicism and to the people. It was in this context that Wojtyla's philosophy began to develop. His mature thought too, reflecting upon the essential theme of action, strikes at the root of the notion that a Marxist philosophy of praxis is higher than a philosophy of conscience.

Wojtyla at the Angelicum and in France—Wojtyla did his doctoral dissertation on St. John of the Cross at the Angelicum from 1946-48. His primary teacher was Fr. Garrigou-Lagrange from whom he received a rigorous training in the most traditional form of Thomism. Even at this time, however, a careful reading of his doctoral thesis indicates that, from the time he began to study philosophy, he had an affinity for a variety of different interpretations of Thomism. He was interested in the work being done at Louvain in Belgium on relationships between Thomism and Kantian philosophy. He was interested in the existential emphasis being given to Thomism by Maritain and Gilson in France, emphasizing Thomas' distinction between essence and existence as well as his legitimation of a certain eidetic intuition in the interpretation of the process of abstraction. Wojtyla's works, however, do not in fact take a direct position on the intellectual controversies which run through

Catholic thought; he limits himself to indications and suggestions within an authentically personal exploration which will eventually flow into an original construction.

Wojtyla also traveled to France at this time and, while having great admiration for French Catholicism (and becoming acquainted with the French worker-priest movement), was all the more shaken to discover that France was only nominally Catholic. What was most needful, Wojtyla reasoned, was for the riches of the faith to become an attitude of life, shaping the fundamental disposition toward existence and establishing a unity between culture, life and faith.

The Cultural Ambience of the Universities of Krakow and Lublin—Though Wojtyla showed a preference for pastoral work after his return from Rome, Cardinal Sapieha insisted that he go on to a second doctorate in philosophy at the University of Krakow. His topic was the possibility of grounding a Christian ethics on Max Scheler's phenomenological system. Although Wojtyla's answer would be negative, this study stimulated the enterprise of a reform of phenomenology which was to form the basis of all his later philosophical work.

One of his major readers was Professor Swiezawski, a proponent of Maritain's existential Thomism, strongly emphasizing the role of intuitive experience in philosophy. Maritain once wrote to Swiezawski: "The misfortune of ordinary scholastic teaching, and above all that of the manuals, is in practice to neglect this essential intuitive element and to replace it with a pseudo-dialectic of concepts and formulas. There is nothing doing so long as the intellect does not see, so long as the philosopher or student philosopher do not have an intellectual intuition of essence." This is perhaps the closest approach which Maritain makes toward a phenomenological position which recognizes the indispensability of a preliminary eidetic intuition for the construction of philosophical knowledge.

Another of the examiners for Wojtyla's second doctoral thesis, destined to have a great influence on his future development, was Roman Ingarden. One of Husserl's earliest students, Ingarden (along with Dietrich von Hildebrand, Edith Stein, and others) always refused to follow his teacher in the idealistic direction, but rather upheld a realistic interpretation of phenomenology. Moreover, Ingarden manifested a particular interest in the intuition of value in ethical and aesthetic life. His phenomenology was a passionate engagement in the life-world, a heroic attempt to encounter the truth and live in accordance with it.

Wojtyla began to teach at the University of Lublin in 1954 and was appointed to the chair of Ethics there in 1956. Both traditional Thomism and existential Thomism with an opening toward phenomenology (through Swiezawski, mentioned above) were present there at the time. Many other thinkers would soon be in evidence there, emphasizing different aspects of Thomism and of realist philosophy: a transcendental Thomist influenced by Louvain (A. Krąpiec), a philosopher of law, an historian of ancient philosophy, an ethicist, a professor of epistemology. Amongst all these divergent approaches, the Lublin school of philosophy was united in a fundamental commitment to the defense of human rights against all theories which would dissolve the unique dignity of human beings in the infinite currents of history, and also in the decision to exhibit the profound alliance between human reason and Christian faith. There was, thus, a fundamentally personalist philosophy, Thomistic in inspiration (in a more rigid sense in Krąpiec's case and a more open one in Wojtyla's) but welcoming dialogue with any thought which took seriously the problem of being human.

Pastoral Engagement—In 1958, Wojtyla was named auxiliary bishop of Krakow and had to leave his university situation and apostolate among the students. But it is important to say a word about the method and the particular quality of his pastoral work with young people. Inspired by his journey through France, he saw that faith must become life. This can only happen through a fellowship which shares with young people all the events of their lives, and which contains a fundamental concern for their truth and human authenticity. Through such a fellowship which awakens the human in man, one is led to the awareness of the greatness of his own vocation and to engage both creativity and patient generosity, progressively extending the presence of a youthful ambience in the Church.

Wojtyla began his pastoral work (although it would be better to speak of friendship for life than of pastoral work) with some, and gradually this friendship/pastoral work embraced the entire nation. The young students called him "Uncle," which makes one think of a parental spirituality which is very discreet but also very demanding. In a special way Wojtyla was intent upon accompanying young people at the moment of their passage into adulthood, at their encounter with work, and at the creation of a family.

—from *KAROL WOJTYLA: The Thought of the Man Who Became John Paul II* by Rocco Buttiglione

The Dramatic Works

The Theater of the "Living Word"

Although the central intuitions of Wojtyla matured in their proper time, they seem already to have received a certain shape and impetus when, in 1939, the young Karol set about his higher studies at the Jagiellonian University in Cracow. He took up the study of Polish letters, language, and history. As we know, 1940-45 were some of the darkest years of Poland's heritage. Wojtyla's interests leaned toward the record of that history as given expression by its poets and national heroes. Thus, word and deed formed an interplay here. Further, with his religious interests came also an older history, biblical history.

Wojtyla's first works for the theater gave expression to the blending of themes in these different histories. In his first dramatic works and in a time of national suffering, he forged a convergence that deliberately overrode the difference in times between the events of ancient Israel, of Poland's past, and the awful events of during the Nazi occupation.

A first play, no longer extant, was entitled *David.* A second was *Job* (1940). A third (also 1940), was called *Jeremiah* and was sub-titled *A National Drama in Three Acts.* In Poland, as in some other cultures (more so than in our own), it seems that the word has a special weight—perhaps as the last bastion the nation could fall back on in defense of its identity (perhaps parallels to Ireland). Certainly, the young Wojtyla was fascinated by the word—spoken, written, and proclaimed. Less than a month after the beginning of WWII and the Nazi (and later Soviet) occupation, Wojtyla wrote in a letter to a fellow dramatist: "Let theater be a church where the national spirit will flourish." He was inviting the man, Mieczylaw Kotlarczyk, to come to Cracow to form a theater company.

Wojtyla worked at this time in a quarry and later in a chemical factory, while pursuing his university studies. During this time, he joined with Kotlarczyk in a clandestine theater of what they called the "living word." In the cramped quarters and sparse conditions of occupied Poland, the Rhapsodic Theater Company (as it became known) produced 7 plays from 1941-44, giving 22 performances and holding hundreds of rehearsals under the most dangerous conditions. Wojtyla was later to say of these times: "Of all the complex resources of the theatrical art, there remained only the living word, spoken by people in extrascenic conditions, in a room with a piano. That unheard-of-scarcity of the means of expression turned into a creative experiment."*

---

* Editor's note: Quotes concerning theater are from *Karol Wojtyla, The Collected Plays and Writings on Theater,* ed. and

A theater critic has referred to the Rhapsodic Theater as "a theater of the imagination, a theater of the inner self." In *The Jeweler's Shop,* Monica imagines her forthcoming wedding day "like rehearsals in a theater: the theater of my imagination and the theater of my thought." Even after the war, Wojtyla's own plays continued to employ sparse staging, symbolic background music and dance, and a chorus giving emphasis to the ethical implications at decisive points. Wojtyla remarks: "The Rhapsodic Theater asks young actors to subordinate themselves to the great poetic word. This can be felt particularly when the word is developed in immaculately spoken choruses. A group of people collectively, somehow, unanimously, subordinated to the great poetic word, evoke ethical associations; this solidarity of people in the word reveals particularly strongly and accentuates the reverence that is the point of departure for the rhapsodists' work and the secret of their style." But all these non-verbal "add-on" dimensions (staging, music, dance, chorus) of the plays are subordinated to what Ken Schmitz calls the "inner discipline" of the word and its meaning. Wojtyla himself distinguishes the theater of the word from more traditional theater by the different roles played out by the word in each: "The position of the word in a theater in not always the same. As in life, the word can appear as an

---

intro. by Boleslaw Taborski; quoted in Kenneth Schmitz, *At the Center of the Human Drama.*

integral part of action, movement, and gesture, inseparable from all human practical activity; or it can appear as 'song'—separate, independent, intended only to contain and express thought, to embrace and transmit a vision of the mind."

So, in traditional theater the word "accompanies" the other elements which surround it as part of the total theatrical action, whereas in the theater of the word it is the word that frames the whole. And it is the word that draws out of its own meaning whatever movement, gesture, and background complements its expression. That's why, as far as possible, the staging and music, every gesture of an actor, chorus, or dance group, turns upon and works with the turn of the words. While traditional theater tells a story through the impact of event upon character, the theater of the word sets forth a problem, an issue of importance: (Wojtyla) "The problem itself acts, rouses interest, disturbs, evokes the audience's participation, demands understanding and a solution." The word and its meaning "mature in spare, simple, rhythmic gesture," and the movement, sounds, and staging arise out of the reservoir of meaning contained in the words and in the problem they articulate. Such a drama of the work is outspokenly intellectual: "The new proportions between word and movement, between word and gesture, doubtless reach even further, in a sense beyond theater and into the philosophical concept of man and the world. The supremacy of word over gesture indirectly restores the supremacy of thought over movement and impulse in man."

Such presentation is not static, however, but moves with the dynamics of thought and of the issue at stake, which "the living human word grasps and makes into a nucleus of action." The theater of the word, according to Wojtyla, "does not infringe on the realist standpoint but enables us to understand the inner base of human action, the very fulcrum of human movement." He insists that the Rhapsodists "not only derive the word from the immediate need of concrete life but also refer to that life from the world of thought. Not—it must be stressed—the world of fantasy, but the world of thought." These inner dramas then must draw on concrete and relevant issues and refer them to the world of thought (again, not fantasy). Thought must be grounded in concrete, immediate reality-contact and thought (so grounded) must then be the basis for the word. In his last play, *Radiation of Fatherhood, A Mystery*, the figure of the mother says: "At no point can the world be fiction, the inner world even less than the external world.... It is no metaphor, but reality (that is played out on stage). The world cannot depend on metaphor alone, the inner world even less that the external world." She goes on to affirm that, as the radiation of the Fatherhood of God, creation is neither fiction nor metaphor. The primacy of truth as normative principle of reality recurs throughout the play, together with the caution never to separate truth from love.

And so, the theater of the word aims at being a theater of reality—at a "symbolic" realism.

By slowing the pace of the action and reducing the external surrounding, such a drama intends to effect a catharsis, as all drama must; it is a catharsis, however, more of meaning than of feeling. Paradoxically, such a reduced external structure permits the dramatic presentation of themes too broad for a traditional stage, even though the traditional stage is physically more spacious. The traditional stage achieves marvelous effects in its own way, but is more bound to the particularities of it setting and plot, so that it is too narrow to do justice to the larger, even eternal, themes that only a drama of thought can encompass. Wojtyla says: "The word, however, must not be divorced from thought. The specific base of theatrical realism discovered by Mieczyslaw Kotlarczyk with his company opens wide the horizons of theatrical practice to encompass works that by their nature could not otherwise be the object of theatrical production.... Perhaps other great works of the human mind, for instance the works of philosophers, could, thus, be adapted for at least some audiences."

To illustrate, let's look at some of the significant themes in Wojtyla's dramas. *Job* was composed early in the brutal Nazi occupation, while being faithful to the biblical text. It is subtitled *A Drama from the Old Testament*, but shows a convergence of past, present, and future as in the inscription: "The action took place in the OT before Christ's coming. The action takes place in our days in Job's time for Poland and the world. The action takes place in the time of expectation, of imploring judgment, in the time of longing for Christ's testament, worked out in Poland's and the world's suffering." Poland as a collective Job is reiterated in the Epilogue: "Behold, my people—and listen to the Word of the Lord, you who are downtrodden, you who are flogged, you who are sent to camps, you—Jobs—Jobs." However, Wojtyla changes the biblical situation to enhance the idea of the coming of Christ. So, one of Jobs friends, Elihu, prophesies in the play: "He is coming—I know he lives…I see that the redeemer lives." In place of the speeches of Yahweh, we find more the voice of Christ in Gethsemane and, with that, the suffering takes on a more positive meaning, a redemptive meaning.

In the next drama, *Jeremiah,* parallels to Polish history are even more explicit. It is set in the 17th century, during crisis and invasion, but resonating with 1940 and with Jeremiah's lamentations: "The city has fallen…. The enemies have struck Judah…. For the temples of Zion have been entered by the unclean band of armed heathen." A great theme here is the primacy of truth compared to propaganda: "One must throw truth across the path of lies. One must throw truth into the eye of a lie." For "in truth are freedom and excellence," but in untruth, only slavery. We find parallels here to Wojtyla's later philosophy: a tremendous interest in inner human experience, but with a primacy to objective truth. Moreover, in the play, Father Peter also says "words are not enough, not enough. One must catch hearts to kindle them, furrow hearts as with a plough and root up the weeds—root them out." The emphasis here anticipates *The Acting Person.* And another character adds: "At the feet of truth one must erect love; at the foundations, low in the ground, it will take root even in a wilderness, will build, uplift, and transform all things"—anticipating *Love and Responsibility.*

The postwar plays deepen the religious themes and the accent is placed even more on the "inner space" of the drama. The path within is the place to search out the truth in the midst now of Stalinist propaganda. It involves the central character's "spiritual struggles and his progress toward sanctity." In *Our God's Brother,* we have a study of Adam Chmielowski, a 19th century Polish saint who deeply influenced Wojtyla. Chmielowski was first a partisan fighter, then an artist, then founder of congregation of religious brothers and sisters, working with the poor in Cracow as Brother Albert, later canonized under that name by JPII himself in 1989.

Wojtyla tells us that his intention is not just to recount the psychological experiences of the characters in the play, but to follow up a line that is "inaccessible to history…an extrahistorical element in man lies at the very sources of his humanity." This anticipates later philosophical themes of transcendence, of the phenomenological approach as accessing truth not just impressions, of the ineffable and irreducible in each human being (especially in moral decision and action), reverberating in eternity and before God. The aim, Wojtyla says, is "to participate in the same multifarious reality in which [the character] participated—and in a way similar to him." Thus, the drama's inwardness is not just "an epic of introspection," rather "the drama does more than analyze [the heroes'] experiences and recreate the stream of their dramatic consciousness."

The drama turns around questions of the social responsibility of art as a seeking after expression of truth and participation in reality [the artist as seeker]. Subjectivism is rejected as leading to isolation and loneliness—anticipating later themes of loneliness in modern life and fragmentation of society. Art is both a seeking and a being sought, a dialogue with reality. Adam says "something in me keeps opening up…it's chasing me." It is a painful, "gradual elucidation." However, the answer is neither revolutionary excess in the name of justice nor Enlightenment rationalism involving mere understanding. Here later political themes are prefigured, the rejection of both Marxism and of rational humanism. Rather the answer is a deeper level of love and commitment taking one beyond artistic expression to the building of something beautiful in oneself, the other, and society—ultimately in the name of God, as with Mother Teresa and doing "something beautiful for God." So Adam begins truly to find himself and his own salvation when he helps a poor man whom he notices leaning wretchedly against a lamp post on a cold dark street. There is an autobiographical undercurrent here for Wojtyla, not only in the Christian response to social collectivism on the one hand and Enlightenment individualism on the other, but also in Wojtyla's own renunciation of art as his principal way of life.

The best know of the plays is of course *The Jeweler's Shop: A Meditation on the Sacrament of Matrimony, Passing on Occasion into a Drama.*" Taborski calls it a poetic drama and suggests that the subtitle doesn't do justice to the dramatic power of the work. The structure is interesting in itself. In addition to the Old Jeweler, the Chorus, and the Christ figure of the bridegroom, there are seven protagonists: three couples and a somewhat mysterious figure whom we learn is named Adam and who represents a sort of Everyman. He is recognized at the very end as "a common denominator of us all—at the same time a spokesman and a judge." The Old Jeweler is also a shadowy figure; perhaps speaking for Divine Providence or as the voice of conscience.

The drama is divided into three acts, each of which contains, for the most part, alternating monologues, as if spoken out loud but spoken into an enveloping, mysterious, and receptive silence. In the first act, we meet Teresa and Andrew during their courtship and impending marriage. It is a short but happy marriage, and the widowed Teresa keeps the presence of Andrew alive within her after he is killed in battle. In the second act, we meet Anna and Stefan whose marriage has been broken by mutual disillusion and anger. In the third act, we meet Monica, the daughter of the separated couple, and Christopher, the son of the first couple. The young people are planning to marry. In sum then, we have the exploration of married love and the challenge life-long commitment (and the vocation to love) in and through a brief but happy marriage at once both sad and joyful; a failing marriage treated sympathetically and without quick judgment; and a coming marriage trembling with fear and hope.

Two great themes might be mentioned here. First, love is presented as an interplay between mind and reality, between consciousness and existence, with both noetic and ontological dimensions. Later themes are anticipated here on the relation between phenomenology and metaphysics. Love is at once something intensely conscious, private, personal, and intimate yet it is also something objectively real. It cannot be reduced to just one side of the equation: marital love is not just a set of subjective impressions (which, if so, could just be replaced by other impressions) but it is also not just the objective, legal bond (which, if so, could be resented or rejected as an imposition). Love has legitimate inner and outer sides.

A second great theme has to do with the relation in love between the surface and the depth and the fact that we often live on the surface but have to recall ourselves to—and see others in light of—the depth. Christopher urges Monica to look more deeply into her (separated) parents relationship in order to see the love with which they have nourished her: "People have their depths, not only the masks on their faces." Adam too speaks of the paradox of love: "There is no other matter embedded more strongly in the surface of human life, and there is no matter more unknown and more mysterious. The divergence between what lies on the surface of the mystery of love constitutes precisely the source of the drama. It is one of the greatest dramas of human existence. The surface of love has its current—swift, flickering, changeable. A kaleidoscope of waves and situation full of attraction. This current is sometimes so stunning that it carries people away—women and men. They get carried away by the thought that they have absorbed the whole secret of love, but in fact they have not yet even touched it. They are happy for a while, thinking they have reached the limits of existence and wrested all its secrets from it, so that nothing remains. That's how it is [in their view]: on the other side of that rapture nothing remains, there is nothing left behind it." Then Adam pauses, and with a new vehemence, adds: "But there can't be nothing; there can't. Listen to me, there can't. Man is a continuum, a totality and a continuity—so it cannot be that nothing remains."

The conversation then turns to the relation between the temporal surface of love and its eternal depth. Love is less a matter of time than of eternity. Teresa earlier has offered a hint at this quality of eternity about love when she recalls the moment Andrew proposed to her and says: "At such moments one does not check the hour, such moments grow in one above time." So love is not just an adventure of the passing moment, because it is shot through with a vertical axis that "cuts across every marriage." Adam's reflection on the source of love highlights the contrast between surface and depth, adventure and drama, the empty and the full, the part and the whole, the momentary "now" and the eternal "forever." The contrast invites the connection between human love and its source. Adam says to Anna: "Ah, Anna, how am I to prove to you that on the other side of all those loves that fill our lives there is Love." In his last speech on the rift between Anna and Stefan, he observes: "The thing is that love carries people away like an absolute, although it [human love] lacks absolute dimensions. But acting under an illusion, they do not try to connect that love with the Love that has such a dimension."

Adam concludes: "Every person has at his disposal an existence and a love. The problem is how to build a sensible structure from it. But this structure must never be inward looking. It must be open in such a way that, on the one hand, it embraces other people, while, on the other, it always reflects the absolute Existence and Love; it must always, *in some way,* reflect them. That is the ultimate sense of your lives." Again, many later themes of Wojtyla's philosophy are prefigured here, themes of community, of exemplary causality, of personalism, and of the person in dialogue with reality, with others, and with God.

In the *Radiation of Fatherhood,* we find again a character named Adam representing everyman in the loneliness and isolation that results from the fallen situation of man. Adam says: "It is easier to for me to feel lonely than to think about death,...easier to feel lonely than guilty of sin." Thus, a certain lethargy or sloth is revealed here as part of the human situation and challenge. Excusing himself before God, Adam says, "leave me my loneliness" and admits to "continually evading Your Fatherhood and gravitating toward my loneliness." But it is not so much a conflict between Adam-with-God and Adam-without-God (impossible); rather, it is more a conflict between two images of how to be like God: self-subsistence vs. relatedness. He wants to be the image of God as self-subsistent, self-sufficient, autonomous rather than the actual image God has conferred on him: relatedness, through a community of shared love, realized ultimately in the Trinity. Self-subsistence (and consequent loneliness) is not what God intended for human nature.

Because of Adam's state here, he finds actual human fatherhood (and with it the invitation to participate in God's own fatherhood) not so much a gift as a burden, an intrusion on his loneliness—for his daughter Monica surely has a claim on his inner life. He comes to realize that loneliness is not the final word in him, "not at the bottom of my being at all." Ultimately, of course, there is a deep fissure in his being which only God can fill.

His opening a relation to his daughter would be a step toward opening to God. He says: "We return to the Father through the Child." Here he also discovers himself anew as a child of God: "To absorb the radiation of fatherhood means not only to become a father but, much more, to become a child."

Throughout the drama, the Mother remains a mysterious figure. She seems to stand for Eve, and for everywoman, while in the last part of the play she seems also to stand for the Church and for Mary. She speaks of herself as the least obtrusive of the servants of history, calling to mind the Magnificat. She herself is not the light, since that light radiates from the Father, but she both reflects and protects as she radiates to the children of Adam. Each time, she counsels: "Adam, accept the radiation of fatherhood; Adam, become a child." But Adam also sees that accepting the commitment of human love (fatherhood) means that our lives and our loves must pass through suffering and death (even as did Mary through and with her Child), yet with the hope of resurrection; so, he is brought back to the realization of his own mortality and lack of self-subsistence. He ends up in a quandary between the loneliness of his own self-isolation and the adopted "fatherhood-childhood" that must pass through suffering and death. We are left at the close of the drama with an indecisive Adam, a sort of universal Hamlet; he needs something more than the knowledge he has gained: he needs *to decide and to act.* We notice parallels to Brother Albert in *Our God's Brother* ("knowledge without love" is not enough), and to *Jeremiah* (when Fr. Peter cries out "words are not enough"). Here we find again in dramatic form Wojtyla's concern with ethical action and its foundations.

—adapted from *At the Center of the Human Drama: The Philosophy of Karol Wojtyla/Pope John Paul II (Michael J. Mcgivney Lectures of the John Paul II Institute)* by Kenneth L. Schmitz

Wojtyla

Philosophical Formation

Wojtyla and St. John of the Cross—Wojtyla's first doctoral thesis on *The Doctrine of Faith According to St. John of the Cross* came about partly through Jan Tyranowski in Poland who introduced him to Carmelite spirituality and partly through the influence of his primary teacher in Rome Fr. Garrigou-Lagrange. The latter is usually remembered as a defender of a rather rigid and plodding Thomistic orthodoxy, but he also had a great interest in St. John of the Cross. In light of the Spanish mystic, Lagrange was working to define a new priestly spirituality in a world left devastated by the war. He continually and urgently sought the presence of the absolute within everyday life, *a presence of mystical contemplation in the world.* The problem lies in trying to reconcile the dogmatic (St. Thomas) and the mystical (St. John) conceptions of faith. Wojtyla attempts such a reconciliation on the basis of his personalism; Lagrange is more comfortable with traditional Thomistic language. Thus, Lagrange objects that Wojtyla refuses to use the term "divine object" to speak about God. While not denying the validity of such terms, Wojtyla strongly emphasizes the personal character of the encounter between God and man, which engenders faith: God as Personal Subject. Faith then is not just an intellectual virtue in relation to its object. It is a personal encounter, a unitive faith involving all man's faculties and virtues. It involves a particular gift of the intellect but is also an organic part of the intentional tendency of the person toward God. The intellect is engaged at the highest level but there realizes its insufficiency before God: one cannot objectivize one's knowledge of Him, cannot "comprehend" Him with our mind and our concepts. One recognizes that God does not become known as an object is known, but as a person is. As a person, he can be known only in a reciprocal relation of self-giving: the human being dwelling within God's personal interior and God within him. The goal of every human being, according to St. John of the Cross, is to become "God by participation" in this way. The young Wojtyla read the writings of St. John as a phenomenology of mystical experience and shied away from objectivistic language about God (without denying its validity) for fear of obscuring the fundamental interpersonal relationship which obtains in knowledge of God through faith, expressed in its highest mode in mystical union. He develops the subjective side to the problem but sees the latter not as autonomous but as tightly bound to the objective side. The subjective side of faith revealed in experience is shown to be, so to speak, absolutely objective and related to truth. This perspective is the key to Wojtyla's later encounter with Scheler and phenomenology. His point of reference in his engagement with Scheler would always be Aquinas, yet Aquinas understood through St. John of the Cross; St.

Thomas was, thus, given an experiential and existential dimension which made it easier to link his thought with phenomenology. St. John's phenomenology of mystical experience takes man toward the irreducible core of the human person and shows the necessity of transcending this core toward that truth who is God himself, by responding to the initiative of God toward human beings. This divine initiative, which traverses natural human structures, illuminates and, in a certain sense, makes the irreducible core of the human person experienceable; this core is normally left out of phenomenological method. Faith is, thus, the key to the comprehension of human beings, permitting an experience deeper than the human truth, reaching its height in subjective experience in mysticism. For this reason, if one wants to understand the human condition, one has to begin from mystical experience.

However, for St. John of the Cross the night in which all human sentiment is silent is also the experience of the absolute distance of God, the incomprehensibility of God. With Aquinas, he argues that no positive knowledge of God is possible (i.e., even our highest positive concepts cannot be directly applied to God in the way we understand them, they are inadequate to him, they cannot comprehend him). Nonetheless, human faith truly encounters God, and God himself becomes the form of the human intellect. This happens not because the human person comprehends God, but because he welcomes God into himself and is welcomed by

Him: one knows God through a personal relation with Him, one of reciprocal giving. Both the ineffability and the personality of God are revealed. Wojtyla draws three conclusions from this analysis of St. John: (1) Human beings can know that God exists, but they cannot know God as an object in the sense of comprehending him. (2) Faith is not an intellectual grasp of what God is but a personal encounter with God which is real though in this life always remains in an obscurity or mystery. But this aspect of God for faith is part of the essence of his person and of his personal relation with us, part of the very form of our personal relationship with God which he initiates. (3) Understood in its purest form, the personal encounter with God in mystical experience occurs in an "absence" of emotion, i.e. goes beyond the emotional level to envelop the intellect and the will of the person.

But since the understanding of man is rooted in his relation to and resemblance to God, if we have no comprehensive knowledge of God, then we also have no comprehensive knowledge of man. The mystery of the human being is rooted in the yet greater mystery of God. Still, we are not left in absolute ignorance. We know that God and human beings resemble one another precisely in being essentially persons and, thus, not reducible to objects or to instrumental means or to mere collections of emotional states. The most profound experience of a person touches his ontological nucleus through conscience: the acting person responsible for his attitudes and deeds. In these latter thoughts we find the ground for the personalist norm: the prohibition against violating in oneself and in others the mystery of the person, the treating of a person as an object. Thus, the very incomprehensibility of God together with man's likeness to Him gives rise to positive norms: (1) the very mystery of the human being reveals a being which is in itself a high value as resembling God and called to relate to him; (2) as an embodied being relating to the world and to others through the body, it is necessary to treat of the human body as a dimension and aspect of the human person in all his mystery and value. While acknowledging the mystery of the human being, and our lack of absolute knowledge of our own essence, such an approach still yields a foundation for ethics based in respect for human freedom and the safeguarding of human dignity, opposing all objectivization and exploitation. Thus, the engagement with St. John of the Cross strengthened Wojtyla in the conviction of the eminently personal character of Christian certainty in faith. It yields an anthropology which elevates and gives value to the person.

Wojtyla and Max Scheler—In a comprehensive assessment of Wojtyla's theoretical interests, the figure of Max Scheler stands near St. John of the Cross. He came to this interest partly through Roman Ingarden, perhaps also through the works of Edith Stein. Ingarden maintained a fundamentally realist interpretation of phenomenology as a method of philosophical inquiry. This was also Scheler's path (in the main body of his works), leading him away from the idealism of the later Husserl. For Scheler the experience of reality is always charged with affectivity, an attraction or repulsion connected with a value or disvalue. Thus, phenomenology is a method of analyzing experience which permits one to grasp values, and this can be a basis for a material ethics of values based in personal experience. This is contrasted to Kant's "formalism" in ethics, wherein the mind gives itself absolute theoretical commands which have not been grounded in subjective experience. Further, Scheler elaborates the role of "following" or "imitating" in apprehending values. It is by appropriating another man's ethos that one can identify with the values and qualities to which his life testifies. These are not transmitted by intellectual teaching. Closely linked to the concepts of value and of following is Scheler's concept of the person. Through the experience of value, one identifies the unique emotional center which is the person; the latter comes about in time (it is only slowly that the child is able to identify with its own emotional reasoning, as distinct from the world around it) and through specific structures. Through empathy and sympathy, the person can grasp the other's experience as the experience of another, and in a certain way he makes it his own even if he recognizes that it belongs to the other. The person is precisely the experienced human "I"—

when one does not abstract from its concrete cognitive and emotional contents—and it is that which characterizes its unrepeatable individuality (and experiential incommunicability as Wojtyla emphasizes). But this is an individuality for Scheler which is nonetheless open to reality, through sympathy. This is Scheler's break with solipsism.

Wojtyla is enthusiastic about Scheler's approach and appropriates much of it, but with three qualifications or criticisms.* (1) First, Scheler's phenomenology makes only emotional values evident. Value never appears as the goal of a conscious action directed toward its realization. Moreover, the value is simply ascertained, not elaborated by conscience into an objective order as a foundation for ethics. The highest value is that which the subject responds to most intensely. Moral value (or the good of the person) is not the end or purpose of an action but is manifested *on the occasion of an action.* In his reaction against a moralism which would not accept the assistance of the experience of value in the moral life, Scheler becomes too polemical and contradicts moral experience by depreciating the role which the judgment of conscience makes about the truthfulness of the affective experience of values. (2) Second, concerning

---

*Editor's note: In his criticisms of Scheler, Wojtyla takes particular account of the objections formulated from a phenomenological point of view by Dietrich von Hildebrand, see ftnt. 28 of Buttiglione's book.

"following," there is again an emphasis on the aesthetic and emotional following of a master, but not so much on the individual judgment and conscience of the disciple. What is neglected is the question of truth and of verification in one's own life and experience of the values absorbed from the master. (3) Third is the question of the nature of the person. For Scheler, the person is the place in which values are made manifest. It is not, however, the center of a judgment and of actions which turn toward the realization of value. Value is understood in relation to a single act, and not to the person as a whole, who is the subject of actions which unite and cohere with the actions which follow them. Such a person lacks ontological consistency. Both a deeper phenomenology of the person in action through his conscious judgments and decisions and an ontology or metaphysics of the person based in more than phenomenological description are needed for an adequate understanding of the person.

Wojtyla concludes: "The ethical system constructed by Max Scheler is not at all suitable as a means of formulating a scientific Christian ethics." He states further: "Scheler in his system has decisively cancelled the normative character of ethical acts, and this is an understandable consequence of his distancing of values from the acting person. If Scheler's phenomenology analyzes acts of consciousness without converging upon a living relation to the person in respect of ethical values, this is for reasons which lie outside his phenomenology. The reason is the 'emotionalist' premises from which he begins." Phenomenology is not to blame for the defects of Scheler's ethical system. A phenomenology of the person can indeed contribute to and enhance the ontological enterprise, starting with the concrete reality of the person and not just with the abstract notion of the subject.

Kant and Scheler—Wojtyla's approach is to try to retrieve from modern thought all elements which are true and to recover a wholeness and balance from different extremes. If in Kant's philosophy, the sole object of ethics is the abstract form of duty and responsibility, then Scheler reacts by excluding the legitimate aspect of this from the sphere of ethics. His philosophy opposes an ethic of pure duty to an ethic of pure value.

The problem begins with Kant's split between the "phenomenal" man (as a part of the determined, causally related material world) and the "noumenal" man (necessarily hypothesized as possessing freedom of the will, as a necessary condition for ethics). Kant tries to save both freedom and causality, but now they have no connection with one another. Thus, also a split occurs in ethics: man must detach himself from any particular situation or good (even his own good) or phenomenal content if he is to turn toward pure duty. Kant's formalism, his divorce of ethics from present goods in favor of the "pure" devotion of the will to duty, may have a certain mystical element to it with some parallels to St. John of the Cross: beyond all phenomenal reality and beyond all emotions lies a supreme value worthy of complete subjugation of the will. But in St. John of the Cross the sphere of sensible experience is simultaneously judged and transcended, while the mystical experience is above all passive or receptive before the real presence of God. By contrast, in Kant sensible experience is disregarded rather than transcended, and the experience of duty as the supreme object of moral willing entirely lacks the receptivity and availability to the presence of value which St. John emphasizes. But in Kant, since sense experience is disregarded ethically (as belonging the sphere of external, causal relationships), it can never be the starting point for the themes of liberty and of the ethical action of the person. Scheler criticizes this aspect of Kant's thought and thereby opens a road toward the rediscovery of the classical, Aristotelian and Thomistic, conception of knowledge. But the full recovery of classical ethics requires the recognition that the person appears simultaneously as the subject and object of action: I decide and bring an act into being and at the same time this act registers in me in its effects. Since Scheler lacks the notion of potentiality and actuality, it is impossible for him to grasp that the person directed toward a value which is external to himself is simultaneously realizing a potential value which is internal to himself, and which is making the person intrinsically better or worse. Furthermore, Scheler so opposes Kant's formalism about ethical duty that he leaves it out of the equation, even as founded in value. "Scheler," Wojtyla writes, "could not bear to think that duty could constitute the objective content of an experience, and his system does not even allow for the idea that it can be born of value itself...." This negation of duty is tied to a certain irrationalism. Values are always tied to emotional feelings. Though Scheler's notion of aspiring to values is an opening toward a deeper conception, he never makes this point clear. But Wojtyla observes that the essence of ethical experience does not consist in emotions but in willing: "Scheler has not noticed the most elemental and fundamental thing, he has not seen that what we call ethical value is solely that value which has as its efficient cause a person's action." In other words, the person is not limited to registering and following an emotion and moving his will according to it. The person judges the emotion and acts upon the basis of that judgment, an act of the whole person involving his intellect and his freedom even if founded deeply in the emotional perception. The experience of bringing about a genuine action through an authentic volition is the fundamental experience of ethical life and the ground of every possible theory of responsibility. Kant's divorce of the pure ethical willing of duty from the ethical experience of goods and values is not really overcome by Scheler, he just emphasizes the other side. The solution requires the reestablishment of the unity of the ethical act and of the real relation of its emotive and cognitive aspects. Phenomenology provides an access to this authentic unity because it begins from a unified experience which is there before abstraction. Wojtyla writes: "There is contained within ethical experience not only value as an objective content (Scheler's emphasis), but also the normative moment (Kant's "duty," but now anchored in reality and experience) in which values are reorganized and given as a task to be realized." (Editor's inserts in parenthesis). Moreover, ethical action must be anchored in the classical notion of potentiality and actuality.

Scheler and St. Thomas—Wojtyla's reading of St. Thomas takes the latter's ethics and anthropology as points of departure, through which one comes in contact with Thomas' metaphysics, rather than the other way around. This is an original and decisively innovative interpretation of St. Thomas: using his ethics to form a complete vision of his philosophy. The philosophy of being is qualified from the beginning as a philosophy of the good, for *ens et bonum convertuntur*. God is the summit and source of the order of the good and of that of being, and the investigation of being is wholly animated by a movement which leads to a personal encounter with God. This dimension of St. Thomas' thought emphasized by Wojtyla draws parallels that of St.

Bonaventure and the Franciscan tradition.* Philosophy then begins with personal experience (of the good) and not just from being (as the most general concept proposed to intellectual reflection). Thus, the fundamental categories of Thomistic metaphysics are retained on the basis of and illuminated through a reflection on the moral experience of the person, as conducted with the phenomenological method. The moral core of the starting point, anchored in metaphysical reality, saves man from being treated merely as a subject understood purely intellectually. The starting point in St. Thomas ethics and anthropology also allows one to reappropriate such great Catholic thinkers as Pascal with his starting point in the examination of the human condition (and the notion that the truth of being is revealed only in that man who is interiorly inclined toward the good). To begin from the phenomenology of moral experience and to graft metaphysical reflection into the matters and the problems which phenomenology emphasizes (but cannot resolve on its own), permits one to arrive at the question of being from the question of man, through the question of the good. This involves a reformulation of St. Thomas' thought which emphasizes certain Platonic and Augustinian elements, especially the idea of participation. God, autonomous subsisting being, is the source of the existence of

* Editor's note: As also Dr. Josef Seifert has pointed out, see ftnts. 47&48 in Buttiglione's book.

accidental beings, which possess being by participation. But since participation in being is inseparable from participation in value, He is also the source of all their goodness and value: He is the exemplar of each created being, and each created being is reflective of Him according to its proper place and species. This provides the objective metaphysical foundation for an ordering of being, a hierarchy of values intrinsic to the things themselves as imitative of God. Wojtyla states: "It is here that we find the nucleus of the normative order." Every being, therefore, has its truth in God and it approaches Him by imitating the divine perfection. The metaphysical measure of being is bound to the divine exemplarity and to its imitation by particular beings. Moreover, since God is personal and addresses man through this hierarchy of values, mere contemplation of the good (even the eternal contemplation of an order of ideal essences) is not the heart of ethics. Rather, the realization of values within existence is called for. The fundamentally practical nature of ethics is, thus, recognized, as it was by Aristotle, but with a criticism of the Aristotelian position insofar as Wojtyla here recognizes that moral goodness is of a higher value that intellectual cognition as such.

Since man is personal, we can see that the object of ethics is properly the person's coming to maturity through his freedom and not simply his fitting himself in with a given order. This approach allows St. Thomas to avoid the two pitfalls described above: (1) that of a notion of the good completely cut off from experience (Kant) and (2) beginning with a notion of experience deprived in advance of any normative dimension, that element of good which alone qualifies it as ethical (Scheler). The normative order which is based in divine exemplarity is not an externally imposed formalism, but the internal rule of goodness within any being; it is objective for man and at the same time contains the ultimate truth of man's subjectivity: he is called to respond and to act appropriately. The exemplarity of God is the basis of the entire normative order; it is therefore not abstract but personal.

This objective ethical order can become a part of a person's awareness and be realized in it, but only through the free consent of the person, which, one hopes, will reorganize his affective perception of reality in the light of objective truth. Objectivity without the person's free consent cannot realize the ethical good because the human moral good comes about only through the act of a person. And yet, the objective moral order does not lose its genuine objectivity if it is not recognized.

Concerning the proofs for God's existence, Wojtyla was partial to St. Thomas' third and fourth ways, arguing from contingent being to necessary being and from limited and participated value (the Good, the True , the Beautiful) to the fullness thereof. The third and fourth ways have as their point of reference the ethical and ontic experience of the person. The metaphysical depth of Wojtyla's ethics is built upon these ways. In this perspective all the positive features of Scheler's thought are retained but carried to a greater level of profundity. Considered through the concept of participation and posed as the ultimate root of the ethical order, God's exemplarity radicalizes Scheler's notion of "following" in the ethical life while divesting it of its irrationality. That which one follows is ultimately the perfection of God, which must be reproduced in the person. Norm and value, therefore, have the same root. Thus, emotional intensity is not the guide; rather, acknowledgement of the truth is. Man is made for the truth, and no values can be lived out which are not illuminated by truth.

Moral knowledge for St. Thomas is a knowledge which introduces us to the truth about being and is based in man's experience. This aspect of things has been lost in much of modern philosophy which tends to reduce "experience" to mere sensation. Phenomenology, by allowing a recapture of the original and founding dimension of experience, rediscovers the co-implication of ethics and metaphysics. Man is "an individual substance of a rational nature" (Boethius). But that which has access to an immaterial knowledge cannot be defined as an object within the material order. Rather it is defined by a relation with the truth and has a personal character. Wojtyla states: "The rational nature does not have a genuine autonomous existence as nature; it subsists as a person. The person, therefore, is an autonomous subject of existence and of action, which otherwise could not be attributed to the rational nature. Note well: this is why God must be a personal being." Thus, God is not, as in Aristotle's naturalistic interpretation, a kind of place of ideas. God is, rather, a person, and as such is a subjective agent who puts ideas into being through his creative work. The affirmation of God as Creator is directly connected with that of the personality of God; here we see St. Thomas' innovation in relation to Aristotle most clearly. But personality, being a person, is also the mark which man shares with God, an original resemblance of which the Scriptures speak.

Wojtyla returns to the central foundations of the anthropology and ethics of St. Thomas, not by simply acquiring and repeating his principles, but by constructing on their basis a new philosophy able to provide a way into the truth of being which is adequate to the people of our times. This is a truly creative return, as Leo XIII called for. How is it necessary to innovate in relation to St. Thomas? He provides the fundamental principles for an adequate understanding of the human person and his situation, yet in a way which is above all objectivist. But the side of subjectivity lacks adequate development, as founded in human experience. Wojtyla notes: "At this point we can observe how far the conception of the person which we find in St. Thomas is objectivist. He appears not to analyze conscience and self-consciousness as genuine and specific symptoms of the subject-person.... Therefore in St. Thomas, we can see very well the person in his objective existence and action, but it is difficult to catch sight of the living experience of the person." Scheler's phenomenology (amended in the sense which Wojtyla indicates) allows us to develop on the basis of personal experience a reflection which concludes in the confirmation of the Thomistic ontology of the person.

—from *KAROL WOJTYLA: The Thought of the Man Who Became John Paul II* by Rocco Buttiglione

Crossing the Threshold of Hope

"The Pope": A Scandal and a Mystery—The notion of "the Pope" seems to involve a lively faith and a certain anxiety. In answer I state right from the outset, with Christ and the Church, "Be not afraid!" We should not fear the truth about ourselves: that we are sinners and imperfect, as are all our systems. Do not be afraid of God: Father, Son incarnate (the sacrament of the invisible God) and Son crucified (in his humiliation), and Holy Spirit (in whom we have confidence). What is important is giving authentic witness to Christ, as Paul and Peter did. Christ Himself is the rock, and Christ builds his Church on Peter—on Peter, Paul and the apostles. In is in this context that words like "Supreme Pontiff," "Your Holiness," and "Holy Father" are to be understood. Do not be afraid of them. Having faith in a crucified God is a tremendous mystery, splitting monotheism (Christianity compared to Judaism or Islam). The Pope also is a mystery, a challenge, a sign that will be contradicted. In the face of this, one must choose, as Peter did. Do not be afraid of God's mystery and his love; do not be afraid of man's weakness or of his grandeur. Christ is personally present in his Church and this is represented when the Pope is called "Vicar of Christ." But Christ is present in each Christian, called to be *another Christ*. This is the dignity of the baptized. A title like Vicar of Christ, however, alludes to service more than dignity, and this title is held also in union with the college of bishops. Thus, if with this title one wants to refer to the dignity of the Bishop of Rome, one cannot consider it apart from the *dignity of the entire college of bishops,* with which it is tightly bound, as it is to the dignity of each bishop, each priest, and each of the baptized. "I am a bishop for you, I am a Christian with you."

Praying: How and Why—We do not know how to pray as we ought, but the Spirit comes to the aid of our weakness. Prayer is a conversation, involving an "I" and a "Thou." The Thou is more important, because our prayer begins with God. Prayer reflects all created reality; it is in a certain sense a cosmic function. Man is the priest of all creation; he speaks in its name, but only insofar as he is guided by the Spirit. In prayer, then, the true protagonist is God: Christ who constantly frees creation from slavery to corruption and leads it toward liberty and the Holy Spirit giving us the initiative to pray which restores us to our true humanity and our unique dignity. One can and must pray in many different ways, but the Book of Psalms is irreplaceable. Prayer is always a work of glory completing creation. Man achieves the fullness of prayer not when he expresses himself, but when he lets God be most fully present in prayer, as the history of mystical prayer (East and West) testifies.

How does the Pope pray?—As the Holy Spirit permits him to pray. He prays for "the joy and the hope, the grief and the anguish of the people of our time." The Gospel is an invitation to joy, a grand affirmation of the world and of man. God is the primary source of joy and hope for man. The Gospel, above all else, is the joy of creation. Good is greater than all that is evil in the world. Evil, in fact, is neither fundamental nor definitive. It must be clear for those who accept Revelation, and in particular the Gospel, that it is better to exist than not to exist. And because of this, in the realm of the Gospel, there is not space for any nirvana, apathy, or resignation. Instead, there is a great challenge to perfect creation—be it oneself, be it the world. This essential joy of creation is completed by the joy of salvation, the joy of redemption., proclaiming victory over evil. The work of redemption is to elevate the work of creation to a new level. The Pope is a witness to this joy and hope in Christ and in the victory over evil but with a realistic awareness of the existence of evil in the world and in every man. To overcome evil, Christian morality can be nothing but extraordinarily demanding. Therefore, the joy of good and the hope of its triumph in man and in the world do not exclude fear for this good, for the disappearance of this hope. The Pope, like every Christian, must be keenly aware of the dangers to which man is subject and the struggle required for victory. It is precisely from this struggle for the victory of the good in man and in the world that the need for prayer arises. The Pope's prayer is a universal prayer for all the churches and the problems that trouble the world today. At the year 2000, we see the ever expanding mystery of sin but more so the superabounding grace which is its response. Prayer, entrusted to one and to all, is the easiest way to make God and his redeeming love present in the world. The Pope prays especially for the missionary dimension of the Church, for vocations, for the suffering, and for the dead. Prayer is a search for God, it is also a revelation of God. Through prayer God reveals himself above all as Mercy.

Does God really exist?—Pascal's distinction between the God of the philosophers (the object of rational proofs) and the God of Jesus Christ must be discussed here. Only the God of Jesus Christ is the living God. Nonetheless, with St. Thomas and his five ways for proving God's existence, we must not abandon the philosophers' approach, as the theology of some of the early Fathers tended to do. In the end, all rationalist arguments follow the path indicated in the book of Wisdom and the Letter to the Romans—passing from the visible world to the invisible Absolute. However, the question of God's existence is not only an issue which touches the intellect; it is, at the same time, an issue that has a strong impact on all of human existence and is intimately united with the purpose of human existence. Not only is it a question of intellect; it is also a question of the will, even a question of the human heart (the *raisons du coeur* of Blaise Pascal). St. Thomas should be read on these subjects. It is not good that his thought has been set aside since the council; he remains the master of philosophical and theological universalism.

"Proof": Is it Still Valid?—I would say, today more than ever. Positivism is fading. Contemporary man has rediscovered the sacred, even if he does not always know how to identify it. Knowledge begins with the senses but the limits of these "senses" are not exclusively sensory. Man knows not only aspects and parts of things but he knows objects globally, including himself (yes, man as a person). He knows, therefore, extrasensory truths or, in other words, the transempirical. We can speak from a solid foundation in human experience, moral experience, religious experience. God is reflected in the good, truth, beauty and existence of the visible world. He is revealed in man's interior world as well: in man recognizing himself as an ethical being capable of good and evil (Kant). Man also recognizes himself as a religious being, capable of putting himself in contact with God. The philosophy of religion (Eliade) is very important here, as well as the return to metaphysics through an integral anthropology. Man depends on God for his very existence. Moreover, this relationship is personal, between an "I" and a "Thou" (Buber). This is a fundamental dimension of man's existence and of our faith, which is always a coexistence in communion with this eternal Thou.

If God exists, why is he hiding?—This type of question stems from a "rationalism" and is characteristic of modern thought, which wants human reason to be the measure of reality. Yet it is not thought which determines existence, but existence, "esse," which determines thought. And the fullness of existence is He Who Is, the absolute uncreated mystery. If he were not mystery, there would be no need for God to reveal himself. However, such questions may also stem from contemporary agnosticism, and echo certain dimensions of the Old and New Testaments. Our knowledge of God and his ways is limited. His wisdom bestows itself on all creatures, while at the same time not revealing to them all His Mystery. However, God's self-revelation comes about in a special way by his "becoming man." The challenge comes from God himself to recognize and accept him incarnate and crucified: the revelation of the invisible God in the visible humanity of Christ. Let's try to be impartial in our reasoning: *Could God go further in His stooping down, in His drawing near to man,* thereby expanding the possibilities of our knowing Him? In truth, *it seems that He has gone as far as possible. He could go no further.* In a certain sense God has gone too far in this closeness to man and has generated protests against it. This great protest has precise names—first it is called the Synagogue, and then Islam.

Is Jesus the Son of God?—Christ is absolutely original and absolutely unique, the one mediator between God and man. He is divine (and holds within himself the entire intimate world of the Trinity), yet he is so human! Thanks to this, the entire world of men, the entire history of humanity, finds in Him its expression before God. He is not just a promulgator of religious discipline (Muhammad), nor just a wise man (Socrates), still less is he similar to Buddha with his denial of all that is created. He is the eternal witness to the Father and to the love that the Father has had for His creatures from the beginning. Hence the Christological focus from the beginning of the faith, together with an accompanying Marian dimension. "He was conceived by the Holy Spirit and born of the Virgin Mary." But, again, Christ is totally original and unique, *the only Son* of the Father Almighty. This comes directly from the apostolic heritage, from Paul and John. The Christology of the New Testament is "explosive." The Fathers, the great Scholastics, and later theologians did nothing other that return, with renewed wonder, to that heritage which they had received. My first encyclical, *Redemptor Hominis,* aims to be a great hymn of joy for the fact the man has been redeemed through Christ—redeemed in spirit and in body (male and female).

What has become of the "history of salvation"?—Let us begin with a look at the history of European thought after Descartes, who inaugurated the great anthropocentric shift in philosophy and the turn toward rationalism. He distanced us from the philosophy of existence, and this distance was expanded throughout modern thought. This has finally ended in modern immanentism and subjectivism. But already 150 years after Descartes, all that was fundamentally Christian in the tradition of European thought had already been pushed aside and rationalism held sway, as in the Enlightenment and the French Revolution and Reign of Terror. Nevertheless, a God *outside the world* (the God of the deists) was never denied. It was God the Redeemer, the one true God, who was denied. Man was supposed to live by his reason alone, as if God did not exist. A God outside the world could be left as an unverifiable hypothesis, but it was crucial that such a God be expelled from the world.

The Centrality of Salvation—With such a way of thinking and acting, the rationalism of the Enlightenment strikes at the heart of Christian soteriology (salvation and redemption). Christ challenges the assumptions of the Enlightenment in every word of his response to Nicodemus. "God so loved the world"—challenges the presumption that the world does not need God's love, that it is self-sufficient and can make man happy, perhaps through modern science and technology. "That he gave his only Son, so that everyone who believes in him might not perish"—makes us realize that this world in not the source of man's ultimate happiness, rather it can become the source of his ruin. This world, with its riches and its wants, needs to be saved, to be redeemed. The world is not able to free man from suffering or from death. *The entire world is subject to "precariousness."* Eternal life can be given only by God; it can only be His gift. Christ comes to save the world deserving of condemnation because of sin. But post-Enlightenment thought refuses to accept the reality of sin and, in particular, it refuses to accept original sin. Convincing the world of sin means creating the conditions for its salvation. To save means to embrace and lift up with redemptive love, with love that is always greater than any sin. The history of salvation is very simple: beginning with the first Adam, through the revelation of the second Adam, Jesus Christ, and ending with the ultimate fulfillment of the history of the world in God, when He will be "all in all." At the same time, this history embraces the life of every man. This history, while it reveals the redemptive will of God, also reveal the mission of the Church. The history of salvation continues to offer new inspiration for interpreting the history of humanity. But it not only addresses the question of human history but also confronts the problem of the meaning of man's existence. The history of salvation is, thus, both a history and a metaphysics, and even the most integral form of theology, the theology of all the encounters between God and the world.

Why is there so much evil in the world?—The Cross remains constant while the world turns. Yet, the question of evil is a source of recurring doubt of God's goodness and even His existence. How could He permit so much evil? Can He truly be Love, Who places such burdens on His creatures and leaves them to such a bleak picture, as has found expression in both ancient and modern literature? God created man as rational and free, thereby placing Himself under man's judgment. The history of salvation is also the history of man's continual judgment of God, as we see in the Book of Job (where we also see intervention and "judgment" of God's actions by the evil spirit). And then we discover the mystery and the scandal of the Cross. Could it have been different? Could God have *justified Himself* before human history, so full of suffering, without placing Christ's Cross at the center of that history? The biblical Job bows before God's Omnipotence. But God who besides being Omnipotence is Wisdom and Love, desires to justify Himself to mankind. He is not the Absolute that remains outside of the world (as the Enlightenment held). He is Emmanuel, God-with-us, a God who shares man's lot and participates in his destiny. His wisdom and omnipotence are placed, by free choice, at the service of creation. If suffering is present in the history of humanity, one understands why His omnipotence was manifested in the omnipotence of humiliation on the Cross. The scandal of the Cross remains the key to the interpretation of the great mystery of suffering, so much a part of the history of mankind. The crucified Christ is proof of God's solidarity with man in his suffering.

Why does God tolerate suffering?—In a certain sense, one could say that *confronted with human freedom, God decided to make Himself "impotent."* In other words, man is really free and God respects his freedom and even pays the price for it himself. He places himself before the judgment of man, even before the illegitimate tribunal of Pilate who finds "no guilt in him" but orders his crucifixion, washing his hands of the issue and returning the responsibility to the violent crowd. Therefore, the condemnation of God by man is not based on the truth, but on arrogance, on an underhanded conspiracy. Isn't this the truth about the history of humanity, the truth about our century? A condemnation repeated by oppressive totalitarian regimes as well as by democracies where laws are regularly passed condemning to death a person not yet born? God is always on the side of the suffering. He stayed on the Cross—and loved—to the end, bearing our infirmities and the guilt of us all, enduring all things. In the end, before Christ Crucified, the man who shares in redemption will have the advantage over the man who sets himself up as an unbending judge of God's actions in his own life as well as in that of all humanity. Thus, we find ourselves at the center of the history of salvation. The judgment of God becomes a judgment of man. "There is no salvation through anyone else, nor is there any other name under heaven given to the human race by which we are to be saved." Christianity is a religion of salvation—a soteriological religion, focused on the Paschal mystery.

What does "to save" mean?—To save means to liberate from evil. This means from social and natural evils, but also from *radical, ultimate evil.* Death ceases to be an ultimate evil, it becomes subject to the power of life through the work of the Redeemer. The world cannot save man from death. *Only God saves, in Jesus ("God who saves").*

An even more radical evil is God's rejection of man, that is, *eternal damnation* as the consequence of man's rejection of God. Damnation is the opposite of salvation. Both are associated with the destiny of man to live eternally. And what is eternal life? It is happiness that comes from *union with God.* The vision of God "face to face" allows enjoyment of the absolute fullness of truth and the encounter with the absolute fullness of good and fullness of life: eternal communion with the Father, the Son, and the Holy Spirit. The death and resurrection of Christ allows us to share in this intimate life of God. But each of us will be judged by the works of charity, fulfilled, or neglected. As a result of this judgment, the just are destined to eternal life. There is a destination to eternal damnation as well, which consists in the ultimate rejection of God, the ultimate break of the communion with the Father and the Son and the Holy Spirit. *Here it is not so much God who rejects man, but man who rejects God.* God "wills everyone to be saved and to come to knowledge of the truth." Christianity is a religion of salvation. Everyone who looks for salvation, not only the Christian, must stop before the Cross of Christ. Will he be willing to accept the truth of the Paschal mystery or not? Will he have faith? The mystery of salvation is an event which has already taken place. The Paschal mystery is by now grafted onto the history of humanity, onto the history of every individual. Christian soteriology is one of the fullness of life, truth, and love—Divine Love. Love above all possesses saving power. The fact that Christianity is a religion of salvation is expressed in the *sacramental life of the Church.* Christ discloses for us the sources of life through the Paschal Mystery of His Death and Resurrection. Linked to this are Baptism and the Eucharist, which create the seeds in man of eternal life, and the Sacrament of Reconciliation, with its regenerative power of forgiveness. That Christianity is a religion of salvation is also expressed in *worship:* at the center of the *work of praise* is the celebration of the Resurrection and of life, especially in the Eastern Church. The Western church, while maintaining the primacy of the Resurrection, has gone further *in the direction of the Passion.* But Christianity, and especially Western Christianity, has never become a religion indifferent to the world. It has always been open to the world, to its questions, to its anxieties, to its hopes.

Why so many religions?—There are many, but we must also look at the common fundamental element and the common root of these religions. Christian revelation views the spiritual history of man as including, in some way, all religions, thereby demonstrating the unity of humankind with regard to the eternal and ultimate destiny of man. Men turn to various religions to solve the mysteries of the human condition and various peoples have shared an awareness of that enigmatic power present throughout the course of things and throughout the events of human life, and, in which, at times, even the Supreme Divinity or the Father is recognizable. In the great cultures of the East, missionary activity is ongoing but difficult. These peoples come from traditions which antedate Christianity and which remain very strong. They are sometimes put off by the image of life in Western society (the so-called Christian society). But the Catholic Church rejects nothing that is true and holy in these religions, e.g., Hinduism in its attempt at freedom from the anguish of our human condition, Buddhism in its recognition of the radical inadequacy of this malleable world, Taoism in its strong emphasis on good and evil, animism in the veneration of ancestors (a sort of preparation for the Christian faith in the communion of saints). These are rays of the truth which enlightens all men, *semina Verbi*. The Holy Spirit works effectively even outside the visible structures of the Church, and we recognize in these *seeds of the Word* a common soteriological root present in all religions. Thus, instead of marveling at the fact that Providence allows such a great variety of religions, we should be amazed at the number of common elements found within them. Christ came into the world for all these peoples. He redeemed them all and has His own ways of reaching them in the present eschatological phase of human history. In fact, in those regions, many accept Him and many more have an implicit faith in Him. However, the Church proclaims, and is bound to proclaim that Christ is the way and the truth and the life.

Buddha?—Buddhism may seem like Christianity in that both involve a doctrine of salvation. However, in Buddhism we find only a negative soteriology: the world is bad and is a source of evil and suffering for man. Thus, we must break our ties to the world as we find them in human nature, in the psyche, and in our bodies. By the highest indifference (nirvana) to the world we are freed from suffering. But do we draw near to God in this way? This is not mentioned. Buddhism is in large measure an "atheistic" system. This detachment as an end in itself is not at all comparable to Christian detachment. St. John of the Cross, in the *Dark Night of the Soul,* proposes not merely detachment from the world, but detachment in order to unite oneself to that which is outside the world, with a personal God who comes to us not just through purification but through love. Carmelite mysticism begins at the point where the reflections of the Buddha end. The Christian vision of the world as created and returning to God also is fundamentally different from the Buddhist view of the world as bad, as fundamentally contrary to the development of both man himself and the world. The created and redeemed world is such as to call for a positive approach to it and for participation in its transformation and perfection. Thus, we must caution against an uncritical acceptance of certain ideas and practices originating in the East. First, one should know one's own spiritual heritage well and consider whether it is right to set it aside lightly. One must also be careful of the return of Gnostic ideas under guise of the so-called New Age. Gnosticism is that attitude of the spirit that, in the name of a profound knowledge of God, results in distorting His Word and replacing it with purely human words.

Muhammad?—As a result of their monotheism, believers in Allah are particularly close to us. Yet, whoever knows the Old and New Testaments, and then reads the Koran, clearly sees the process by which it completely reduces Divine Revelation. In Islam all the richness of God's self-revelation, through the prophets and through His Son, has definitely been set aside. Some of the most beautiful names in the human language are given to the God of the Koran, but He is ultimately a God outside of the world, a God who is only Majesty, never Emmanuel, God-with-us.

Islam is not a religion of redemption. There is no room for the cross and resurrection. Thus, not only the theology but the anthropology of Islam is very different from Christianity. Nevertheless, the religiosity of Muslims deserves respect, their fidelity to prayer remains a model for all those who invoke the true God. Further, we must continue to seriously dialogue with the followers of the "Prophet," for the benefit of mankind. Nevertheless, fundamentalist movements, imposing their religion on all, make for a terribly disturbing situation for Christians in these countries.

Judaism?—Certainly the people of God of the Old Testament espouse a religion that is closest to our own. The Church cannot forget that it received the revelation of the Old Testament through the people with whom God made the Ancient Covenant and that the Church continues to draw sustenance from that root. Thus, mutual understanding, respect, and fraternal discussion must dominate our relations with the Jewish people. This has been my personal experience as well, starting with my childhood friendships, through the horrors of the Second World War (and the persecution of the Jewish people), through the days of my pastoral experience as Bishop in Krakow, and during my pontificate. I have spoken of the Jews as our *elder brothers in the faith.* We must never forget, in such reminders as Auschwitz, that anti-Semitism (and indeed all racial hatred) is a great sin against humanity. Israel has paid a high price for its "election." Perhaps because of this, Israel has become more similar to the Son of Man, who, according to the flesh, was also a son of Israel. The two thousandth anniversary of His coming to the world will be a celebration for Jews as well. The New Covenant has its roots in the Old. The time when the people of the Old Covenant will be able to see themselves as part of the New is, naturally, a question to be left to the Holy Spirit. We, as human beings, try only not to put obstacles in the way.

A Minority by the Year 2000—Statistics about Hindus or Muslims outnumbering Catholics provide a somewhat simplistic view of the situation. We are speaking here of *values which are not quantifiable.* No statistic aiming at a quantitative measurement of faith will get to the heart of the matter. Current popularity and statistical measurements do not tell us which religion has a future ahead of it. Christ said, "Do not be afraid any longer, little flock, for your Father is pleased to give you the kingdom." He also asked, "When the Son of Man comes, will he find faith on the earth?" These statements reflect a solid foundation for the faith together with a profound realism: the Gospel is not a promise of easy success, yet we must have faith in the Father even in the midst of opposition and persecution. The Gospel contains a fundamental paradox: to find life, one must lose life; to be born, one must die; to save oneself, one must take up the cross. This is the essential truth of the Gospel, which always and everywhere is bound to meet with man's protest. The Gospel is a challenge to human weakness, and yet this is also its power: man wants such a challenge and feels the inner need to transcend himself in order to become fully human (Pascal).

What is the "New Evangelization"?—Evangelization of course is the essential task of the Church and her call in every age of her history. "Woe to me if I do not preach the Gospel!" (St. Paul). Paul carried this message to Europe, to Greece (with holy stubbornness), to Rome, to his death. Other martyrs followed. Evangelization involves first the proclamation of the faith, then catechesis or formation in the faith, and also the entire wide-ranging commitment to reflect on the faith as the fathers of the church and the early councils did. The history of evangelization is the history of the encounter of the Gospel with the culture of each epoch and with each new generation. It requires setting about the work of inculturation: making the Gospel accessible to each new age. This has occurred with the Slavic peoples centuries ago, with the discovery of America as a new world, with the peoples of the East, with Africa. Vocations are growing in Asia and Africa even as they are diminishing in Europe. Truly there are no grounds for losing hope. We are involved in a struggle for the world's soul, even where the spirit of the world seems strongest in the realms of science, culture, and the media. But *Christ is forever young* and his Church constantly goes out to meet new generations. The new spring of evangelization refers to the urgent need which our world feels for the Gospel. Perhaps we feel this need precisely because the world seems to be distancing itself from the Gospel (the "Old World"—Europe), or rather because the world has not yet drawn near to the Gospel (much of Asia, the Far East, Africa). These are the new challenges which the contemporary world creates for the mission of the Church. Remember that evangelization cannot be reduced to mere restoration or proselytism (as if the Church were just a social or political power), nor can evangelization be condemned on grounds of pluralism or tolerance. The mission of evangelization is essential to the mission of the Church. There are many ways and methods of genuine evangelization, but one is certainly the rebirth and rediscovery of the authentic values found in popular piety, e.g., pilgrimages. There is a need for a proclamation of the Gospel capable of accompanying man on his pilgrim way, capable of walking alongside the younger generation.

Is There Really Hope in the Young?—There is something in man which never changes, especially in the young. Yet today's youth are also different from those who came before. The WWII generation was called to acts of great heroism in situations of constant danger, recognizing the preciousness of each life even in the midst of the horrors of war and of the concentration camps. Today's young people are certainly growing up in a different context. They live in freedom, which others have won for them, and have yielded in large part to the consumer culture. And yet, today no less than yesterday, idealism is present in young people. My most memorable experience from my pastoral activities was *the discovery of the fundamental importance of youth.* It is a time given by Providence to every person and given to him as a responsibility. He searches, like the young man in the Gospel, for the answers to life's basic questions, for his own concrete way in life. This characteristic is something that every parent, every mentor, must recognize and love as a fundamental aspect of youth. But young people need guides in their search for purpose and for love. Youth is when we come to know ourselves. It is also a time of *communion.*

Young people, whether boys or girls, know they must live for and with others, they know that their life *has meaning to the extent that it becomes a free gift for others.* Here is the origin of all vocation—whether to priesthood or religious life, or to marriage and family. It is this vocation to love that naturally allows us to draw close to the young. As a young priest, I learned to love human love. If one loves human love, there naturally arises the need to commit oneself completely to the service of "fair love," because love is fair, it is beautiful. After all, young people are always searching for the beauty in love. They want their love to be beautiful. If they give in to weakness, following models of behavior that can rightly be considered a "scandal in the contemporary world" (and these are, unfortunately, widely diffused models), in the depths of their hearts they still desire a beautiful and pure love. This is as true of boys as it is of girls. Ultimately, they know that only God can give them this love. As a result, they are willing to follow Christ, without caring about the sacrifices this may entail. Young people await answers and, even if they are demanding answers, the young are not afraid of them. In the young there is an immense potential for good and for creative possibility. We need the enthusiasm of the young, we need their joy of life. This has been the origin of the extraordinarily successful World Youth Days. It was the young people themselves who created them! It is necessary that *the young know the Church, that they perceive Christ in the Church*, Christ who walks through the centuries alongside each generation, alongside every person as a friend. An important day in a young person's life is the day on which he becomes convinced that this is the only Friend who will not disappoint him, on whom he can always count.

Was God at Work in the Fall of Communism?—Certainly God is always at work. Christianity is not a religion of knowledge, of contemplation. It is a religion of God's action and of man's action. In one sense, God is silent, *because he has revealed everything.* In the Son He said to us all that He had to say. But in another sense, he still speaks to us in human history. Today, despite how things might appear, there are many who find the way to experience *God who is at work,* e.g. flourishing movements in the Church, like World Youth Day. Such movements involve the mind, the will, and the heart, and issue into action. Yes, Christianity is a great action of God. The action of the word becomes the action of the sacraments. In this light it is truly difficult to speak of the silence of God. One must speak rather of the desire to stifle the voice of God and even in carefully planned ways. Many will do just about anything so that His voice cannot be heard, so that only the voice of man will be heard, a voice that has nothing to offer except the things of this world—which often brings with it destruction of cosmic proportions as we have seen this century. We must see the fall of communism in this light but be wary of oversimplification as well. Communism was a reaction to injustice—a protest on the part of the great world of workers, which then became an ideology. Unfortunately, as Leo XIII prophesied, this cure became worse than the disease itself. Prophecies were also made at Fatima about the fall of communism. The fact that the Pope came from "a faraway country" and that an assassination attempt was made on the anniversary of Fatima, perhaps all these are signs of a God who is always at work. But, not to oversimplify, one must also say that in a certain sense communism as a system fell by itself, as a consequence of its own mistakes and failures, due to its own inherent weakness. The fall of Communism opens before us a retrospective panorama of modern civilization's typical way of thinking and acting, especially in Europe. It is a civilization that constantly equips itself with power structures and structures of oppression, both political and cultural (especially through the media), in order to impose similar mistakes and abuses on all humanity. Man is responsible for such systems, and the responsibility lies with the struggle against God, the systematic elimination of all that is Christian. Marxism is nothing but a "cheap version" of this plan. Will man surrender to the love of God, will he recognize his tragic mistake? Will he see through the deceits of "the father of lies" and listen once more to the word by which God has said everything to humanity? God's essential work will always remain the Cross and Resurrection of Christ.

Is Only Rome Right?—Here we need to explain the Christian doctrine of salvation and of the mediation of salvation. There is salvation only and exclusively in Christ. The Church, inasmuch as it is the body of Christ, is simply an instrument of this salvation. Man is saved in the Church by being brought into the Mystery of the Divine Trinity. But the Church is a living body and is more than just its visible aspect. Thus, Vatican II is far from proclaiming any kind of *ecclesiocentrism.* Its teaching is *Christocentric* in all of its aspects. In Christ, the Church is a communion. Its character as a communion renders the Church similar to the communion of the Divine Trinity. Thanks to this communion, the Church is the instrument of man's salvation. But it is Christ Himself who is the active subject of man's salvation through the shedding of His own blood. Those who are formal members of the Church but who do not persist in charity—even if they remain in the Church in "body," but not in "heart"—cannot be saved. But besides formal membership in the Church, the sphere of salvation can also include other forms of relation to the Church. This doctrine is extremely open. It cannot be accused of an *ecclesiological exclusivism.* Although the Catholic Church knows that it has received *the fullness of the means of salvation*, the Church, precisely because it is Catholic, is open to dialogue with all other Christians, with the followers of non-Christian religions, and also with all people of good will. We wish to become true worshippers of God, those who worship Him in spirit and in truth. But the mystery of the Church is larger than the visible structure and organization of the Church. Structure and organization are at the service of the mystery and there is even a mystical element here to the fullness of the Church. The spiritual, mystical dimensions of the Church are much greater than any sociological statistics could ever possibly show.

In Search of Lost Unity—We must first speak of positive forces. The Second Vatican Council set the Church on the path to ecumenism. My own country of Poland is deeply rooted in ecumenical traditions, being a crossroads of east and west, with many nationalities and religions. Tolerance and openness have always been a trait of Polish culture. There have been disappointments in ecumenical dialogue, but more powerful than these is the fact that the path to Christian unity has been undertaken with renewed vigor. Our divisions are contrary to the will of Christ. Further, "what separates us as believers in Christ is much less than what unites." This is the heart of ecumenical thinking. Indeed, the first seven ecumenical councils were held for the first millennium of Christianity. So there is a basis for dialogue and *for the growth of unity,* a growth that should occur at the same rate at which we are able to overcome our divisions—divisions that to a great degree result from the idea that one can have a monopoly on truth. Our different approaches to understanding and living out one's faith in Christ can, in certain cases, be complementary; they do not have to be mutually exclusive. However, there is also need to determine where the genuine divisions start, the point beyond which faith is compromised. We must recognize where the doctrinal divisions are narrow (with the Orthodox) or wider (with the Reformation churches). We must acknowledge that difficulties of a psychological and historical nature play a great role beyond the doctrinal differences. And yet there is a growing desire to work for Christian unity. The road itself is a process which is difficult. It is necessary to rid ourselves of stereotypes, of old habits. And above all it is necessary to recognize the unity that already exists. Much prayer will be needed, as well as great commitment to the task of profound conversation. The true protagonist remains the Holy Spirit. We Christians need to be more united, as in the first millennium of the faith, as we approach the third millennium. We can trust that "the one who began this good work in us will bring it to completion."

Why Divided?—There are well-known historical reasons of course, but there are also metahistorical reasons. A more negative one would see in these divisions the bitter fruit of sins committed by Christians. Yet God can bring good out of evil. Thus, could it not be that these divisions have also been a path continually leading the Church to discover the untold wealth contained in Christ's gospel and in the redemption accomplished by Christ? More generally, we can affirm that human knowledge and human action require a certain *dialectic.* It is necessary for humanity to achieve unity through plurality, to learn to come together in the one Church, even while presenting a plurality of ways of thinking and acting, of cultures and civilizations. Nonetheless, this cannot be a justification for the divisions that continue to deepen! *The time must come for the love that unites us to be manifested.* Certainly, mutual respect is a prerequisite for authentic ecumenism. Further, preserving the unity of the flock is a specific pastoral duty conferred on Peter. *The Petrine ministry is also a ministry of unity.* Therefore, the successor of Peter must not create obstacles but must open up paths. You are able to strengthen others only insofar as you are aware of your own weakness. The great truth of God, meant for man's salvation, cannot be preached or put into practice except by loving. To live the truth in love: this is what is always necessary.

The Church and the Council—Despite different perspectives concerning its effects, the Second Vatican Council was a great gift for the Church, but we must interpret it correctly and defend it from tendentious interpretations. I regard it as a special gift from God that I was able to take part in the Council from the first day to the last. On the basis of my experience at the Council I wrote *Sources of Renewal,* an attempt to repay the debt to the Holy Spirit incurred by every Bishop who participated in the Council. It was a unique occasion for listening to others, but also for creative thinking. I was a member of the working group that prepared the document *Gaudium et Spes,* working with Cardinal Garrone, Yves Congar, and Henri de Lubac. The Council was a great experience for the Church; it was—as we said at the time—*the "seminary of the Holy Spirit."* The words of the Holy Spirit always represent a deeper insight into the eternal mystery and point out the paths to be walked by those entrusted with the task of bringing this mystery to the contemporary world. Even the fact that those men were called together by the Holy Spirit and formed, during the Council, a special community that listened together, prayed together, thought and created together, has a fundamental importance for evangelization, for the *new evangelization, which originated precisely at the Second Vatican Council.*

A "Dialogue of Salvation"—Vatican II was not so much a defensive one, to oppose a particular heresy, as in earlier cases. Rather it was set in motion by a double process: on the one hand, overcoming the divisions in Christianity which had multiplied throughout the second millennium; on the other, as much as possible in common, the preaching of the Gospel on the threshold of the third millennium. Its style was *ecumenical,* with a great openness to dialogue, a dialogue described by Pope Paul VI as a "dialogue of salvation"—for Christians, for non-Christians, indeed for the whole modern world including those who do not believe. *Truth in fact cannot be confined.* Truth is for one and for all. And if this truth comes about through love, then it becomes even more universal. This style and spirit will be remembered as the essential truth about the Council, not the controversies between "liberals" and "conservatives"—controversies seen in political, not religious terms—to which some people wanted to reduce the whole Council. The Council will continue to be a challenge and a duty for all Churches and for each person for a long time to come. This challenge has been taken up at different levels in the Church. For example, the post-conciliar Synods of Bishops with the Pope and of priests and laymen with their Bishops have become a means for expressing the responsibility of each person toward the Church. This sense of responsibility is certainly a source for renewal which will shape the image of the Church for generations to come. Again, out of the Synod of Bishops came the *Catechism of the Catholic Church*, despite the fact that some theologians, at times whole groups, thought such a thing was obsolete. Similarly, the new Code of Canon Law has been a timely initiative which met a need within the Church. The Catechism was also indispensable, in order that all the richness of the teaching of the Church following the Second Vatican Council could be preserved in a new synthesis and be given a new direction. It became a best-seller worldwide. *The world, tired of ideology, is opening itself to the truth.* If we consider how much has been accomplished and how much is being accomplished, it is clear that the Council will not remain a dead letter. The Spirit who spoke through the Second Vatican Council did not speak in vain.

A Qualitative Renewal—Did the Council throw open the doors so that people today could enter the Church, or so that individuals and groups could begin to leave the Church? Such a question reflects a certain truth, especially if we look at the Church in western Europe (even though there are now also many signs of religious renewal there). But we must also take into consideration all that is happening in the rest of the world: central and eastern Europe, North and South America, mission countries, Africa, India and the Pacific, Asia, including China. In many of these countries, the Church has been built on the witness of martyrs and is growing with ever-increasing vigor, even if still in a minority. Since the Council, we have been witnessing a qualitative renewal, religious movements are being born and are flourishing. The new movements are oriented, before all else, toward the renewal of the individual and involve for the most part lay people, who are married and have professions, while also including consecrated religious. The ideal of the world's renewal in Christ springs directly from the fundamental duty of baptism. Moreover, it would be wrong to speak only of people leaving the Church. There are also people who come back. Above all, there has been a very radical transformation of the underlying model, from a quantitative to a more qualitative model. This also is the result of the Council. The post-conciliar Church has difficulties in the area of doctrine and discipline (though not serious enough to present a real threat of new divisions), but it is marked by an intense collegiality among the world's bishops. In a divided world, the unity of the Catholic Church, which transcends national boundaries, remains a great force, as is acknowledged even by its enemies. Not everyone is comfortable with this force, but the Church continues to speak with the Apostles: "It is impossible for us not to speak about what we have seen and heard."

The Reaction of the "World"—The phrase refers to the reception of the Church's teaching in today's world, especially in the area of ethics and morals. Is the Pope (and the Church) out of touch on morality, especially as regards sexual ethics? The world is going in the direction of an ever greater freedom of conduct. Is the Church moving backward, being left behind? This opinion is widespread, but I am convinced that it is quite wrong. The encyclical *Veritatis Splendor* demonstrates this and addresses the great threat posed to Western Civilization by *moral relativism.* With Pope Paul VI in *Humanae Vitae,* we must battle against such relativism for the sake of the essential good of man, whether it be convenient or inconvenient. "The time will come when people will not tolerate sound doctrine," says St. Paul, and unfortunately that seems to characterize the situation today. The media have conditioned society to listen to what it wants to hear. An even worse situation occurs when theologians, and especially moralists, ally themselves with the media, which obviously pay a great deal of attention to what they have to say when it opposes "sound doctrine." Indeed, *when the true doctrine is unpopular, it is not right to seek easy popularity.* The Church must be honest about what it takes to gain eternal life; the road is not broad and comfortable, but narrow and difficult. The truth, even the most demanding truth, is better than an appearance of truth, which creates only the illusion of moral honesty. Moreover, the idea that the world is growing toward a greater freedom of behavior while the Church is supposedly at a standstill hides that relativism which is so detrimental to man. Not only abortion, but also contraception, *are ultimately bound up with the truth about man.* Moving away from this truth does not represent a step forward and cannot be considered a measure of "ethical progress." Concerning faith in the Church, remember that in the Creeds we say, *I believe in the Church.* We place the Church on the same level as the Mystery of the Holy Trinity and the mysteries of the Incarnation and Redemption, but with this difference: *that we not only believe in the Church but at the same time we are the Church.* Our faith in the Church has been renewed and deepened by the Council and once again entrusted to us as a duty. Furthermore, each of the baptized participates, albeit at his own level, in the prophetic, priestly, and kingly mission of Christ. Therefore, we are talking not only about changing concepts but also of renewing attitudes. The Church is a teaching Church, but it is also a learning Church through the individuals within it and their participation in its mission. For a long time, the Church paid more attention to its institutional and hierarchical dimension and neglected somewhat its fundamental dimension of grace and charism, which is proper to the people of God. But let us return to the current religious situation in Europe. The fall of Communism did not lead to an instinctive return to religion at all levels, as some hoped. And yet in many instances, in Russia and central Europe, there has been a return to the practices of the Orthodox Church and—thanks to a new religious freedom—a rebirth of the Catholic Church, as well as a new influence of Protestant communities and *Western Sects* (with great economic resources at their disposal). But where does the true power of the Church lie? With her saints and with her martyrs who witness to the world. These saints have never been lacking and have been numerous in this century: true martyrs and authentic saints faced with oppression and ready to die for Christ—among Catholics, Orthodox, and Protestants as well. They have completed in their death as martyrs the redemptive sufferings of Christ and, at the same time, they have become the foundation of a new world, a new Europe, and a new civilization.

Does "Eternal Life" exist?—Though it is true that in recent pastoral practice some of the emphasis on the individual in relation to the "last things" (death, judgment, heaven, and hell) has been lost, it is nonetheless present in Vatican II (*Lumen Gentium*) and must never be lost. Traditional spirituality has reminded the individual of the last things, and in this it has been profoundly personal: you as an individual will be judged before God on your entire life, your actions, your words, your thoughts—even the most secret. This goes to the heart of man's inner world, stressing the freedom and responsibility before God which constitutes man's greatness. To deny these things, or to no longer speak of them, constitutes a threat to this basic greatness of man and to his call to heroism and holiness, which is universal and profoundly personal for every member of the Church. Now to this *individual eschatology,* profoundly rooted in Divine Revelation, the Council added or emphasized an *eschatology of the Church and the world.* It must be admitted that this eschatological vision was only faintly present in traditional teaching, and yet it is an original, biblical teaching. The eschatological tradition, which centered upon the so-called *Last Things,* is placed by the Council in this fundamental biblical vision. Eschatology, as I have already mentioned, is profoundly anthropological, but in light of the New Testament, it is above all centered on Christ and the Holy Spirit, and it is also, in a certain sense, cosmic. The question, or the problem, is whether man as an individual might not end up getting lost in this cosmic dimension. And *to a certain degree man does get lost;* so too do preachers, catechists, teachers; as a result, they no longer have the courage to preach the threat of hell. And perhaps those who listen to them have stopped being afraid of hell.

In fact, people of our time have become insensitive to the Last Things. This is partly due to secularization and a consumer mentality oriented toward the enjoyment of earthly good; perhaps it is also partly due to an insensitivity to evil, humiliation, and contempt after the experience of the concentration camps, gulags, bombings, and catastrophes of this century. Nonetheless, *faith in God, as Supreme Justice,* has not become irrelevant to man; the expectation remains that there is Someone who, in the end, will be able to speak the truth about the good and evil which man does, Someone able to reward the good and punish the bad. No one else but He is capable of doing it. This is a common denominator for all monotheistic religions, as well as for others. In Christ we discover that this God who is the just Judge is, above all, Love. Not just Mercy, but Love. But this requires a certain change in focus with regard to eschatology. *Eschatology has already begun with the coming of Christ,* with His redemptive death and resurrection, proclaiming forgiveness and the beginning of "a new heaven and a new earth." In Christ, God revealed to the world that he desires everyone to be saved. In light of this, the question arises, can anyone be damned? Theologians beginning with Origen and continuing through von Balthasar today have grappled with this problem, yet the ancient councils rejected the idea of a final regeneration of all, which would indirectly abolish hell. The words of Christ are unequivocal; He clearly speaks of those who will go to eternal punishment. Who will these be? This is a mystery, truly inscrutable. Yet is not hell in a certain sense the ultimate safeguard of man's moral conscience? Is not God who is Love also ultimate Justice? Can He tolerate these terrible crimes, can they go unpunished? Isn't final punishment in some way necessary in order to reestablish moral equilibrium in the complex history of humanity? We also have the question of purgatory. The holy scriptures include the concept of the *purifying fire.* The "living flame of love," of which St. John of the Cross speaks, is above all a purifying fire. Here we do not find ourselves before a mere tribunal. We present ourselves before the power of Love itself. *Before all else, it is Love that judges.* God, who is Love, judges through love. It is love that demands purification, before man can be made ready for that union with God which is his ultimate vocation and destiny. The Church still has its eschatological awareness, leading men to eternal life, essential to its vocation.

What is the Use of Believing?—The usefulness of faith is not comparable to any good, not even one of a moral nature; it lies precisely in the fact that a person believes and entrusts himself, responding to God's word. Nevertheless, God absolutely does not want to force us to respond to His word. It is part of the dignity of man that we are bound to search for the truth, above all religious truth, and then to arrange our lives according to such truth. But in keeping with man's dignity, this search must be free: man cannot be forced to accept the truth. This has always been the teaching of Christ and the Church, elaborated well by such thinkers as Aquinas and Newman. The conscience may err out of invincible ignorance without losing its dignity and authority. But this cannot be said of the man who does very little to search for the truth and good, or when through the habit of sin conscience itself becomes almost blind. Thus, what is not permitted is that a man culpably indulge in error without trying to reach the truth. Ultimately, the usefulness of faith consists in the fact that, through faith, man achieves the good of his rational nature, as is his duty not only to God but also to himself. Thus, with many others in the Church and in history, we must protest against those who attempted to force faith, "making conversions by the sword." Christ certainly desires faith of man and for man, but He wants this in full respect of human dignity. In the very search for faith an implicit faith is already present, and therefore the necessary condition for salvation is already satisfied. However, in such a case, if a life is truly upright it is because the Gospel (not known and therefore not rejected on a conscious level) is in reality already at work in the depths of the person who searches for the truth with an honest effort and who willingly accepts it as soon as it becomes known to him. This is a manifestation of grace and of the work of the Spirit who blows where He wills and as He wills. This clarification is necessary to avoid the Pelagian interpretation that even without Divine grace man could lead a good and happy life. Ultimately, only God can save man, but He expects man to cooperate. This is the doctrine of *synergism* in the Eastern tradition. With God, man "creates" the world; with God, man "creates" his personal salvation. The divinization of man comes from God. But here, too, man must cooperate with God.

Human Rights—Human rights were inscribed by the creator in the order of creation; so we cannot speak of "concessions" on the part of human institutions when those rights are recognized. The Gospel is the fullest confirmation of all of human rights. The Redeemer confirms human rights simply by restoring the fullness of the dignity man received when God created him in His image and likeness. This issue gradually became central for me. First in the polemic against Marxism, the Marxists themselves made man and his moral life the center of their arguments. My book *The Acting Person* was first noticed and attacked by the Marxists; they recognized it as an unsettling element in their polemic against religion and against the Church. However, the book did not arise out of disputes with the Marxists. I had long had an interest in man as a person. Through literature I became fascinated with man as creator of language and as subject of literature; later in my priestly vocation man became the central theme of my pastoral work. In those years, my greatest involvement was with young people, who asked me *about how to live*, how to face and resolve problems of love and marriage, not to mention problems related to work. Out of this grew the book *Love* *and Responsibility*, in which I formulate the concept of a *personalistic principle: the person is a being for whom the only suitable dimension is love.* We are just to a person if we love him (God or man). This excludes the possibility of treating him as an object of pleasure, as Kant so clearly saw in response to utilitarianism. But Kant did not fully interpret the commandment of love, but only expressed it negatively. It requires more; it requires the *affirmation of the person as a person.* The true personalistic interpretation of the commandment of love is found in the words of the Council: "Man, who is the only creature on earth that God wanted for his own sake, can fully discover himself only by the sincere giving of himself." Here the principle that a person has value by the simple fact that he is a person finds very clear expression, yet he can only realize himself though love, through a sincere gift of self. Man affirms himself most completely by giving of himself. If we deprive human freedom of this possibility, then this freedom can become dangerous. If we cannot accept the prospect of giving ourselves as a gift, then the danger of a selfish freedom will always be present. Kant, Scheler, and others who shared his ethics of values fought against this danger, but a complete expression of all this is already found in the Gospel. We can find in the Gospel a consistent declaration of all human rights, even those that can for various reasons make us feel uneasy.

The Defense of Every Life—For man, the right to life is the *fundamental right:* the right to be born and then continue to live until one's natural end. A part of our contemporary culture has wanted to deny that right, turning it into an "uncomfortable" one that has to be defended. The question of conceived but unborn children is a particularly delicate yet clear problem. The *legalization of the termination of pregnancy* is none other that authorization given to an adult, with the approval of established law, to take the lives of children yet unborn and, thus, incapable of defending themselves. It is difficult to imagine a more unjust situation. This is not a question of a woman's right to *free choice.* It is not possible to speak of the right to choose when a clear moral evil is involved, when what is at stake is the commandment *Do not kill!* Might this commandment allow of *exception?* The answer in and of itself is no. The hypothesis of legitimate self-defense (wherein in any case one must choose the option that does the least damage and if possible saves the life of the aggressor) does not fit here. *A child conceived in its mother's womb is never an unjust aggressor;* it is a defenseless being waiting to be welcomed and helped. However, it is necessary to recognize that, in this context, we are witnessing true human tragedies. Often the woman is the victim of male selfishness. Therefore, in firmly rejecting "pro choice" it is necessary to become courageously "pro woman," promoting a choice that is truly in favor of women. It is precisely the woman, in fact, who pays the highest price, not only for her motherhood, but even more for its destruction, for the suppression of the life of the child who has been conceived. The only honest stance, in these cases, is that of *radical solidarity with the woman.* Yet we cannot afford forms of permissiveness that would lead directly to the trampling of human rights and the destruction of values fundamental to individual lives, families, and society itself. This is the *culture of death.* But the opposite of the culture of death is not irresponsible global population growth (its growth rate must be taken into consideration), but responsible parenthood—the necessary condition for human love and for authentic conjugal love, because love cannot be irresponsible. The most effective way to be at the service of the truth of responsible parenthood is to show its ethical and anthropological foundations. Here I must mention Emmanuel Levinas and his personalism and philosophy of dialogue. For him, the face reveals the person. It is through his face that man speaks, and in particular, every man who has suffered a wrong speaks and says the words "Do not kill me!" *The human face and the commandment "Do not kill" are ingeniously joined in Levinas, and, thus, become a testimony for our age.*

The Mother of God—Totuus Tuus ("I am completely yours, O Mary") is the motto of my papacy and is more than just an expression of piety or devotion. Thanks to St. Louis de Montfort, I came to understand that true devotion to the Mother of God is actually Christocentric, indeed, it is very profoundly rooted in the Mystery of the Blessed Trinity, and the mysteries of the Incarnation and Redemption. Further, devotion to Mary not only addresses a need of the heart, a sentimental inclination, but it also corresponds to the objective truth about the Mother of God. The Second Vatican Council in *Lumen Gentium* (Ch. 8) made great strides with regard to Marian doctrine and devotion. These teachings reflected all my youthful experiences: stopping before the image of Our Lady of Perpetual Help, the tradition of the Carmelite scapular, the pilgrimages to the shrine of Kalwaria, the Black Madonna of Our Lady of Jasna Gora, Queen of Poland—a source of special and new evangelization and of great events in the life of Poland. The present Pope's attitude is one of *total abandonment to Mary.*

Women—Marian devotion is not only a form of piety, it is also an attitude—an attitude toward woman as woman. If our century has been characterized by a growing feminism, this trend is a reaction to the lack of respect accorded each woman. I was brought up in a time of great respect and consideration for women, especially for women who were mothers. I think that a certain contemporary feminism finds its roots in the absence of true respect for woman. Revealed truth teaches us something different. But in our civilization woman has become, before all else, an object of pleasure. It is very significant, on the other hand, that in the midst of this very situation the authentic *theology of woman* is being reborn. The spiritual beauty, the particular genius, of women is being rediscovered. The bases for the consolidation of the position of women in life, not only family life but also social and cultural life, are being redefined. And for this purpose, we must return to the figure of Mary, and devotion to her, as a powerful and creative inspiration.

"Be Not Afraid"—This was an exhortation addressed to all people, to conquer fear in the present world situation; fear of what they themselves have created and produced; ultimately, fear of themselves. Why should we have no fear? Because man has been redeemed by God. *The power of Christ's Cross and Resurrection is greater than any evil which man could or should fear.* We return here too to the Mother of God. First in Poland, through Jasna Gora, and then later when I inherited the Ministry of Peter in Rome, I saw again *Mary's participation in the victory of Christ.* This became clear to me above all from the experience of my own people. But on the universal level as well, if victory comes it will be brought by Mary. *Christ will conquer through her, because He wants the Church's victories now and in the future to be linked to her.* I held this conviction even though I did not yet know very much about Fatima. And then came the events of May13, 1981, when I was wounded by gunshots in St. Peter's Square, on the exact anniversary of Mary's appearance to the three children at Fatima. With this event, didn't Christ perhaps say, once again, "Be not afraid?" At the end of the second millennium, we need these words more than ever. Peoples and nations of the entire world need to hear these words. *Their conscience needs to grow in the certainty that Someone exists who holds in His hands the destiny of this passing world; Someone who holds the keys to death and the netherworld; Someone who is the Alpha and the Omega of human history.* And this Someone is Love, who became man, was crucified and is risen, and is present among men—Eucharistic love—the infinite source of communion. It is He who says "Be not afraid!" Yet the Gospel is certainly demanding, and Christ certainly does not say "Be not afraid" in order to nullify in some way that which He has required. Rather, by these words, He confirms the entire truth of the Gospel and all the demands it contains. At the same time, however, He reveals that *His demands never exceed man's abilities.* To accept the Gospel's demands means to affirm all of our humanity, to see in it the beauty desired by God, while recognizing, in light of the Power of God Himself, our own weaknesses. "What is impossible for men is possible for God." These two dimensions cannot be separated: the moral demands God makes of man and, by the gift of His grace, the demands of His saving love to which God in a certain sense has bound Himself. God desires the salvation of man; He desires that humanity find that fulfillment to which He Himself has destined it. *It is very important to cross the threshold of hope*, not to stop before it but to let oneself be led.

Crossing the Threshold of Hope—"The fear of the Lord is the beginning of wisdom." We need to cultivate this true fear of the Lord as a gift of the Holy Spirit and pray the people everywhere will receive this gift as the beginning of wisdom. But this is not the fear of a slave. It is filial fear, not servile fear. The authentic and full expression of this fear is Christ Himself. He has come into the world to set man free through love, which drives out all fear. Every sign of servile fear vanishes before the awesome power of the All-powerful and all-present one. Its place is taken by filial concern, in order that God's will be done on earth. But is contemporary man moved by a filial fear of God, a fear that is first of all love? One might think—and there is no lack of evidence to this effect—that Hegel's paradigm of the master and the servant is more present in people's consciousness today than is wisdom. But in the Gospel of Christ, the paradigm of master-slave is radically transformed into the paradigm of *father-son.* The father-son paradigm is ageless. Yet the "rays of fatherhood" meet a first resistance in the obscure but real fact of original sin. *This is truly a key for interpreting reality.* Original sin attempts to abolish fatherhood, destroying its rays which permeate the created world, placing in doubt the truth about God who is Love and leaving man only with a sense of the master-slave relationship. As a result, the Lord appears jealous of His power over the world and over man; and consequently, man feels goaded to do battle against God. In sum, then, we face the following paradox. *In order to set contemporary man free from fear* of himself, of the world, of others, of earthly powers, of oppressive systems, in order to set him free from every manifestation of a servile fear before that "prevailing force" which believers call God, *it is necessary to pray fervently that he will bear and cultivate in his heart that true fear of God which is the beginning of wisdom.* This fear of God is the *saving power of the Gospel.* It is constructive, never destructive. It creates people who allow themselves to be led by responsibility, by responsible love. It creates holy men and women—true Christians—to whom the future of the world ultimately belongs. "Be not afraid."

—adapted from *Crossing the Threshold of Hope* by Pope John Paul II

The Acting Person

Introduction

1. THE EXPERIENCE OF MAN

The Meaning of Man's "Experience"—Man's experience of anything outside of himself is always associated with the experience of himself, and he never experiences anything external without having at the same time the experience of himself. Experience is not just a set of sensations or emotions subsequently ordered by the mind ("phenomenalistic"). I myself emerge from all the moments and am present in every one of them in experience and understanding.

Experience as the Basis of the Knowledge of Man—We also have both experience of other men as objects and knowledge about men through various domains of learning, but such knowledge and the sharing of it ultimately springs from one's own experience while also influencing the latter.

The Ego and Man in the Field of Experience—Everyone is the object of his own unique experience and no external relation to any other human being, no matter how close, can take the place of the experiential relation that the subject has to himself.

Experience and Comprehension—There is a unity to human experience above the level of mere sensing (the level of animals) based on the participation of mind in the acts of human experience. There is an indispensable intellectual element in the formation of experiential acts and in the experience of oneself as a man.

Simultaneity of the Inner and Outer Aspects in the Experience of Man—I experience myself from within and others from without but these aspects complement and compensate each other in the totality of cognition. Thus, the complexity of the experience of man is dominated by its intrinsic simplicity. The complexity itself shows that the whole experience, and consequently the cognition of man, is composed of both the experience that everyone has relatively to himself and the experience of other men, the experience had both from the inside and from the outside.

2. COGNITION OF THE PERSON RESTS ON THE EXPERIENCE OF MAN

The Empirical Standpoint is not Identifiable with Phenomenalism—The "empirical" approach adopted in this work means a return to the truths given in man's immediate experience. This is not at all to be identified with the "phenomenalistic" conception of experience reducing the latter to the functions and content of sense alone. This would lead to deep contradictions and serious misunderstandings about man. It is not just sense impressions alone or some mere surface aspects but man himself, man with his conscious acting or action, which is given in experience.

The Argument Begins with the Fact that Man's Acting is Phenomenologically Given— Experience is indicative of the directness of cognition itself, of a direct cognitive relation to the object. We grasp the fact of man's acting, not just some preliminary set of sense data which the mind then organizes and calls the "acting person." On the contrary, it seems that the mind is engaged already in experience itself and that the experience enables it to establish its relation to the object, a relation that is also, though in a different way, direct.

Action as a Special Moment of Insight into the Person— In every human experience there is also a certain measure of understanding of what is experienced. This is contrary to phenomenalism but fits very well with phenomenology, which stresses more than anything the unity in the acts of human cognition. Man manifests or reveals himself in a particular way through acts of the person ("man-acts"). Man has this ability to manifest himself to himself and this ability is confirmed in the content of experience, the experience of the person acting on innumerable occasions. Traditionally it has been understood that human action in the proper sense of the word presupposes a person. However, what we wish to stress as our starting point is that action *reveals the* person, and we look at the person through his action. We experience man as a person, and we are convinced of it because he performs actions.

The Moral Modality of Human Actions—But our experience and our intellectual apprehension of the person in and through his actions are derived in particular from the fact that our actions have a moral value: they are morally good or morally bad as an intrinsic feature. Moreover, only the acting in which the agent is assumed to be a person—we have stressed earlier that only such acting deserves to be called "action"—has moral significance. Thus, there is an essential connection between ethics and anthropology or the philosophy of man. Good and evil manifest themselves in actions and by actions they become a part of man. The more philosophical reflection becomes comprehensive, the more anthropological questions tend to appear.

Moral Value Deepens our Insight into the Person—Actions reveal the person and are the most adequate starting point for comprehending the dynamic nature of the person. But moral values as the inherent property of actions and in their actual "becoming" through actions give us an even better and deeper insight into the person. Through good or evil actions, man himself becomes good or evil. The person emerges more completely into view in moral action than in non-moral or so-called "pure" action.

Anthropology and Ethics Rest on the Unity of the Experience of the Moral Man—The source of our knowledge of the reality that is the person lies in action, but even more so in the dynamic or existential aspects of morality. The real objective unity of the experience of moral value and the experience of man is, thus, the fundamental condition of apprehending and then progressively comprehending the person.

Ethics as the Common Factor—We focus on the person-action relation as if pulled out of brackets in order to reveal itself more fully in its own reality as revelatory of the person but also for a deeper understanding of human morality.

3. THE STAGES OF COMPREHENSION AND THE LINES OF INTERPRETATION

Induction and the Unity of Meaning—The experience of man, actions revealing the person, is multiple (composed of innumerable data) and complex (given from the outside with others, from the inside with myself). Grasping the essential sameness within the data (grasping the same person-action relation within each action) is achieved by induction: grasping mentally the unity of meaning from among the multiplicity and complexity of phenomena. The person is revealed and grasped by the mind within the wealth and diversity of factual data.

Reduction Allows Us to Explore the Experience of Man—The rich inductive experience of man revealing the person through action also stimulates the need for discussing it and provides the basis for the discussion. This is the step toward reductive understanding through which experience is explored. "Reductive" here does not mean diminishing or limiting the wealth of the experiential object, but rather is a cognitive process in which the original apprehension of the person in action is brought out more fully.

Reduction and Interpretation Lead to a Theory Issuing from Human Praxis—Our question is not how to act consciously but what conscious acting or action really is, how the action reveals the person and how it helps us to gain a full and comprehensive understanding of the person. Each individual experience of the person in action has a subjective and an objective component and induction reveals that practical cognition or understanding (praxis) necessary and sufficient for a man to live and to act consciously.

Issues Relevant to Adequate Interpretation—*From the vast wealth of inductive experience about the person, we move to reduction. To reduce means* to convert to suitable arguments and items of evidence *or, in other words,* to explain and interpret, *advancing step by step to trace the object given us in experience and in the manner in which it is given. We seek to penetrate something which actually exists and the arguments explaining this existence have to correspond to experience. Intellectual understanding is intrinsic to human sensuous experience but also transcends it. To experience is one thing and to understand and interpret is quite another. The aim of interpretation is to produce an intellectual image of the object, an image that is adequate and coincident with the object itself.*

The Understanding and Interpretation of the Object—The understanding itself also matures only gradually from the initial apprehension of the acting person to the final and complete interpretation and presentation in a manner communicable to other people. One of our main tasks will be to integrate correctly the two aspects of man's experience of the person-action relation: the immanent experience in relation to the ego and the outer experience extending to all men other than myself.

4. THE CONCEPTION OF PERSON AND ACTION TO BE PRESENTED IN THIS STUDY

Attempt to Approach the Subjectivity of Man—On the ground of the integrated experience of man, in contrast to the behavioristic approach, the person is revealed through action, because in this experience man is given us from the inside and not only outwardly. This yields new possibilities for interpretation and integration of the inner and outer aspects of human experience. Much more important than any attempt to attribute absolute significance to either aspect of human experience is the need to acknowledge their mutual relativeness.

The Aspect of Consciousness—Our study will not deal with consciousness alone but with conscious action as that dynamic reality itself which simultaneously reveals the person as its efficacious subject. Action as the moment of the special apprehension of the person always manifests itself through consciousness—as does the *person,* whose essence the action discloses in a specific manner on the ground of the experience of man, particularly the inner experience. We must deal first (Chapters 1&2) with the interrelation of consciousness and the efficacy of the person, then (Chapters 3&4) with the specific transcendence disclosed by the person's action.

Transcendence and Integration of the Person—Our first and chief concern is to educe from the experience of action (that is, of "man-acts") that evidence which shows man to be a person or "brings the person into view." But the understanding of the transcendence of the person in action also allows us to perceive simultaneously the moment of the integration of the person in the whole of the psychosomatic complexity of the human person. In Chapters 5&6 we shall analyze this complexity. Finally, in Chapter 7, we shall deal in an introductory fashion with the notion of subjectivity by participation in relation to others and to community.

The Significance of Personalistic Problems—Man has made many tremendous advances and discoveries in culture and civilization, but he must never cease to wonder at the mysterious being which he is himself. Having conquered so many secrets of nature the conqueror himself must have his own mysteries ceaselessly unraveled anew. Since man is the first, closest, and most frequent object of experience, he is in danger of becoming usual and commonplace to himself, too ordinary even for himself. This must be avoided. Our study attempts to oppose such a falling into the rut of habit and to rediscover wonderment at the human being. Man should not lose his proper place in the world he has shaped himself.

PART ONE

CONSCIOUSNESS AND EFFICACY

CHAPTER ONE: THE ACTING PERSON IN THE ASPECT OF CONSCIOUSNESS

1. THE HISTORICAL WEALTH OF THE EXPRESSION "HUMAN ACT"

The Act in Its Traditional Interpretation—It is only man's deliberate acting with purpose that we call an act or action. In the Aristotelian-Thomistic tradition, this is the *actus humanus* with its corresponding *potentia.* This considers man as the subject who acts and his potentiality as the source of acting. More precisely, this is also the *actus voluntarius,* indicating the power (of free will) that serves as the dynamic basis in conscious acting, the basis of action.

Action as Peculiar to the Person—Human act implies conscious acting and such action may serve as a source of knowledge of the person. The potentiality is that of the personal being, so that action is to be interpreted not only as the human action but also as the action of a person. "Action," in the sense it is used here, is equivalent to the acting of man as a person. Rather than assume the person as the source of action as the tradition does, we will attempt to bring into full view the person revealed in his actions.

Voluntariness as Indication of Consciousness—By "action" is meant the conscious acting characteristic of the will. So a human act must be conscious and voluntary. We will have to gradually unfold the implications of these different aspects while never taking a mere aspect for the whole. The whole is the complex reality of the human person as revealed in his actions.

2. THE ATTEMPT TO DISCERN CONSCIOUSNESS IN THE "HUMAN ACT"

Is this Analysis Possible and Necessary?—A distinction can be made between conscious acting and the consciousness of acting. For man not only acts consciously, but also has the consciousness that he is acting and even that he is acting consciously. Our discussion will henceforth concentrate on this consciousness of acting and consequently on the consciousness of the acting person. It is possible and even necessary to discern, in that dynamic whole, consciousness as such, and to examine it as a special aspect. But our analysis will always be of the consciousness of the person acting and will, thus, be an avenue toward revealing the dynamism and efficacy of the whole human being.

How is Consciousness Implied in the Human Act?—We want to bring out the fact that consciousness constitutes a specific and unique aspect in human action. In the scholastic approach the aspect of consciousness was on the one hand only implied and, as it were, hidden in "rationality" while on the other hand contained in the will (understood as *appetitus rationalis)* and expressed by *voluntarius.* Our task is to go farther and to exhibit consciousness as an intrinsic and constitutive aspect of the dynamic structure, that is, of the acting person. Man's awareness of his own acting and that it is he who is acting is simultaneous with conscious acting and, so to speak, accompanies it. But man's consciousness is also present before and after each particular acting. Every action finds consciousness, if one may say so, already there. This accompanying presence of consciousness is decisive in making man aware of his acting and of his acts as the acts of a person and requires exposition.

In What Sense is Consciousness Used Here?—"Contained" (i.e., mirrored or reflected) in consciousness in its own specific manner is the whole man, as well as the whole world accessible to this concrete man—the man who is me, that is, myself. It lies in the essence of cognitive acts performed by man to investigate a thing, to objectivize it intentionally, and in this way to comprehend it. In this sense, cognitive acts have an intentional character, since they are directed toward the cognitive object. But consciousness as such is restricted to mirroring what has already been cognized. As "consciousness" we understand then "reflecting consciousness"—that is, consciousness in its mirroring function. Thus, we attribute to consciousness the specific quality of penetrating and illuminating whatever becomes in any way man's cognitive possession.

Consciousness Is not an Autonomous Subject—Looking at consciousness, however, we see it not as a separate and self-contained reality (this would lead toward idealism) but as the subjective content of the being and acting that is conscious, the being and acting proper to man. Consciousness itself does not exist as the "substantive" subject of the acts of consciousness; rather it is a concomitant "being aware" or mirroring of the action as well as of the person acting. This mirroring function is different from the cognitive objectivization. It is not only cognitively that man enters into the world of other men and objects and even discovers himself there as one of them: he has also as his possession all this world in the image mirrored by consciousness, which is a factor in his inner, most personal life. For consciousness not only reflects but also *interiorizes* in its own specific manner what it mirrors, thus, enclosing or capturing it in the person's ego.

3. CONSCIOUSNESS AND SELF-KNOWLEDGE

Consciousness Conditioned by the Cognitive Potentiality of Man—Consciousness itself is conditioned by the power and the efficacy of active understanding (the cognitive potentiality of man) which allows us to ascertain the meaning of particular things and to intellectually incorporate them (as well as the relations between them) "into" our consciousness. Hence the various degrees of knowledge determine the different levels of consciousness. Self-knowledge consists in the understanding of one's own self and is concerned with cognitive insight into the object that I am for myself. At this point self-knowledge and consciousness come closest together but remain distinct since consciousness itself does not objectivize the ego or anything else. This function is performed by the acts of self-knowledge themselves. It is to them that every man owes the objectivizing contact with himself and his actions. Because of self-knowledge consciousness can mirror actions and their relations to the person. Without it consciousness would be deprived of meanings concerning man's self as the object of direct cognition and would then exist as if suspended in the void (idealism).

Consciousness Opened to the Ego by Self-Knowledge— Owing to self-knowledge the acting subject's ego is cognitively grasped as an object. In this way the person and his action have an objective significance in consciousness. Being the "subject" man is also the "object"; he is the object for the subject, and he does not lose his objective significance when mirrored by consciousness. Self-knowledge has as its object not only the person and the action, but also the person as being aware of himself and aware of his action.

Self-Knowledge as the Basis of Self-Consciousness—What is meant when speaking of "being conscious of an action" is not just the reflection itself in consciousness of a conscious act but intentional self-knowledge. By this phrase we mean that by an act of self-knowledge I objectivize my action in relation to my person. I objectivize the fact that my action is the actual *acting* of my person and not what would only *happen* in my person. Further, my acting is a conscious event (involving free will) and being performed according to the will may have a moral value, positive or negative, and so is either good or evil.

The Specific Position of Self-Knowledge in the Totality of Human Cognition—Every man's ego constitutes, in a way, a meeting point where all intentional acts of self-knowledge (moral, religious, social, etc.) concentrate. Real knowledge of oneself as an integral whole is the goal. Our knowledge of human beings in general can be one source for self-knowledge to make use of, but the goal is not simply generalized knowledge of the human being but the concrete knowledge of one's own being. Here man always finds fresh material for cognizing himself. *Individuum est ineffable.*

4. THE TWO-FOLD FUNCTION OF CONSCIOUSNESS AND THE EXPERIENCE OF SUBJECTIVENESS

Mirroring and Experience—Consciousness in its mirroring function permeates and illumines all that it mirrors, including self-knowledge (the self as the object of understanding). The decisive factor for unraveling the problem of the consciousness-self-knowledge relation is the objectiveness and simultaneous subjectiveness of man. Consciousness is the "ground," on which the ego manifests itself in all its peculiar objectiveness (being the object of self-knowledge) and at the same time fully experiences its own subjectiveness. Thus, we cannot restrict our analysis of consciousness solely to its mirroring. Consciousness allows us not only to have an inner view of our actions (immanent perceptions) and of their dynamic dependence on the ego, but to *experience these actions as actions and as our own.* Objective self-knowledge as well as knowledge of the "world" with its objective content are themselves "subjectified" (mirrored in consciousness).

Experience of the Ego Conditioned by the Reflexive Function of Consciousness—In consciousness we have not only the reflective function mirroring the cognized object in relation to the self, but also a reflexive trait of consciousness denoting that consciousness, so to speak, turns back naturally upon the subject. The subjectiveness of the subject is brought into prominence in experience. We discern clearly that it is one thing to *be* the subject, another thing to *be cognized* (that is, objectified) as the subject, and still a different thing to *experience* one's self as the subject of one's own acts and experiences. This last distinction we owe to the reflexive function of consciousness: the concrete man has the experience of himself as the subject and, thus, of his subjectivity, allowing designation of himself by means of the pronoun *I*. The ego is the real subject having the experience of its subjectiveness or, in other words, constituting itself in consciousness.

The Ego Constituted as Subject—It is impossible to detach the experiential ego from its ontic foundations. Every human being is given in a total or simple experience as an autonomous individual real being, as the subject of existing and acting. But every man is also given to himself as the concrete ego, and this is achieved by means of both self-consciousness and self-knowledge. Self-knowledge ascertains that the being, who objectively is I, subjectively constitutes my ego, because in it I have the experience of my subjectiveness. Consciousness in intimate union with the ontically founded being and acting of the concrete man-person does not absorb it itself or overshadow this being, its dynamic reality, but, on the contrary, discloses it "inwardly" and thereby reveals it in its specific distinctness and unique correctness. This disclosing is precisely what the reflexive function of consciousness consists in.

The Experiential Manifestation of Human Spirituality—Consciousness, as long as it only mirrors and is but a reflected image, remains objectively aloof from the ego. When, however, it becomes the basis of experience, when experience is constituted by its reflexiveness, the objective aloofness disappears and consciousness penetrates the subject shaping it experientially every time an experience occurs. Without consciousness there is no human experience; this is part of the meaning of the word "rational" in the traditional conception of man as an individual substance of a rational nature.

Furthermore, consciousness opens the way to the emergence of the spirituality of the human being and gives us an insight into it. The spirituality of man's acts and action manifests itself in consciousness, which allows us to undergo the experiential innerness of our being and acting.

Consciousness and the Experience of Action in the Dimension of Moral Values—The human being experiences his acting as something thoroughly different from anything that only happens, anything that only occurs in him. It is only in connection with his acting (that is, action) that man experiences as his own the moral value of good and bad. He is not only conscious of the morality of his actions but he actually experiences it, often very deeply, in an attitude that is at once emotional and appreciative. Objectively, both action and moral values belong to and depend upon a real subject. Consciousness, owing to its mirroring function closely related to self-knowledge, allows us, on the one hand, to gain an objective awareness of the good or evil that we are the agents of in any particular action—while, on the other hand, it enables us to experience the good or evil in which its reflexiveness is manifested. What we are considering here has a reflexively inward direction that makes of the action itself as well as of the moral good or bad the fully subjective reality of man: he thereby experiences himself as the one who is either good or evil.

How Does the Ego Help in Understanding Man?—There is no denying that the sphere of self-experience and self-comprehending serves as a privileged vantage point, a point specially productive of meanings in experience and in the understanding of man. From the very start we take, as it were, a double stance: beginning "inside" ourselves we go out of our ego toward "man" and at the same time we proceed from "man" back to the ego. Thus, our knowledge of man proceeds in cycles.

5. THE EMOTIONALIZATION OF CONSCIOUSNESS

The Element of Consciousness and the Emotive Element in Man—The free exercise of the will, having an essential significance for actions, is variously modified by the emotive side of the human psyche. In relation to the body, both dimensions of consciousness are present. Man is conscious of his body, and he also experiences it; he has the experience of his corporality just as he has of his sensuality and emotionality. The world of sensations and feelings in man, who is a feeling creature and not only a thinking creature, has an objective wealth of its own. The differentiation of feelings is not merely quantitative but also qualitative, and in this respect they come in a hierarchical order. Feelings of qualitatively "higher rank" participate in man's spiritual life. The emotional life of man exerts a tremendous influence in the formation of his actions. Emotions may in some respects enhance our actions, but in others they have a restraining or even crippling effect on what in acting is essential, namely, the exercise of free will.

What Does the Emotionalization of Consciousness Consist in?—The essence of the problem consists in that emotions are not only reflected in consciousness but also affect in their own specific way the image that is formed in consciousness of various objects, including of course man's ego and his actions. Diverse feelings emotionalize consciousness, and this can be overwhelming due either to the intensity, changeability, and rapidity of emotions or due to a lack or inefficiency in one's self-knowledge and self-understanding. The task of self-knowledge is to prevent the emotionalization of consciousness from going too far, to protect consciousness from being deprived of its objectivizing relation to the totality of emotive occurrences.

Emotionalization and the Twofold Function of Consciousness: Mirroring and Reflexivity—When over-emotionalization occurs, the mirroring function of consciousness continues but the unifying core of consciousness—the ego—is rushed to the background while the enhanced feelings behave as if they were uprooted from the soil on which their unity develops. Emotions and passions are then not "experienced" by the human being but "undergone" by him or, strictly speaking, allowed to grow in him and prevail upon him in some primitive and, as it were, impersonal fashion; for "personal" signifies only that experience in which also the experienced subjectiveness of the ego is to be discerned. The reflexive function of consciousness than also loses its decisive role: subjectiveness is no longer experienced in a way that brings into prominence the personal ego as the source of experiences, as the center governing emotions. Man, then, only undergoes his emotions and allows them to dwell in him according to their own primitive forms of subjectivity, but does not experience them subjectively in a way that would bring out the personal ego as the true pivot of experience.

6. SUBJECTIVITY AND SUBJECTIVENESS

Subjectivity Inherent in the Reality of the Acting Person—We must distinguish clearly between man's "subjectivity" (which we are here considering together with the analysis of consciousness) and "subjectivism" as a mental attitude. The latter can be a mere bias, just as there can be a narrow and one-sided objectivism—neither taking into account the full reality of the human person. But to demonstrate the subjectivity of the human person is fundamental for the realistic position of this study. Without outlining an explanation of man's subjectivity, it would be impossible to grasp the full depth of the dynamic interrelation of person and action. This interrelation is not only mirrored in consciousness, as if it was reflected in an inner mirror of man's being and action; in addition, it is owing to consciousness that it obtains in its own way its final, subjective form. The form is that of experience, the experience of action, the experience had of the efficacious interrelation of person and action, and of the moral value that germinates in this dynamic system. All these are objective data, but data that hold their objectivity and reality status only and exclusively in the subjectivity of man.

The Difference between Subjectivity and Subjectivism—Subjectivism as here considered seems to consist (1) in a complete separation of experience from action, and (2) in reducing to the mere content of consciousness the moral values that, as we have figuratively put it, germinate in this action as well as in the person. However, when consciousness is absolutized it at once ceases to account for the subjectivity of man, that is to say, his being the subject, or for the subjectivity his actions; it becomes a substitute for the subject. Ultimately consciousness itself ceases to be anything real, it becomes but the subject of mental contents wherein *to be = to be perceived.* The path of subjectivism ends in idealism. On the other hand, the boundary of objectivism and realism in the conception of man—in our case this applies to the person-action totality—is marked out by the assertion of self-knowledge. In spite of its specifically conscious character, consciousness integrated by self-knowledge into the whole of a real person retains its objective significance and, thus, also the objective status in the subjective structure of man. In this perspective and due to this status, consciousness appears but due to the subjectivity of man, and so in no way can serve as the basis for subjectivism. It owes its role in human subjectivity to its being the condition of experience, in which the human ego reveals itself (experientially) as the object.

Conclusions Leading to the Analysis of Human Efficacy—Now that we have examined the aspects of consciousness in the acting person we are ready for the next step, and we can embark upon an analysis of efficacy. Even if in the course of our discussion we placed the aspect of consciousness somewhat apart and in isolation, the effect aimed at was to show off more sharply the presence of consciousness in the person's action. The features of human efficacy differ from those of consciousness though obviously the specificity of the former cannot be grasped apart from or in isolation from the latter. Each of them in its own specific manner determines both person and action.

CHAPTER TWO

AN ANALYSIS OF EFFICACY IN THE LIGHT OF HUMAN DYNAMISM

1. THE BASIC CONCEPTION AND DIFFERENTIATION OF HUMAN DYNAMISM

Introductory Remarks on the Relation of Dynamism to Consciousness—The fact that man acts is given first in the experience of "I act." We ourselves are placed, as it were, right inside this fact. Hence, when "you," "he," or "anybody else" acts, their acting can be understood on the ground of experiencing our own acting, in "I act." But not everything belonging to human dynamism is reflected in consciousness (e.g., vegetative or organic processes in the human body). Thus, we must go beyond the evidence of consciousness and investigate the total experience of man and his dynamism.

The Juxtaposition of "To Act" and "To Happen" as the Experiential Basis of Activeness and Passiveness—We may say that man's actions ("I act" as the experiential basis of activeness) and all that "happens in him" (as the experiential basis of passiveness) are not only mutually opposite but also distinctly correlated in the sense of a certain parity of both facts or both structures. In both cases man stands as the dynamic subject and unity "from within."

Note that something happening with man by external force is not at all the same as something happening in man by internal dynamism.

The Potency and Act Conjugate as Conceptual Homologue of Dynamism—The traditional metaphysics of potency and act remains the only adequate language to render the dynamic essence of (relative) change. Every actualization contains in itself both the possibility and the act, which is the real fulfillment of the possibility. It contains them not as two entities but as two interrelated forms of existence. What exists as a possibility may, because it, thus, exists, come into existence as an act; conversely, what came into existence in the act did so because of its previous existence as a potentiality.

The Ambiguity of the Concept of "Act" and Differentiation of the Experiences of Acting and Happening—"Act" in the sense of "fulfillment of a potency" applies both to "man-acts" and to "something-that-happens-in-man." Each is a concrete manifestation of the dynamism proper to man. However, this is not yet enough to adequately reveal the specific nature of "action."

2. THE DEFINITION OF EFFICACY

The Definition of Efficacy and the Differentiation of the Experiences of Acting and Happening—We can distinguish a "human act" from an "act of man." It is the moment of efficacy (having the experience of "being the actor") that determines this fundamental difference. When acting I have the experience of myself as the agent responsible for this particular form of the dynamism of myself as the subject. When there is something happening in me, then the dynamism is imparted without the efficacious participation of my ego.

The Experience of Efficacy and the Causal Relation of Person and Action—In human action ("man-acts"), there is between person and action a sensibly experiential, causal relation which brings the person (that is to say, every concrete human ego) to recognize his action to be the result of his efficacy. I am the efficient cause. Thus, I must accept such actions as truly my own. This is the domain of moral responsibility.

The Experience of Efficacy and Man's Transcendence of His Acting—The moment of efficacy, the experience of efficacy, brings forth first of all the transcendence of man relative to his own acting (I am experienced as the cause of my own acting). This is the difference between "man-acts" and "something happens in man." The man who is the ego has the experience of himself as the agent, not just as passively undergoing something.

The Experience of Efficacy and the Differentiation of Action out of Various Activations—Every dynamism of man, in which he is not active as the concrete ego, that is to say, he does not have the experience of his efficacy, we shall call *activation.* There is activation whenever something only happens in man, derived from the inner dynamism of man himself.

Man "Creates" Himself in Action: the Roots of Human Ethos—Efficacy and transcendence bring with them a special dependence of acting upon the person. Man is not only the agent of his acting, he is the creator of it. In a sense, acting is a work created by man. If it is in acting that man forms his own moral value—wherein is contained an element of the specifically human creativity—then this additionally confirms that man, the actor, himself shapes his acting and his actions. Man is here both the "creator" and the "raw material" being shaped. There is no doubt that action always consists in overcoming human passiveness in one way or another.

3. THE SYNTHESIS OF EFFICACY AND SUBJECTIVENESS. THE PERSON AS THE SUPPOSITUM.

The Differentiation between Acting and Happening Contrasts Efficacy with Subjectiveness in Man—What does *subject* really mean? On one sense, man has the experience of himself as the *subject* when he is "subjected to" something happening in him; this is contrasted to his experience of acting, when he has the experience of himself as the "actor." These are two separate structural levels of experience. But both are united in the human being, as the dynamic subject, who is their origin. This is the second sense of *subject.*

How the Subject is the Ontic Support of Action—Acting depends upon the being-who-acts (the suppositum, the ontic support). It is, thus, that man underlies all his actions and everything that happens in him. The *suppositum* indicates the fact itself of being the subject or the fact that the subject is a being. *Operari sequitur esse:* for something to act it must first exist. The entire dynamism of man's functioning (whether the "acting of" or the "happening in" the dynamic subject) simultaneously proceeds from (but also enacts) the initial dynamism owing to which a being exists at all.

Man as the Ontic Support of Action—Man is indeed an individual substance of a rational nature (Boethius) but this definition focusing on individuation within a species does not express fully the concept of man as a person. He is "somebody" not just "something." The person, the human being as the person, is the subject of both existence and acting. The existence proper to him is personal, thus, the acting (all the dynamism of man including his acting as well as what happens in him) is also personal.

Differences between Efficacy and Subjectiveness and their Synthesis—Once we see the man-person's status as the suppositum, we can see in him a synthesis of those experiences and those dynamic structures which we have distinguished in this chapter: man as efficacious agent and man as subjected to what-happens-in-him. The human being as personal, as subject, is simultaneously both the basis and the source of the two different forms of dynamism.

4. THE PERSON AND NATURE: THEIR OPPOSITION OR INTEGRATION?

The Significance of the Problem—The person and with him his ontic support have here been conceived not only as the metaphysical subject of the existence and the dynamism of the human being, but also as, in a way, a phenomenological synthesis of efficacy and subjectivenness. Thus, *nature* has to assume to some extent a double sense.

Nature Defines the Subjective Basis of Acting—"Nature" denotes literally everything that is going to be born (from the Latin *nascor).* It can be used as a noun (human nature) but does not denote a real and actual subject of existing and acting, but an abstract subject. We prescind from every human being in whom it actually exists and conceive it as an abstract being which stands in relation to all men. Thus, it points to the specific traits common to all by the very fact of their being human, to what is essentially human.

Nature Determines the Manner of Acting—Birth is the beginning of existence—it contains the initial and basic dynamism caused by existence (esse)— from which will issue all the subsequent dynamism of functioning. Hence, in the case of man the consequence of birth would be the whole synthesis of acting and happening which we have been tracing in this chapter. Nature here can mean either the whole human being or just a certain domain of human dynamism (what happens in man).

Why the Antagonistic Conception of Nature and Person?—If nature is regarded as the sphere of what-happens-in-man, that is, the dynamism which is directly and solely the consequence of birth itself (inborn, innate, determined in advance by its properties), then this is in contradistinction to the realm of actions which show him to be a person. Being contained in actions, efficacy brings into view a concrete ego as the self-conscious cause of action. It is this that is the person. So conceived, the person would differ from the nature in man and would even be its opposite. However, we must strive to grasp the transition between man's nature and his person and to grasp their integrity.

Arguments in Favor of the Integration of Nature in the Person—The different aspects of experience must not be raised above its total significance. The total experience, which gives both a simple and a fundamental perception of the human being (as one and the same ontic support for both the acting and the happening in man), supplies the evidence for the unity and the identity of the man-subject. Phenomenology and metaphysics agree here.

5. NATURE AS THE BASIS FOR THE DYNAMIC COHESION OF THE PERSON

Efficacy of the Person and Causality of Nature—How is the integration of nature (as an activation undergone) in the person accomplished? It is in man, the personal "somebody," that the activations that happen in him have their origin just as much as it is from him that spring the actions he as the actor performs. What takes place in myself in the form of the various activations is the property of my ego and, what is more, issues from my ego, which is its only appropriate substratum and cause, though then I have no experience of my causality, of my efficacious participation, as I have in my actions.

The Meaning of the "Priority" of Existence over Actions—Nature in the metaphysical sense is equivalent to the essence of any being, where essence is regarded as the basis for the dynamism of this being. In order to act it is first necessary to exist and the existence of acting flows from and is subsequent to the existence of man: it is its consequence or effect. Thus, nature provides the basis for the essential cohesion of the subject of dynamism with all the dynamism of the subject.

Personal Existence as the Basis of the Dynamic Cohesion of Man—The experience of man's coherence with all his dynamism, with his acting as well as with what happens in him, allows us to understand how nature is integrated in the person. The first and foremost dynamization of any being is derived from its existence, from its *esse*. Dynamization by personal *esse* must lie at the roots of the integration of humanness by the person. Hence, every form of dynamization of the subject (whether in acting or in happening-in-me) if really related to humanness, to nature, must really be personal.

Person as the Real Existence of Human Nature—Humanness or human nature is equipped with the properties that enable a concrete human being to be a person. It prevents him from being and acting otherwise. No other nature has any real (that is, individual) existence as a person—for this pertains to man alone. Acting and happening are both human insofar as they derive within the person from nature, from the humanness of man. It is the person himself that is human and so are his actions. The efficacy of the human ego pertaining to action reveals the transcendence of the person, without, however, separating the person from nature.

6. POTENTIALITY AND ITS RELATION TO CONSCIOUSNESS

The Nature-Person Relation in the Potentiality of the Man-Subject—Humanness and personality (the fact of being a person) are two different things integrated by the unity and identity of the human being as subject. This nature-as-humanness comes into our analysis but only as if it was its background. In the foreground there is nature as the basis of causation for the human being. In other words, we are interested in the relation of nature to the person from the point of view of the potentiality of the man-subject.

Potentiality Indicates the Source of the Inner Dynamization of the Subject—The dynamism of the subject is derived from his potentiality; for potentiality consists in having at one's disposal certain powers inherent in the subject. What is given to human experience directly in the dynamization of the man-subject (whether by acting or merely happening to) reveals indirectly the potency: the particular, clearly defined dynamic source for one or other form of the dynamization of the subject. This requires interpretation and reasoning but is strictly connected with the overall object of experience.

The Different Basis of Activity and Passivity in the Potentiality of Man—The structure of something happening in man indicates a different basis for the potentiality of the man-subject than for the structure of man's acting. We may suppose that if the difference in the forms of the dynamism itself is so striking, then there has to be a corresponding difference in the potentialities, which means that different faculties must lie at the dynamic roots of acting and happening, of action and activation. Following the basic intuition of the person as it manifests itself in actions, our aim is to develop a more precise conception of the relation of consciousness to potentiality in man.

The Relation of Consciousness to Psycho-emotive Potentiality—Concerning the experience of man as only the subject and not as the actor, there are two levels in the dynamism as well as in the potentiality: the psycho-emotive and the somato-vegetative. These two differ in various ways. One great difference is in terms of awareness: the acts of the emotive sphere are clearly mirrored in consciousness, inherently accessible to consciousness.

The Relation of Consciousness to Somato-Vegetative Potentiality—The acts of the vegetative sphere (that dynamism proper to the human body as an actual organism) do not on the whole attain man's awareness, and they even seem to be inaccessible to consciousness, though we have an awareness of the body and of sensations related to it.

7. THE RELATION OF POTENTIALITY TO CONSCIOUSNESS EXPRESSED BY THE SUBCONSCIOUS

Potentiality Comes before Consciousness—Man who is the actor, who performs actions, is also the dynamic subject of everything that happens in him whether at the emotive or vegetative level and whether or not accessible to consciousness: the subject is that person, that "somebody." But this shows clearly that consciousness alone is inadequate for a comprehensive analysis of the human being, the acting person. There is a dynamic unity of life in the human suppositum including the somato-vegetative dimension, the subconscious dimension, that is more comprehensive than that accessible to the field of consciousness alone. Thus, there is a priority of potentiality with regard to consciousness (the latter does not fully encompass the former).

Consciousness and the Delimitation of the Psychical and the Somatic—The dividing line between the emotive sphere (the various sensations and emotions vividly experienced by man) and the data belonging to the somato-vegetative life (which are not consciously experienced) coincides to some extent with the line dividing the psychical from the somatic. Though not perfectly parallel, the latter division adopts some criteria from the former.

Introducing Subconsciousness into the Analysis—Besides those dimensions of man's dynamism open to conscious awareness and those inaccessible to consciousness, there is also the sphere of the subconscious. Here there is not merely inaccessibility to consciousness (as in the case of vegetative processes) but a different source of the content of human experience than the source that feeds consciousness. The content of this human experience is connected with instincts or drives, such as the sexual instinct or the ego instinct. Again, we must conclude that we have here a priority of potentiality with regard to consciousness (the latter does not fully encompass the former). This is just a structural priority, not one of superiority or predominance.

The Relation of Subconsciousness to the Dynamism and Potentiality of Man—The subconscious refers to an inner space to which some objects are expelled or where they are withheld and prevented from reaching the threshold of consciousness. Such "repressed" entities however remain with the subject and press toward consciousness but are opposed entry to consciousness by some dimension of the will. This complex situation reveals both types of dynamism in the subject: something happening in man below the level of consciousness (and perhaps assisted by the vegetative and emotive levels) and an underlying dominant potentiality which keeps watch at the threshold of consciousness.

Subconsciousness Shows Consciousness as the Sphere of Man's Self-realization—Subconsciousness shows (1) the potentiality of the subject in its inner aspect itself; (2) the continuity and cohesion of the subject since the subconscious is a transition point and connector between the vegetative and possibly also emotive activations and what man consciously experiences; (3) with its continual relation to consciousness, the subconscious allows us to see the human being as internally subjected to time and, thus, having his own internal history; and (4) reveals the hierarchy of human potentialities: the constant drive toward the light of consciousness reveals that it is the latter sphere where man most appropriately fulfills himself.

8. MAN IN BECOMING: THE MANIFESTATION OF FREEDOM IN THE DYNAMISM OF THE MAN-SUBJECT

The Being-Acting-Becoming Relation—"Becoming" indicates that aspect of man's acting or of what happens in him insofar as it introduces a process of change. The subject not only participates in such changes but is formed or transformed by them. The original dynamism of the man is his coming into existence. In each subsequent dynamism, something begins to exist in the man-subject that already is: man changes one way or another through action or activation.

The Subject's Differentiated Potentiality and the Corresponding Spheres of Man's Becoming and Development—Two types of becoming correspond to the two levels of potentiality: the somato-vegetative and the psycho-emotive. Concerning the former, the human organism determines its own development almost entirely, and only the conditions of development are established by man. It is the opposite in the psycho-emotive sphere, which itself establishes the conditions and, as it were, supplies the material for its own development. Consequently, the formation of this sphere mainly depends on the human person.

Actions Make Man Good or Bad—The formation of the psycho-emotive sphere brings us to that particular type of human becoming which will next receive our attention. It is man's actions, his conscious acting, that make him *what* and *who* he actually is. This form of human becoming, thus, presupposes the efficacy or causation proper to man, and morality is its fruit. It is man's actions, the way he consciously acts, that make of him a morally good or bad man. The moral quality of actions, which depends on the norm of morality and ultimately on the dictates of conscience, is imprinted upon man by his performing the actions.

Freedom is the Root of Man's Goodness or Badness—It is in the structure of man's becoming, through his actions, morally good or bad, that freedom manifests itself most appropriately. Further, freedom is not only a moment, but a real and inherent component of the structure, and the decisive one for moral becoming.

The Moment of Freedom Emerges from the Analysis of Human Dynamism. Freedom and Efficacy of the Person—Freedom is best visualized by the human being in the experience aptly epitomized in the phrase, "I could but I need not." This is not a matter of a mere content of consciousness but of a manifestation and actualization of the dynamism proper to man and, thus, must have its correlate in the potentiality of the man-subject. This correlate is the *will.* Between the "I could" on the one hand and the "I need not" on the other, the human "I want" is formed and it constitutes the dynamism proper to the will. The distinction into acting and happening (actions and activations) rests on the difference between the real participation of the will and the absence of the will. What only happens in man has no dynamic source; it lacks the element of freedom and the experience of "I could but I need not;" it is dynamized out of inner necessity and not out of the free efficacy of man.

PART TWO
THE TRANSCENDENCE OF THE PERSON IN ACTION

CHAPTER THREE
THE PERSONAL STRUCTURE OF SELF-DETERMINATION

1. THE FUNDAMENTALS OF THE PERSONAL STRUCTURE OF SELF-DETERMINATION

In Self-Determination the Will is Seen as a Property of the Person—Every action confirms and at the same time makes more concrete the relation, in which the will manifests itself as a property of the person, and the person manifests himself as a reality with regard to his dynamism that is properly constituted by the will. It is this relation that we call self-determination. Only the one who has possession of himself and is simultaneously his own sole and exclusive possession (prescinding from the God-relationship) can be a person. *Persona est sui juris.*

Self-Determination Shows the Structure of Self-Governance and Self-Possession as Essential to the Person—Being in possession of himself man can determine himself. Every genuine "I will" reveals, confirms, and realizes the self-possession that is appropriate solely to the person—the fact that the person is *sui juris*, is his own master. This also reveals the relation of self-governance (more than mere self-control): the person is on the one hand, the one who governs himself and, on the other, the one who is governed.

Self-Possession is Presupposed in Self-Governance—The self-governance that is found in the person is possible only when there is self-possession that is proper to the person. Self-determination is conditioned by one as well as by the other. Because of self-determination everyone actually governs himself; he actually exercises that specific power over himself which nobody else can exercise or execute. This constitutes man's inalienability or incommunicability: *Persona est alteri incommunicabilitas.*

2. AN ATTEMPT TO INTERPRET THE INTEGRAL DYNAMISM OF THE WILL

The Reference to the Ego as Object is Essential to Self-Determination—The objectification we are now considering is realized by and also manifested in self-determination. This objectification means that in every actual act of self-determination—in every "I will"—the self is the object, indeed the primary and nearest object: one is determined by oneself as both subject and object. The one as well as the other is the ego. This is true of every intentional "willing" directed toward any object.

Objectification Is More Fundamental than the Intentionality of Volitions—The objectification that is essential for self-determination takes place together with the intentionality of the particular acts of the will and is more fundamental. When I will anything, then I am also determined by myself. The experience of "I will" contains also self-determination and not only intentionality.

Self-Determination and the Distinction between the Experiences of "I will" and "I am willing"—It lies in the nature of the experience of "I will," in the nature of the will itself, that it never consists in something that only happens in man; on the contrary, it always occurs as an instance of "acting," indeed, is the very core of every acting. However, we also experience volitions which are not within the frame of self-determination, such as an appetitive desire. Here I experience only an "I am willing" or an "I want." The latter is a type of volition but it does not contain the true dynamism of the will.

The Experience of "I will" Reveals the Transcendence of the Person in the Action—The dynamism of the will cannot be reduced to volition with its specific intentionality. An essential trait of this dynamism is that it involves the person in its own specific structure of self-governance and self-determination. It is, thus, that every genuine "I will" reveals the person's transcendence in the action. The *actus humanus* is not just a *persona in actu* but a real *actus personae.* That is, the human act, the action, is a real act of the person; for in it not only is an individual rational nature actualized, but also an act is performed—as evidenced in experience—by the unique individual person.

In Self-Determination the Reference to the Ego as Object Is Influenced by Consciousness—The person in his specific structure possessing consciousness lives not only in his own reflection, the mirrored image the person has of himself, but also in that specific self-experience which is conditioned by the reflexive function of consciousness. Man has the experience of each of his willings, of every act of self-determination. So, the person, the acting ego, also experiences that *he is the one who is determined by himself* and that *his decisions make him become somebody,* who may be good or bad

The Will is Governed by the Objectifying Function of Cognition—It is not merely consciousness in either its mirroring or its reflexive function which guides the will (this way leads to solipsism). Rather, the guidance provided by the cognitive function has an objectifying character. Thus, if self-determination and the whole dynamism of the will are to be guided by anything, then this can only be self-knowledge together with man's whole knowledge of the existing reality, in particular, his knowledge of values as possible ends and also as the basis of the norms that he refers to in his acting.

The Dialectics of Objectification and Subjectification Appropriate to the Integral Dynamism of the Will—The acting person reveals himself as a specific synthesis of objectiveness and subjectiveness. As consciousness brings with it subjectification and some inwardness (though not full "subjectification"), so self-determination introduces also some outwardness (though not full "objectification").

The Interior Act is Also an External Manifestation of the Person—Every internal act is also an external manifestation of the person and every external act remains to a certain degree interior to the subject who performs it. Thus, the synthesis of objectiveness with subjectiveness is projected in the dynamic image of the person to the syntheses of externality with interiority.

Self-determination Reveals Freedom as a True Attribute of the Person—The freedom appropriate to the human being, the person's freedom resulting from the will, exhibits itself as identical with self-determination, with that experiential, most complete, and fundamental organ of man's autonomous being. We are, thus, considering freedom as a reality (the experience of "I will" as well as of "I could but I need not"), freedom as the real property of man and the real attribute of his will (not as an idealistic abstraction).

3. FREE WILL AS THE BASIS OF THE TRANSCENDENCE OF THE ACTING PERSON

The Difference between the Dynamisms of Self-Determination and Instinct—The dynamism at the level of nature (instinct as a coordination of activations) is in opposition to the dynamism at the level of the person (self-determined acting). The dynamism at the level of nature lacks that special dependence of the ego which is the characteristic mark of the specific dynamism of the person.

Free Will Signifies the Self-Dependence of the Person—It is the dependence of acting on the ego that serves as the basis of freedom, while the absence of this dependence places the whole dynamism of any individual being (say an animal being) beyond the sphere of freedom. Note that the lack of dependence on the ego in the dynamization of the subject is equivalent to the absence of freedom, or at any rate the absence of the real grounds for freedom to be based upon (as opposed to any abstract or idealistic notion of freedom as "independence from all possible factors").

The Contextual Meaning of the Transcendence of the Person—Transcendence means to go over and beyond a threshold or boundary. Transgressing the subject's limits in the direction of an object—and this is intentionality in the "external" perception or volition of an object—is defined as "horizontal transcendence." But "vertical transcendence" is the fruit of self-determination; transcendence through the fact itself of freedom, of being free in acting. Self-determination, thus, introduces the dominant position of the ego.

The Role of the Objectification of the Ego in the Structure of Freedom—The fundamental significance of man's freedom, of the exercise of his free will, forces us to see in freedom first of all that special self-dependence which goes together with self-determination. Hence the fundamental significance of freedom presupposes the objectification which we discussed earlier. The precondition of freedom is the concrete ego, which while it is the subject is also the object determined by acts of will.

4. THE SIGNIFICANCE OF THE WILL AS THE PERSON'S POWER OF SELF-DETERMINATION

Autodeterminism Conditions Independence in Relation to Intentional Objects of Volition—In relation to intentional objects of volition, the structure of freedom is not confined solely to "I will" but comprises the whole "I will something." Our willing now has a *definite* object and has, thus, been determined. But even here the "I could, but I need not" is somehow continued. This inner independence of the ego in relation to the intentional objects of volition (i.e., the value-end) is justified by self-dependence. Thus, any realistic interpretation of free will must rely on man's *autodeterminism,* not float in the air by stressing merely indeterminism.

The Dynamism of Self-Determination Consists in Man's Use of the Will—The expression "free" will does not mean some kind of independence of will from the person. Rather the will is a property and a power of the person, which is subordinate in relation to the person and does not determine or govern the person. Because of the person's exclusive power over the will, the *will is the person's power to be free.* The interpretation of the will as a power also reveals it as a dynamism with its appropriate potentiality.

The Meaning of the Instinct of Freedom—Within the dynamism appropriate to the person and his acting we may also detect the "instinct of freedom" (used only in a metaphorical sense). It then denotes that, for the person, self-determination is something absolutely proper and innate, even something "natural" (i.e., it is of the nature of the person not to merely follow instinctual nature).

The Meaning of the Phrase "Man's Instinctual Acting"—Probably not even when man himself refers to his acting as instinctive (he *instinctively* turns away from pain or reaches for food) can we regard this as functioning solely at the level of nature. Although self-determination is appropriate and even "natural" to the person, there is in man a certain tension between his will as the power of deliberate choice and decision and his bodily potentiality, emotiveness, and drives. Experience tells us that it is in this tension rather than in simple and pure self-determination that consists the lot of man.

5. DECISION IS THE FOCUS OF THE ACTIVITIES OF FREE WILL

Transcendence versus Appetite—Because of the fact itself of being free—the fact of self-determination and its related ascendancy over the human dynamism—we call this transcendence "vertical." It is more fundamental than the traditionally stressed "horizontal" transcendence involving the will's characteristic urge (appetitus) toward good as its object and end.

Intent, Intendedness, and Intentionality—"Rational appetite" conveys the notion of a striving directed toward an end together with a desire for this end (this latter is more akin to something-happening-in-man). Thus, in the act of will there is an "intent," or "intendedness," which implies tending toward something. This marks a further moment beyond the "intentionality" proper to man's experience (whether in acts of volition or of cognition, of thinking) which consists in being oriented or directed toward an object.

Decision as the Crucial Constitutive Moment in the Experience of "I will"—Choice and decision define the intrinsic essence of volition (of "I will," whether simply as wanting or as choosing). In true willing the subject is never passively directed toward an object. There is a directing of oneself that is appropriate to volition, to the active engagement of the subject. This is due to the moment of decision which brings into full view the person in his efficacy and transcendence: it shows the person as a person.

Readiness to Strive toward Good Underlies All Volitive Decisions—The greater the good the greater becomes its power to attract the will and, thus, also the person. But man's *consent* is necessary. We must stress that all forms and degrees of such foundational absorption or engagement of the will toward the good are made personal by the moment of decision. Decision is an instance of a threshold that the person as a person has to pass on his way toward the good. Moreover, this personal outgoing has to continue throughout his absorption by the good. The more he becomes engulfed, the more fundamental is his decision and vice versa.

6. RESPONSIBILITY IN THE ACTS OF WILL—MOTIVATION AND RESPONSE

What is Motivation?—By motivation we mean the effect motives have on the will. When I want something, the object presents itself to my attention as a good and, thus, shows its value. Presentation is broadly speaking the cognition of values. But motivation means more: we owe to motivation the actuation, the movement of the will toward the object presented—not just a turn toward it but an outright movement. However, motives essentially only stimulate the will. They do not arouse emotions.

The Motivation of Simple Willing and the Motivation of Choice—In simple willing, man desires only one object, one motivating value. However, though choice is unnecessary in such a case, a decision still has to be made. In choice, there are competing goods and a separate process, a deliberation of motives, is necessary before a decision can be made.

The Ability to Decide is Seen as Choosing—In the deliberation of motives, there is the fundamental readiness of striving toward good (which is primary), plus something akin to a momentary suspension of the process of willing. Not until the moment of decision, which in this case coincides with choice, can any one of the potential willings be actualized. Thus, the will is definitely included in vertical transcendence, associated with self-governance and self-possession, and not only with horizontal transcendence.

The Free Will Manifests Itself in an Independent Choice of Objects—More than anything else, freedom is present and manifests itself in the ability to choose; for this ability confirms the independence of the will in the intentional order of willing. In choosing, the will is not cramped by the object, by the value as its end; it is the will and only the will that determines (chooses) its object. This freedom does not, however, abolish the fact that man is conditioned in the broadest sense by the world of objects, in particular, by the domain of values. For his is not the freedom *from* objects or values, but on the contrary the freedom *for* objects or values.

The Dynamic Originality of Acts of Will Disproves Moral Determinism—Determinists claim that the mere presentation of objects to the will thereby determines decision, but this hides a far-reaching oversimplification and the essentials are sacrificed to a schematic pattern of thinking. Here the phenomenological method is of great service. Presentation is but the condition of decision, not the actual cause. The dynamic specificity appertaining to decision (simple willing or complex choosing) is essential to the will and is of the kind that makes impossible any determination.

The Act of Will as the Person's Response to the Appeal of Values—Every instance of "I will" comprises not only a passive acceptance or assimilation of a presented value (something merely happening in man), but constitutes an individual, unique, and authentic response to the value. This remarkable trait of the will's dynamism must not be lost in contemplation of the will as an independent entity in itself. Nevertheless, it is not the objects and values that have a grip of man (as if determining him); on the contrary, in his relation to them he governs himself: he is his own master.

7. "TRUTH ABOUT GOOD" AS THE BASIS FOR THE ACTING PERSON'S DECISION AND TRANSCENDENCE

Dynamic Structure of the Object Common to Cognition and Will—The assertion that the active, dynamic ability to respond to values is a characteristic of the will, however, refers not only to a certain analogy between will and thought but also to the nature of the will itself. According to the traditional view, nothing may become the object of will unless it is already known. The question still remains as to what is the common dynamic structure of the object as already known and again as an object of the will.

The Will's Reference to Truth as the Inner Principle of Decision—It would be impossible to understand choice without referring the dynamism proper to the will to truth as the principle of willing. Thus, in choosing and deciding, will—and, thus, of course the person—*responds* to motives instead of being in one way or another only determined by them. The ability to respond manifested by "free will" presupposes a reference to *truth* and not only a reference to the *objects* which elicit the response.

The Will's Dependence on Truth Gives it Independence from Objects—In its element of choice and decision, every volition manifests its specific dependence on the person from whom it flows, a dependence that may be called the "dependence in truth." It is this essential surrender of the will to truth that seems finally to account for the person's transcendence in action, ultimately for his ascendancy to his own dynamism. Thus, the will is not determined by the object; the person becomes independent of the objects of his own acting through the moment of truth.

Truth about the Good and the Moral Value of Action—Not all particular choices are correct. Too often we seek what is not the true good. But this is not just an error, because errors stem from the mind and not from the will. Choices and decisions which take as their object what is not a real good (especially if contrary to what has been recognized a real good) lead to the experience of guilt or sin. But it is the reality of guilt—of sin or moral evil—known from moral experience that brings to light explicitly the fact that the reference to truth and the inner dependence on truth is rooted in the human will. If choice and decision were to be without their inherent moment of truth, performed apart from the specific reference to truth, moral conduct would become incomprehensible.

8. THE COGNITIVE EXPERIENCE OF VALUES AS THE CONDITION OF CHOICE AND DECISION

Motivation Leads the Will out of Initial Indetermination—Motivation is not to be identified with determination, but it is the condition of autodetermination (the moment of freedom: the self-dependence of the person in relation to the possible objects of willing). Motivation serves to urge the will out of its initial, still undetermined state, though this is achieved by its being not a determining factor but the condition enabling autodetermination.

The Special Nature of Cognition as a Condition of the Will—Knowledge appears then as a condition influencing choice, decision-making, and more generally the exercise of self-determination; it is a condition of the person's transcendence in action, springing from the relation to truth. Lest we be too one-sided, we must also acknowledge that the will influences cognition, not by changing "at will" the nature of the cognized objects or the processes of cognition and thinking: the will acknowledges objects as cognized, but proposes to and imposes certain tasks on cognition and thought.

Truth about Good is Essential in the Experiencing of Values—In the experience of value the moment of truth also seems to play an essential role. It is the truth about this or that object (nutritive value of food, educative value of a book, etc.) which crystallizes this or that moment of good. The relation to truth then evolved in cognition is of such a kind that it may become the principle of willing when a choice or a decision is made.

The Axiological Truth and the So-called "Practical Truth"—The moment of truth contained in the essence itself of choice or decision, thus, determines the dynamism of the person as such. It is the dynamism conductive toward the action. The moment of truth liberates the acting of the person and is the boundary between acting and something merely happening in the subject. This is a cognitive experience of truth belonging to theoretical knowledge and does not belong directly to so-called "practical knowledge."

9. THE CREATIVE ROLE OF INTUITION IS UNDIMINISHED BY THE JUDGMENT OF VALUES

Thought and the Efficacy of the Subject—Alongside the active experience of cognition we also have the experience of thinking, which though of a more passive nature has cognitive significance. The difference between thinking and willing lies in their different directions: willing implies a certain outgoing toward an object (striving). Thinking, or rather cognizing, consists in some sort of introducing of an object into a subject either (1) by perception or imagination through the senses or (2) by comprehension and understanding through the intellect.

In Judgment Man Has the Experience of Himself as the Agent of Thought—Up to a point, thinking only happens in man, and beyond that point it clearly becomes his acting: then man has the experience of being the agent of thought and cognition. This point is evidently reached with the moment of judgment. Judgment presupposes ideation but this function is inherent in the function of judging wherein consciousness manifests itself as the act in which the ego is not merely the subject but also the agent. Besides the outer structure of the sentence, a judgment grasps a truth (this is its inner structure) about the object that is its raw material. Truth is not only essential for the possibility of human knowledge, but it is simultaneously *the basis for the person's transcendence in the action.*

Correspondence of Judgment and Decision—Through judgments the person attains his proper cognitive transcendence with respect to objects, the transcendence due to the truth about the cognized objects (primarily the axiological truth contained in the judgment of the values of objects). There is a correspondence here: whenever the person chooses or decides, he has had first to make a judgment of values. The essence of *judging is cognitive and, thus, belongs to the sphere of knowing* while *the essence of decision is strictly connected with willing.* "To will" means not only to strive toward an end but also *to strive while deciding:* this is what actualizes the proper self-governance and self-possession of the person.

The Creative Role of Intuition in the Discursive Perception of Values—When judging, the ego has the experience of himself as the agent—the one who acts—of the act itself of cognizing. But we may also cognitively experience directly the value of the object of cognition, remaining as if absorbed in this value, contemplating more passively than actively. There is an active moment in this operation, however, inasmuch as it is always accompanied by judgment (and if values are the object of cognition, then a judgment of values). Moreover, intuition can either be the starting point for new discursive reasoning or the endpoint and culmination of previous discursive reasoning with all the active efforts that this implies. The important thing is the moment of truth, for it is the relation to truth that explains all choice and decision.

CHAPTER FOUR

SELF-DETERMINATION AND FULFILLMENT

1. PERFORMING AN ACTION BRINGS PERSONAL FULFILLMENT

The Crucial Significance of Fulfillment in an Action—All the essential problems considered in this study seem to be focused and condensed in the simple assertion of fulfillment in an action. Person and action here are not two separate and self-sufficient entities but—and we have emphasized this from the start—as a single, deeply cohesive reality.

The Inner and Intransitive Effects of an Action—When we speak of "performing an action" we see the person as the subject and the agent while the action itself is a consequence of the efficacy of the agent. This consequence is external with regard to the person, but it is also internal to, or immanent in, the person. Moreover, it is both transitive and intransitive with regard to the person.

Self-Fulfillment in Action Is Presupposed in Morality—At this stage in our discussion we are here primarily, if not exclusively, concerned with action as the inner and intransitive consequence of a person's efficacy. In the inner dimension of the person, human action is at once both transitory and relatively lasting, inasmuch as its effects last longer than the action itself: for, being the performer of an action, man also fulfills himself in it. Human actions once performed do not vanish without trace: they leave their moral value, which constitutes an objective reality intrinsically cohesive with the person, and, thus, a reality also profoundly subjective. Being a person, man is somebody and being somebody he may be either good or bad.

2. THE RELIANCE OF SELF-FULFILLMENT ON THE CONSCIENCE

The Moral Dimension of the Person's Fulfillment in an Action—The significance of moral values for the person is such that the true fulfillment of the person is accomplished by the moral goodness of an action far more than by the mere performance of the action itself. Moral badness on the other hand, always involving a defect, leads to nonfulfillment even though the person is acting.

The Contingency of the Human Person as Revealed by Possible Nonfulfillment—Since the person acts and fulfills himself in and through action, morality evidences a specific ontological contingency of the individual real being: man is a contingent being in the sense embraced by traditional metaphysics. Furthermore, the possibility of being good (fulfilling oneself) or being bad (nonfulfilling oneself) shows a special feature of the contingency of the person: his freedom may be used rightly or wrongly.

Action's Dependence on the Recognition of Moral Goodness as Revealed by the Conscience—Human freedom is not accomplished or exercised in bypassing truth (either in ontological autonomy or in self-centered dependence on the ego) but, on the contrary in realization and surrender to truth. The human person is free, not absolutely, but insofar as freedom is the core of a person's self-dependence that essentially relates to the surrender to truth. It is this moral freedom that more than anything else *constitutes the spiritual dynamism of the person.* The dividing line between good and evil is marked out by truth, the unique truthfulness of the good of which man has the experience in his conscience.

The Person's Transcendence and its Relation to Truth, Good and Beauty—The notion of the "transcendence of the person" may be broadened and examined in relation to all the traditionally distinguished transcendentals: being, truth, good, beauty. Man has access to them through knowledge, and in the wake of knowledge, of the mind, through the will and through action. The action serves the realization of truth, good, and beauty. This is not just an abstract notion: the evidence of experience tells us that the spiritual life of man essentially refers to, and in its strivings vibrates around his experientially innermost attempts to reach truth, goodness, and beauty. We have experience of the transcendentals accompanying the experience of personal transcendence.

The Conscience as the Person's Inner Normative Reality—The function of conscience consists in distinguishing the element of moral good in action and in releasing and forming a sense of duty with respect to this good. *The sense of duty is the experiential form of the reference to (or dependence on) the moral truth,* to which the freedom of the person is subordinate. The appropriate and complete function of the conscience consists in subordinating the actions to the truth that has, thus, become known. This surrender to the good in truth forms a new moral reality in the person. This new reality has a normative character and manifest itself in the formulation of norms and their role in human action.

The Conscience as the Norm of Actions Conditions the Fulfillment of the Person—Only the norms of ethics, which correspond to morality, bear upon man's actions and upon man as a person. It is through them that man himself as a person becomes morally good or bad, with "through" indicating the relation based on a compliance or noncompliance with norms. The norms of logic as well as those of aesthetics never have such a strong effect on man, for they are not norms of acting but only of knowing and producing. Within their scope they do not refer to man as the person but to man's products, to his works.

3. CONSCIENCE DEPENDS ON TRUTH

Why is the Normative Power of Truth Rooted in the Mind?—Thus, fulfillment is connected with the inner, intransitive effect of action. As manifested in man's conscience, the capacity to surrender to truth is rooted in the potentiality of the personal being of man. Because of its ability to grasp the truth and to distinguish it from fallacy, the mind provides the basis for man's peculiar ascendancy over reality, over the objects of cognition. But it is the whole effort of the person (a special striving toward truth as value) directed toward moral truth and not consciousness alone which supplies the basis for the transcendence of the person. Far from being but a passive mirror that only reflects objects, man acquires through truth as a value a specific ascendancy over them.

The Person's Transcendence and Fulfillment Depend on the Truthfulness of the Conscience—The conscience is the necessary condition of man's fulfillment of himself in action. The persistence of action in the person, because of its moral value, derives from and depends on the conscience. The role of conscience is to experience not only truthfulness but also duty (based on truth).

Normative Power as the Union of Truth and Duty—Owing to the role of conscience, it is the normative function of the evaluated and recognized truth to condition not only the performance of an action by the person but also his fulfillment of himself in action. Truthfulness, the normative role of truth exercised by the conscience, is the keystone of the whole structure. Without truthfulness (or while out of touch with it) the conscience or, more broadly speaking, the whole specific system of the moral function and order cannot be properly grasped and correctly interpreted. In each of his actions, the human person is eyewitness of the transition from the "is" to the "should"—the transition from "X is truly good" to "I should do X."

4. THE OBLIGATION TO SEEK SELF-FULFILLMENT

Duty and the Person's Fulfillment in Action—The explanation of the normative power of truth is to be sought in its reference to a sense of duty, while it also explains the sense of duty because of the reference to values. It is most strictly related with the specific dynamism of the fulfillment of the personal ego in and through the action; it is from this point of view that duty is discussed here.

The Truthfulness of Moral Norms—The fundamental value of norms lies in the truthfulness of the good they objectify and not in the generation itself of duties. It is owing to their truthfulness that they become related to the conscience, which then, so to speak, transforms their value of truth into the concrete and real obligation. The real issue is not an abstractly conceived objective truthfulness of norms but experiencing their truthfulness: the deeper the certitude, the stronger becomes the sense of obligation.

The Creative Role of Conscience—Contrary to Kant's conception, the conscience is no lawmaker; it does not itself create norms; rather it discovers them, as it were, in the objective order of morality or law. Yet conscience does have a creative role as well, consisting in the fact that it shapes the norms into that unique and unparalleled form they acquire with the experience and fulfillment of the person. The sense of conviction and certitude, whereby the truthfulness of a norm is molded within the personal dimension, is followed by the sense of duty. Far from abolishing freedom, truth liberates it.

The Transition from Value to Obligation—Insofar as truth is the ultimate point of reference for the transcendence of the person, the traditional definition of the person is right in stressing that this transcendence, especially the transcendence of the person in action, has its source in the mind. It seems, however, that the metaphysical reduction implicit in this definition emphasizes the intellectual nature (i.e., rational nature) rather than transcendence of the person through the relation to the value of moral truth (will and the freedom of the person in their own dynamic way surrender to truth). The cognitive experience of values does not necessarily initiate the willing of values, not to mention the experience of obligation. If a value is to give birth to obligation it needs first to intercept in a special manner and as a specific appeal the path of the person's acting.

The Calling to Self-Fulfillment in Action—Any obligation (arising positively with the acceptance of values, even if only implied through prohibitions) tells in one way or another about the calling of the person. For in every obligation there is an imperative: be good as man—do not be bad as man. All other more detailed callings and vocations, or perhaps we may call them challenges by values, are ultimately reducible to this first, fundamental calling.

The Person's Transcendence Evidenced in the Drama of Values and Obligations—Man's relation to reality then is not merely cognitive (interiorized by consciousness). Obligation goes in the other direction: it introduces the person through his actions into that characteristic drama (of values and obligations) enacted in the context of reality of which it makes of him the subject (*dramatis persona).* He realizes himself neither by the intentionality of volitions nor through self-determination but through *his sense of obligation as the peculiar modification of self-determination and intentionality.*

5. RESPONSIBILITY

Obligation Relates Responsibility to Efficacy—Responsibility informs us primarily about the person performing an action and fulfilling himself in the action. Although we have related responsibility directly to efficacy, its source is in obligation rather than in the efficacy itself of the person. The relationship of responsibility with efficacy implies obligation.

Responsiveness to and Responsibility for Values—Obligation constitutes that mature form of responding to values which is most intimately related to responsibility. Responsibility bears within itself the element of obligatory reference to values, therefore the response to values characteristic of the will assumes in the person and in his actions the form of responsibility for values. The important thing in human striving is its truthfulness—the striving must correspond to the true value of the object.

The Subject's Responsibility for His Own Moral Value is Based on Self-Determination—The responsibility for the value that is appropriate to the object of acting is strictly connected with the responsibility for the subject himself, namely, for the value that in the course of acting is formed in the subject, the concrete ego. Together with the responsibility for the value of intentional objects, the first and fundamental responsibility that arises in acting on the basis of self-determination and self-dependence is the responsibility for the subject, for the moral worth of the ego who is the agent performing the action.

The Relation of Responsibility to Personal Authority—The whole of the reality constituted by responsibility has still another aspect, which we shall here designate as "responsibility to," and which presupposes "responsibility for." For it lies in the nature of responsibility that we are always responsible to somebody and, thus, to a person. On the social level, this implies the juridical power. On the philosophical and theological levels, this responsibility to somebody assumes the religious meaning of being responsible to God (conscience as the "voice of God"). However, responsibility to somebody, regardless of any other appropriate relations, develops and is expressed in relation to its own subject. I myself am also the "somebody" to whom I feel and am responsible. At the ego-person begins the road which leads to other persons seen both in the community of mankind and in religious perspectives.

In His Conscience Man Is Responsible to Himself—The responsibility to somebody when integrated in the voice of the conscience places my own ego in the position of judge over myself. If man as a person is the one who governs and possesses himself, then he can do so also because, on the one hand, he is responsible for himself and, on the other, he is in some respects responsible to himself. For he is at once the one who governs and the one who is governed by himself, the one who possesses and the one who is his own possession. He is also the one responsible as well as the one for whom and to whom he is responsible.

6. HAPPINESS AND THE PERSON'S TRANSCENDENCE IN ACTION

Self-Fulfillment as a Synonym of Felicity—In the notion of "felicity" there is something akin to fulfillment, to the fulfillment of the self through action. To fulfill oneself is almost synonymous with felicity, with being happy. But to fulfill oneself is the same thing as to realize the good whereby man as the person becomes and is good himself.

Truth and Freedom as Sources of Felicity—The fulfillment of the person in the action depends on the active and inwardly creative union of truth with freedom. Thus, felicity has to be identified not with the availability of freedom as such but with the fulfillment of freedom through truth.

Felicity Derived from the Relation to Others—All relations to the social and to the natural world play a role in man's happiness, but man's relation to other persons plays an especial and crucial role. Experience shows that this sort of mutual (specifically personal) participation is the source of a special type of happiness. This is also crucial for felicity in the religious sense (intercourse with God and communion with Him).

The Intrapersonal Profile of Felicity—In our discussion we limit ourselves to what felicity seems to be in the inner and intransitive dimension of the acting person. We do this in order to better understand the other dimension just mentioned. In addition, when in his quest of happiness man reaches out beyond himself, the fact of the quest itself seems to indicate a special correlation between felicity and his own person (i.e., his own structures of freedom, truth, action, self-possession, and self-governance).

Felicity and Its Reverse Belong to the Personal Structure—The personal structure of felicity implies that it may be experienced only by beings who are also persons. Felicity—like its extreme opposite "despair"—seems to be the exclusive privilege of the person, with that special unique structure of the person (fulfillment of the ego through action) which has no analogue in the world of nature.

Felicity Is Not Pleasure—What is strictly related to man's fulfillment (transcendence in action, freedom, truth, conscience) we call felicity but not pleasure. We would seek in vain for pleasure as the element of this integral structure. Is it at all possible to speak of pleasure in having a "clear conscience" or in fulfilling an obligation? We rather speak of joy or satisfaction. Pleasure (or its opposite vexation) are secondary and only *happen* in man. Felicity (or its opposite despair) relate to the personal structure of man.

The Person and Action Remain within the Sphere of Pleasure and Displeasure—Felicity is not just a more intense or deeper form of pleasure on the emotional side of experience (as Scheler holds). The dividing line is between the fundamental experience of "man acts" and "something happens in man," and this notwithstanding the fact that pleasure and displeasure may be the aim of man's acting (this is the basis of hedonism and utilitarianism). Person and action are not "separated" from pleasure and displeasure, but felicity is not to be reduced to pleasure; it is most strictly related to the transcendence of the person.

7. THE TRANSCENDENCE OF THE PERSON AND THE SPIRITUALITY OF MAN

The Various Meanings of "Transcendence"—Metaphysically, transcendence can refer to the transcendentals (being, truth, good, beauty) not being limited to any species or genera. Epistemologically, it can refer to "horizontal transcendence" (certain human acts reaching out beyond the subject) or to "vertical transcendence" (characterizing the dynamic person-action conjugate from within).

"Transcendence" Expresses the Essence of Acting—"Vertical transcendence" means that "man acts" with self-governance and self-possession. This is revealed in experience through the phenomenological method which in no way stops at surface description here but allows deep intuition and explanation. In virtue of his self-governance and self-possession (showing superiority over actual being that is exhibited by the person) man deserves the designation "somebody" regardless of whether he has this distinctive structure actually or only potentially. Thus, man is somebody from the very moment of his coming into existence even when and if something intervenes and prevents his fulfillment of himself in actions.

The Spirituality of Man and the Person's Transcendence in Action—Thus, we come to the conclusion that the evidence of the spiritual nature of man stems in the first place from the experience of the person's transcendence in action. By "spiritual" we mean indeed an immaterial factor which is inherently irreducible to matter. The positive expression of this is to be found in the idea of the transcendence of the person and, since this latter is within reach of the phenomenological insight, the acceptance of the spiritual nature of man in its authentic manifestations is not the result of some abstraction but, if one may say so, has an intuitional shape; spirituality is open to intuition as well as to insight. This shape, the shape of transcendence, is in actuality that of human existence: it is the shape of human life itself.

The Real Immanence of the Spiritual Element in Man—But all the manifestations of the spiritual nature of man lead by the thread of their genesis to a demonstration of the spirit and of the spiritual nature of man. Man could not exhibit the spiritual element of his nature had he not in some way been a spirit himself. This not only confirms traditional metaphysics in its dualistic interpretation of man but, going much further, our analyses have accumulated sufficient evidence of the spirituality of man not only in the phenomenological sense but also, even if indirectly, in the ontological sense.

The Sequence of Comprehensions—The cognition of the spirituality of the human being comes from the transcendence of the person according to the following sequence: (1) we recognize that man is person, (2) that his spiritual nature reveals itself as the transcendence of the person in acting, and finally (3) that only then can we comprehend in what his spiritual being consists. For a spiritual being like man, to be a person is the proper mode of existence: Thus, "spiritual nature" indicates some ontologically grounded permanence of the spiritual being. The person can only partly and only in a certain respect be identified with nature, namely, only in his substantiality. As a whole and in his intrinsic essence he reaches beyond nature. For the personal freedom repudiates the necessity peculiar to nature.

8. THE UNITY AND COMPLEXITY OF THE MAN-PERSON

Phenomenological Intuition and the Unity and Complexity of the Man-Person—The transcendence of the person in action revealing the spiritual nature of man impels us to look more closely into the problem and to discuss the complexity of man as a corporeal and spiritual being. Experience reveals that man is a unity. The disparity in the dynamism of acting and happening does not prevent the unity of man as the person, but reflects a certain complexity. The unity of the person is most completely manifested in the action (through transcendence) in which the person possesses (and is possessed by) himself, governs (and is governed by) himself, and phenomenologically manifests here a specific organic unity, not an unintegrated manifold. Thus, the transcendence of the person in action, understood in the phenomenological sense, seems to lead to an ontological conception of man in which the unity of his being is determined by the spirit.

The Spiritual Potentiality of Man—As the source of the specific dynamism of the person (manifested in efficacy, responsibility, self-determination, conscience, freedom, and reference to truth), the spiritual element itself must be dynamic. But dynamism is proportional to potentiality. We infer from this the presence of the spiritual potentiality in man, the powers of his spiritual nature. Hence the powers of the intellect and the will seem to be partaking of, and exhibiting themselves as, a spiritual element, not reducible to nature alone.

Spirituality Determines the Personal Unity of the Corporeal Man—This notion of "spirituality" may serve as the key to understanding the complexity of man. For we now see man as person, and we see him first of all in his acting, in action. He then appears in the field of our integral experience as somebody material, as corporeal, but at the same time we know the personal unity of this material somebody to be determined by spirit, by his spiritual nature and spiritual life. Indeed the very fact of the personal—as well as the ontic—unity of the corporeal man is ultimately determined by man's spirituality allows us to see in him the ontic composite of soul and body, of the spiritual and the material elements.

The Experience of Personal Unity Helps to Understand Man's Ontic Complexity—Thus, the experience of the unity of man as the person stimulates a need to understand the complexity of man as a being. There is no question but that the conception of man as person—though it is accessible in the original intuition within the frame of phenomenological insight—has to be completed and supplemented by the metaphysical analysis of the human being. Thus, while the experience of the personal unity of man shows us his complex nature, the attempt at a deepened understanding of this complexity allows us in turn to interpret "the human composite" as the one and ontically unique person.

The Experience of the Soul—It is to metaphysical analysis that we owe the knowledge of the human soul as the principle underlying the unity of being and the life of a concrete person. We deduce the existence of the soul and its spiritual nature from effects that demand a sufficient reason, that is to say, a commensurate cause. Thus, we have no direct experience of the soul but an experience of the effects requiring an adequate cause in man's being. What is meant by "experience of the soul" (speaking broadly) is everything in our previous analyses attributed to the transcendence of the person: obligation, responsibility, truthfulness, self-determination, and consciousness—and in and through these, man's entire, as it were, spiritual ego. Thus, the possible knowledge of the soul as the spiritual ego of man seems in its own way to indicate the direction of metaphysical analysis.

PART THREE

THE INTEGRATION OF THE PERSON IN ACTION

CHAPTER FIVE

INTEGRATION AND THE SOMA

1. THE FUNDAMENTALS OF THE PERSON'S INTEGRATION IN ACTION

Integration as a Complementary Aspect of Transcendence—Man manifests his transcendence of nature in self-determination, freedom, self-possession and self-governance. But he who governs himself is at the same time subjected and subordinate to himself. He who possesses himself is simultaneously in possession of himself. We define this aspect by the expression "the integration of the person in action." This is directly complementary to the person's transcendence in action. There is no governance of oneself without subjecting and subordinating oneself to this governance: active possession of oneself requires also a passive response in the structure of the person.

Integration as a Realization of the Person—Every action contains a synthesis of the efficacy (being intrinsically active) and the subjectiveness (a certain passivity: experiencing all that happens in him) of the human ego. Insofar as efficacy may be viewed as the domain where transcendence manifests itself, integration is manifested in subjectiveness. Integration here refers to the manifestation of a whole and a unity emerging on the basis of some complexity. The transcendence characteristic of experience passes over into the immanence of the experience of acting itself: when I act, I am wholly engaged in my acting.

2. THE INTEGRATION IN ACTION AS DISPLAYED IN DISINTEGRATION

The Many Meanings of Disintegration—The word "disintegration," implying a deficiency or lack of integration, is used in many different areas of human learning to connote a falling away from the normal or "integrated" mode of human being. Moreover, the notion of disintegration as used in the human sciences (including medicine and psychiatry) very often relies upon facts that have an essentially ethical nature (morality being an indispensable part of the integral experience of man).

Disintegration as a Structural Defect of Self-Governance and Self-Possession—Disintegration in its fundamental sense signifies what in the structure of self-governance and self-possession of the person appears as a defect or a failing. The lower limit of disintegration is set by all the symptoms that reflect what is in fact a total absence of self-governance and self-possession. While self-determination means that man can govern himself and possess himself, disintegration on the contrary signifies a more or less deep-seated inability to govern, or to possess, oneself.

Disintegration Reveals the Significance of the Person's Integration in Action—There are many forms and degrees of intensity of the problem of disintegration. In Aristotelian-Thomistic philosophy, we distinguish three stages of disintegration: actual (isolated instances in a person's actions), habitual (such instances regularly occurring), and "potential" (if the individual has a defect in what would be considered the normal human potential). Disintegration reveals the subjective ego is "insubordinate" or "unpossessable."

3. THE PERSON'S INTEGRATION IN ACTION IS THE KEY TO THE UNDERSTANDING OF MAN'S PSYCHOSOMATIC UNITY

Psychosomatic Unity and the Integration of the Acting Person—The crucial problem for understanding man's dynamic reality is to establish the fundamental significance of the integration and disintegration of the acting person. Simply to call man a "psycho-physical" unity, thereby revealing man as an object of the empirical sciences, is insufficient. To reveal man as a person manifested in his actions we have to change this approach. In studying "man-acts" we see the transcendence and integration of the person.

The Person-Action Unity Has Precedence over the Psychosomatic Complexity—In action, the whole psychosomatic complexity develops into the specific person-action unity. This latter unity has precedence over the former. Action comprises the multiplicity and diversity of the dynamisms that belong to the soma and to the psyche. In relation to them action constitutes that superior dynamic unity. That is what the integration of the person in the action (as the complementary aspect to transcendence) consists in. Human action is more than the sum of those other dynamisms: it is a new and superior type of dynamism, from which the others receive a new meaning and a new quality that is properly personal.

Integration Introduces Psychosomatic Activations into the Dynamic Unity of Action—Integration in action introduces the various activations of the psychosomatic structure of man into the action. In action, they reach a new and superior unity, in which they play an active part; but apart from action, when they are only the dynamisms of the soma or the psyche, they only "happen" in the man-subject. The function of integration consists in this overstepping of the dividing line between what only "happens" and "acting." Owing to integration these dynamisms play an active role in self-determination and the emergence of freedom.

4. THE INTEGRATION AND THE "INTEGRITY" OF MAN ON THE BASIS OF INTERACTING PSYCHOSOMATIC CONDITIONINGS

The Fundamentals of Man's Psychical and Somatic Dynamisms—The aim of our subsequent analyses is not to gain insight into the dynamisms of man's psychosomatic complexity of the type pursued by the particular sciences, concerned with the details appropriate to their own disciplines. Rather, we will be concerned with the person-action relation as a whole. Man in his psychosomatic complexity constitutes a highly diversified manifold, the particular elements of which are strictly interrelated. The most important of these interrelations is the dependence of the dynamism appropriate to the psyche on the soma.

The Outerness and Innerness of the Human Body—The term "somatic" refers to the body in the outer as well as the inner aspects of the system; thus, when we speak of somatic dynamism we refer both to the outer reality (shape, visible appearance) of the body with its appropriate members and to its inner reality, that is, the organism: the system and the joint functioning of all the bodily organs.

The Principle of Man's Psychosomatic Integrity—The somatic side of man and his psychical side are strictly interrelated. The person's integration in action rests on the conditioning of the psychical by the somatic; it is from the conditioning that man's integrity is derived. Concerning psychical functions conditioned by somatic ones, Aristotelian-Thomistic anthropology distinguishes two alternatives: internal (all sense functions) and external (man's spiritual functions). This is so because spiritual functions are seen as remaining internally independent from matter.

5. THE PERSON AND THE BODY

Reminiscences of Hylomorphism—We cannot discuss the human body apart from the whole that man is, that is, without recognizing that he is a person. So too the human body's dynamisms must be understood in light of the essentials of action and of its specifically personal character. This is done in traditional Aristotelian-Thomistic philosophy's interpretation of the hylomorphic nature of man, but we do not intend to repeat the traditional formulations but to rethink anew the dynamic human reality in terms of the reality of the acting person.

The Somatic Constitution and the Person—Even in the "static" approach, the relation of the body to the human person is seen as strictly necessary: in the definition of man as a rational animal, "animal" denotes the body and corporeality. The body gives man his concreteness, visible and external. His bodily "constitution" also connotes the inner side of the organism and its organ systems. This is even one way of trying to categorize human beings, by body type and consequent temperament.

The Human Body as the Person's Means of Expression—Thus, we pass from the static image of man to his dynamism. What exactly are the links between his visible outwardness and invisible inwardness? The dynamic transcendence (spiritual by nature) of the person finds in the human body the territory and the means for its expression. This common manifestation of the person's integration in the action, that may be thought of as "traversing" the body and being expressed in it, provides perhaps the simplest demonstration of the way the body belongs and is subordinate to the person. The integration of the person in action, taking place in the body and expressed by it, reveals simultaneously the deepest sense of the integrity of man as a person. It is the soul, indeed the spiritual soul, that appears to be the ultimate principle of this integrity. The person is not to identified with the body as such.

The Man-Person Has and Uses His Body When Acting—Whenever the person externalizes himself by means of the body he becomes simultaneously the object of his acting. The objectification of the body then becomes an integral element in the objectification of the whole personal subject, to whom the body "belongs" and of whose subjectivity it forms a structural part. The body is not a member of the subjective ego in the way of being identical with the ego; man *is not* the body, he only *has* it—this statement is the consequence of the belief that man "is" his own self (i.e. the person) only insofar as he possesses himself; and, in the same sense, if he *has* his body. Man as the person "possesses himself" in the experience of his embodiment precisely because it entails the feeling of possessing his body, and he governs himself because he controls his body. It is to this extent that the relation of the person to the body becomes "externally" apparent in the action of the person (with ethical implications).

[Important further considerations here in footnote 64, reproduced in full]—Luijpen, in criticizing view which treats the body as an object of having (he is of course speaking of "having" in a literal sense of the word), says, "My body is Not the Object of 'Having' ...I 'have' a car, a pen, a book. In this 'having' the object of the 'having' reveals itself as an exteriority. There is a distance between me and what I 'have.' What I 'have' is to a certain extent independent of me. ...My body is not something external to me like my car. I cannot dispose of my body or give it away as I dispose of money. ...All this stems from the fact that my body is not 'a' body but *my* body...in such a way that my body *embodies* me." (*Existential Phenomenology,* 3d ed. (Louvain: E. Nauwelaerts, 1963), p. 188. To explain the relation between the conscious subject and the body, Luijpen remarks, "In the supposition that I 'am' my body, I am a thing and wholly immersed in a world of mere things. But then the conscious self is reduced to nothing, and, consequently, also my body as 'mine,' as well as the world as 'mine.' Accordingly, I neither 'am' my body nor 'have' it. My body is precisely midway between these two extremes. It constitutes the transition from the conscious self to the worldly object. It is the mysterious reality which grafts me on things, secures my being-in-the-world, involves me in the world, and give me a standpoint in the world." (*ibid.*, pp. 189-90).

Bergson, on the other hand, is inclined to believe that it is the spirit that uses the body. For instance, he asserts, though in a different context, that "...c'est dire aussi que la vie de l'esprit ne peut pas etre un effet de la vie du corps, que tout se passe au contraire comme si le corps etait simplement utilize par l'esprit, et que des lors nous n'avons aucune raison de supposer que le corps et l'esprit soient inseparablement lies l'un a l'autre." *L'energie spirituelle,* pp. 57-58.

In connection with these different views the present author thinks it necessary to stress that when he affirms, "man *is not* the body, he only has it," this statement is the consequence of the belief that man "is" his own self (i.e., the person) only insofar as he possesses himself; and, in the same sense, if he *has* his body.

6. THE SELF-DETERMINATION OF THE PERSON AND THE REACTIVITY OF THE BODY

The Dynamism of the Body and the Total Dynamism of Man—The external experience does not, however, account fully for the relation that exists between the body and the person, in particular insofar as his acting, or the action, is concerned. The experience has to take us, so to say, to the interior of the body, so as to allow us to feel its own inwardness. It is only then that the relation is seen more completely and its image becomes more mature. But the discrimination of the somatic dynamism in the whole of the human dynamism presents a task that demands a high level of cognitive precision and involves us in questions even of the nature of the soul and its relation to the body.

The Reactivity of the Somatic Dynamism—Because of his body, the man-person genuinely belongs to nature. The close connection existing between the human organism and nature, so far as nature constitutes the set of conditions of existence and life, helps us to define the somatic dynamism of man. The purely somatic dynamism of man (of the human body) can be viewed as being "reactive," and we may also speak of the potentiality lying at its roots as reactive.

Why Can the Somatic Dynamism Be Called Reactive?—Though the term has wider meanings (involving man's emotional life and even the level of choice or decision) we are here restricting the use of the term "reactivity" to the soma, that is, to the dynamism of the body alone, due to the direct connections of the body itself with nature; the psychical and emotive factors are only indirectly connected with nature by means of the soma and its somatic dynamism. At the level of animate creatures, reactivity is a manifestation of life and to some extent even its principle, that is to say, the principle of formation, subsistence, and development. It is also the distinctive feature expressing man's somatic potentialities and consequently his bodily vitality.

The Relation between Reactivity and Vitality of the Human Body—The vitality of the human body is of an essentially vegetative nature; the life of the body itself is vegetative. As an organism, it has innate powers of vegetation and reproduction itself (made possible by sexual differentiation of the human body). The dynamic fabric of all the vegetative vitality of the human body consists of purely instinctive reactions which happen in the person without any special influence of the will or self-determination. The role of instincts will be considered presently. The body, through the nervous system, is also capable of active response to stimuli.

7. ACTION AND MOTION

The Meaning of the Body's Subjectivity—The fact that the body's efficacy (something-happens-in-man) differs from the efficacy of the person (man-acts) brings sharply into evidence the ontic complexity of man. This by no means contradicts man's personal unity but is characteristic of it. There is, intrinsically built into the personal structure of man's unity, a structure that exists and is dynamized according to nature—in a different way than that of the person. The unity of the body with the ontic subjectivity of man cannot be doubted. However, the experience of the subjective ego is related to the reflexive function of consciousness which tends to include only the external aspects of the body and its mobility. The normal course of the whole vegetative vitality and somatic reactivity of man seems to lie beyond the reach of his consciousness.

The Synthesis of Action and Motion—The human body has its own "subjectivity" (dynamism, reactivity) different from the efficacious and transcendent subjectivity of the person. The normal integrity of the human person consists in the "matching" of these two dimensions of man. The realization of every transcendent action, which visibly incorporates the spontaneous bodily dynamism, rests on a specific integration. We see this in the case of bodily motion. It may be merely instinctive (reactive to stimuli, a "reflex" action, without involving human will and freedom) or bodily motion may be as a result of man's free decision and transcendent personal efficacy (e.g. walking to school). The latter requires a specific integration of the two dimensions.

The Moment of Skill in the Action-Motion Synthesis—Man may have a skilled or unskilled body and this is always reflected in his motions. Bodily motions are the territory in which man develops his first skills, earliest motor habits. Some of this is instinctive but very early the process begins to be influenced by the will, the source of motor impulses coming from the interior of the person bearing the mark of self-determination. Developed skill becomes so spontaneous and fluent that we are no longer so aware of it and of causative effect of the will, unless in an exceptional situation (mountain climbing) where we concentrate on the motions needed.

The Somatic Constitution and Human Mobility—In every individual case, man's mobility constitutes a specific phenomenological whole with the structure of the body, that is, with its constitution. Mobility as the manifestation of the somatic reactivity, partly innate and partly acquired through early developed skills, corresponds to and derives from the specific traits of the organism. If due to a purely somatic defect (disability) the body is not whole, this is of physical but of no moral significance. On the contrary, very often a human being with a high degree of somatic disintegration may represent a personality of great value.

8. DRIVE AND THE PERSON'S INTEGRATION IN ACTION

The Complex Nature of Drive—Instincts are indicative of a dynamism (in this case, an immediate particular reaction) appropriate to nature itself, while drive tells of nature's dynamic orientation in a definite direction, e.g. the "drive of self-preservation" or the "sexual" or "reproductive drive." Drives are part of the somatic dynamism of man but also have a psycho-emotive character, e.g. in the urge to self-preservation or in the sexual urge, creating an incitement or an objectively felt necessity with a somatic ground.

The Relation of Drives to Somatic Reactivity—The body's specific reactivity conditions drives. The human organism is equipped with the necessary mechanisms (even on the vegetative level) of self-preservation which function automatically according to the rules of nature without engaging conscious awareness. Its contact with consciousness is maintained by means of the "bodily sensations" by which we say "I'm fine" or "I'm sick." These words may refer to spiritual conditions but usually describe one's physical state. The sensations of hunger and thirst also spring from the drive for self-preservation. Clearly this drive is not restricted to the somatic but constitutes a dynamic trait of the human being and existence as a whole.

The Drive of Self-Preservation—At the origin of the drive of self-preservation there is a metaphysical principle and a fundamental value: existence itself. Even the vegetative level expresses this compulsion to exist and the "subjective necessity" to exist pervades the whole dynamic structure of man. This feeling meets the intellectual affirmation of existence, the awareness that "it is good to exist and to live" while it would be "bad to lose one's existence and one's life." Here the instinct of self-preservation becomes a consciously adopted attitude. This drive does not control man; the suicide substitutes negation in place of affirmation. Yet even here the negation may not be of existing *at all* but only a rejection of existence in a way that seems unbearable.

The Drive of Sex and Reproduction—The drive of sex, which relies on the momentous division of mankind into male and female individuals, also stems from the somatic ground and also penetrates deeply into the psyche and its emotivity, thereby affecting even man's spiritual life. The desire for sharing with another human being, springing from both the close similarity and the difference due to the separation of the sexes, is based on the sexual drive. The latter also becomes the source for the propagation of life; hence it is simultaneously the drive of reproduction preserving the species. This natural desire is the basis of marriage and through marital life becomes the foundation of the family. The reproductive, procreative trait at the somatic level of drive to some extent automatically or spontaneously *happens* in man. However, these reactions remain sufficiently conscious to be controllable by man and this control consists in the adaptation of the body's dynamism to its proper end. Though possible, the control of the sexual drive may and often does raise many difficult problems, especially for individuals whose sexual desire is unusually strong. This involves not only somatic reactions but also a special psychical urge of the emotive type. (See *Love and Responsibility*).

The Correct Interpretation of Drives—The problem of drives is not a purely somatic one. Though drives in man are part of the more general problem of the integration of the dynamism of the body, the full solution of the question of the integration of drives requires a broader look at the psycho-emotive element. Moreover, the significance of drives is not only as a subjective force based in somatic reactions but also, and more significantly, as the outcome of the objective value of ends to which they urge and direct.

CHAPTER SIX

PERSONAL INTEGRATION AND THE PSYCHE

1. THE PSYCHE AND THE SOMA

The Fundamentals of the Psychical Component—The person's integration in action depends upon the surrender to the will's transcendence through self-determination and efficacy and, thus, by complementing transcendence, it plays its own role in shaping the structure of self-possession and self-governance. In the preceding chapter, we investigated this integration with regard to the soma, now we must do so with regard to the psyche.

The Meaning of the Term "Psyche"—"Psyche" refers to that which makes man an integral being, indeed, to that which determines the integrity of his components without itself being of a bodily or somatic nature. "Psyche" or "psychical" apply to those elements of the concrete human being that in the experience of man we discern as in a way cohesive or integrated with the body but that in themselves differ from it. The disclosure of what is distinctively psychical but simultaneously related to what is somatic in man provides the groundwork for conclusions to be drawn, first, about the relation between soul and body and, second, on a still more distant plane between spirit and matter.

Man's Psychical Functioning and His Somatic Constitution—Man's integrated psychical functioning is the basis for the integration of the person in action; it does not, however, exteriorize itself in the same way as does somatic functioning. The psyche is essentially different from the body. It is neither "matter" nor "material" in the sense that the body is material. The functions of the psyche are "internal" and "immaterial" and while internally they are conditioned by the soma with its own proper functions, they can in no way be reduced to what is somatic.

2. A CHARACTERISTIC OF THE PSYCHE — EMOTIVITY

Etymological Interpretation of Emotivity and Emotion—The words "emotive" and "emotivity" (from the Latin *movere,* to move) point to a movement or actuation whose external origin is indicated by the prefix *ex.* Thus, though the psychical actuation depends to some extent on the body and is in various ways conditioned by the somatic, it does not belong to the body, and differs from it and its somatic dynamism. We have to stress the irreducible nature of emotions to reactions and of emotivity to reactivity. An emotion is not a somatic reaction but a psychical event distinctive in its nature and qualitatively different from a bodily reaction.

Emotivity and Reactivity—Since emotivity is so deeply rooted in and conditioned by reactivity we often speak of "psychical reactions" or of someone "reacting is such and such a way," by which we mean not only his somatic reaction but his comportment as a whole in an action that includes also his conscious response to a definite value. Due to integration, even a response that is a choice of a decision appropriate to the will comprises some elements of somatic reactivity. Man in action is a complex unity.

***Emotivity and the Conscious Response of the Will*—** The integration of the person in action includes somatic reactivity and psychical emotivity into the unity of the action, into the unity with the transcendence of the person expressed by efficacious self-determination that is simultaneously a conscious response to values. This conscious response to values takes place in a specific way, through the integration of the whole psycho-emotivity of man which is, moreover, indicative of a specific sensitivity to values. Because of this specific sensitivity to values the emotive potentiality supplies the will with, so to speak, a special kind of raw material: for in choice and decision an act of will is always a cognitively defined, intellectual response to values. Here we gain a better insight into the meaning of transcendence, for it is in the transcendence and not in the integration of the human emotivity itself that the deepest meanings of the spirituality of the person are manifested, and it is there that we find the most adequate basis for asserting the spirituality of the soul. The psychical is also emotive and sensuous.

3. FEELINGS AND CONSCIOUSNESS IN THE EXPERIENCE OF THE BODY

Emotive Dynamism as a Concentrator of Experiences—The psychical strand in emotivity may be seen as running between corporeality and spirituality, but far from dividing them it interweaves with the one and the other bringing them together. All that determines and constitutes the spiritual transcendence of the person—his attitude toward truth, good, and beauty with the accompanying faculty of self-determination—stimulates a very deep emotive resonance in the human being. Thus, it would be impossible to reach a sound understanding of the person's integration in action without an analysis of emotivity.

The Affective and the Motor Response—The *ability to feel* at the somatic level (closest to the reactivity of the body concerned with motor stimuli) also consists in the reception of stimuli from material objects; but their effect is not somatic and does not consist in a movement of the body: their effect is psychical and expressed in feelings, completely transcending the somatic reaction.

Feeling Places Psychical above Somatic Subjectivity—Feeling response differs essentially from motor response though they very often come together (e.g., the hand is instinctively jerked away from a hot object). Our inner motor responses (the "subjectivity of the body") are not normally felt, but sensation allows man to emerge from and above this unfelt level. For feeling as such constitutes a cognitive sensuous reflex of the body, which, thus, becomes accessible to consciousness—because of feeling the body becomes an objective content of consciousness and is reflected in it.

Feeling Underlies the Consciousness of the Body—There is the feeling of one's own body: its different states and movements are the source of sensations which play a decisive role in enabling man to have an experience of his own body. The range of consciousness of the body is, so to speak, currently determined by the field of feeling. Thus, the vegetative dynamism of the body is normally beyond the reach of the body, unless something penetrates into the field of consciousness, such as bodily pain.

Self-Feeling—The habitual experience of one's body is the resultant of many sensations and feelings connected with the body and its reactive-motor dynamisms. These sensations reveal to every man not a separate "subjectivity" of the body but the somatic structure of the whole subject that he is, of the whole ego. They reveal to what extent he is a body, to what extent his soma participates in his existence and his acting. The direct and proper object of self-feeling is the whole somatic ego, which is not isolated from the personal ego but is, on the contrary, intrinsically cohesive with it. Moreover, how well we feel and even how efficiently our body functions on the motor-reactive level can condition the efficiency of our "higher psychical functions." This shows how intrinsically cohesive is our somatic ego with the whole of the personal ego, how strict is their mutual union.

"Precedence" of Consciousness over Feelings in Personal Dynamism—The feeling of one's body is a necessary condition for experiencing the integral subjectivity of man. The relation between senses and mind is bilateral because a feeling we have of our own body allows us to establish an objective contact with it and at the same time reveals the psychical subjectivity integrated with the somatic body-subject. Feeling "happens" psychically within the human ego, revealing subjectivity to consciousness, which—except in extreme cases when emotions overcome consciousness—retains a certain "precedence" over feelings. This precedence of consciousness and "subordination" of feelings is the condition of self-determination and, thus, also of self-governance and self-possession: it is the condition of the realization of the action, of really personal dynamism.

4. SENSITIVITY AND TRUTHFULNESS

The Consciousness of Feelings and Man's Individual Sensitivity—Man not only feels his body but he also has a more integral feeling of himself, he feels what determines his own ego and his dynamism. Further, we ascertain in man not only a feeling of his body or of bodies in general—to which he has cognitive access through sense—but also some aesthetic, religious, and moral feelings, Thus, we have evidence that the emotive element in him somehow corresponds to what is spiritual, not merely sensual.

Sensitivity and Personal Experience of Values—"Sensitivity" can refer to sense stimuli, but on another level it can refer the different intentional directions of human feeling deeply rooted in man's spiritual life. But it is to values that all feelings or sensations are intentionally directed. This is why a feeling or sensation becomes in man, so to speak, the nucleus or the crystallization of an experience of value. M. Scheler goes so far as to say that feelings are the *only* source of man's cognitive relations to values. In any case, we note that the experience of values based on the integration of feelings through consciousness is not itself sufficient; in view of the person's transcendence in action still another integration is necessary, namely, the integration through "truthfulness." Therefore, the experience of values has to be subordinated, within the dimension of the acting person, to the reference to truth. Such an understanding of the notion of "authenticity"—based on truthfulness—may sometimes be contrary to its understanding based on sensitivity alone. Indeed, self-determination and the closely related self-governance often require that action be taken in the name of *bare truth* about good, in the name of values that are not felt. It may even require that action be taken against one's actual feelings.

Sensitivity as a Source of Enrichment of the Psyche—Sensitivity to values is itself a great enrichment of human nature and the basis of many human talents. Emotionalists are right when they contend that this ability in man is unique and irreplaceable. No intellectual approval of values leading to their objectively correct appreciation will ever by itself result in so expressive an experience as when it is guided by feeling. Neither can the intellect impart to man that closeness to a value and concentration on it as feeling does. However, the more there is truthfulness in man's awareness of all values, and their relations and order, the more complete is his self-governance and mature is his self-possession.

5. DESIRE AND EXCITEMENT

Concupiscent Appetite and Irascible Appetite—In Aristotelian-Thomistic philosophy, sensuousness and rationality are distinct but strictly related. The senses provide the raw material for the mind, though intellectual cognition extends far beyond that which is given in experience. Similarly, the sensitive appetite supplies material or objectives for volition. St. Thomas distinguishes between the "concupiscent appetite" (in which the objective is but an object of desire) and the "irascible appetite" (in which the objective can only be attained by overcoming obstacles or opposition). Thereby he distinguishes different types of sentiments and even different types of human individuals: concupiscence is a dominant trait in some people and irascibility in others.

Excitement as a Distinctive Emotive Fact—Excitement "happens" in the subject and thereby reveals his psychical potentiality; it is an emotive instance that differs from feeling, to which we have rightly attributed a certain cognitive intentionality. No such cognitive tendency of the psyche is present in excitement, whose character is never cognitive. Further, though indirectly excitement has an appetitive bent, what we observe in such states directly is simply excitement and not appetite. Excitement is always shown in a definite reaction of the body, a chain of reactions of the organism (blood circulation, breathing, quickened heartbeat, etc.).

The Difference between Excitement and Elation—But to reduce excitements to sensuousness would be an oversimplification. The source of excitement may come from the experience of a value entirely inaccessible to sense or from a wholehearted acceptance of ideals; then, however, we tend to speak of "elation" rather than excitement. Elation, being spiritual in nature, may be accompanied in the subject by sensuous or even bodily excitement of greater or lesser degree (showing the need for integration).

Excitability—Integration must comprise not only *the* particular excitements but the whole of human excitability. Excitability is closely associated with but distinct from man's sensitivity. It constitutes what in man may be called the "explosive sphere" of emotions (i.e., an awakening of emotions often rather sudden and therefore characterized as explosive). The source of emotions is then seen as irrational and their experience is in itself "blind"—features we attribute to passions. Excitement establishes certain forms of human emotions and feelings, but obviously it does not exhaust their enormous wealth of tone and variation.

Excitability as a Constituent of Drives—Sensuous-emotive excitability appears to particularly well rooted in the soil of human drives, with both a somato-reactive layer and a psychosomatic center to them, as previously discussed (e.g., sexual drive or drive for self-preservation). But this aptitude for excitement is insufficient to exhaust the notion of "drive." Both reactivity and excitability remain at the disposal of the powerful forces of nature that steer them in the direction of the most elemental and fundamental value, that is existence itself.

6. "STIRRING EMOTIONS" AND EMOTIVITY

"Stirring Emotions" Differ from Excitement—Mere excitement must be distinguished from deep, stirring emotions and there must be no reduction of the latter to the former. There is a difference of depth and kind of experience here and not only of intensity. Though both are accompanied by some kind of somatic reaction, excitement is more embedded in this reaction than very deep emotions.

In the latter, bodily feelings may appear to yield priority to spiritual feelings, moreover, the content of such emotions is strictly related to the spiritual life of man, e.g., aesthetic emotion before the beautiful, cognitive emotion arising from the discovery of a truth, and deep emotions connected with the sphere of the good. Scheler stresses the latter as providing examples of deep emotivity in relation to conscience: remorse, repentance, justification, conversion, mental peace, deep joy, spiritual bliss.

The "Stir of Emotion" as the Core of Human Affectivity—At the root of human emotions is a "stirring of emotion" which then radiates internally, spreads to the whole of man's psychical sphere, and produces different emotional experiences. In this way an emotion springs forth and develops in man and fades away. However, an emotion may also become fixed in what we may call an "affective state." The latter however involves an original emotive stirring that has since been taken over by the will. The question of the penetration of emotions to the realm of the will and, thus, also of the transition from emotional states to "*affective attitudes*" is of great importance in any discussion on the integration of the psyche, which is precisely the theme of this chapter.

The Multifarious Richness of Emotions—When we try to characterize and name emotions, we in fact distinguish between *the different ways emotions are stirred,* e.g., feelings of sorrow, joy, anger, tenderness, love, or hatred. The world of human emotions is rich and diversified, like the colors, tones, and shades on the palette of a painter. Moreover, emotions, like colors, can be mixed; they overlap and interpenetrate; they also enhance or complete or destroy one another. Since emotions *happen* "in" man (in their emergence, growth, and passing away), subjectivity is here understood in the particular sense that has been distinguished earlier in this study. Emotional dynamism is at least to a large extent independent of the efficacy of the person. Already the Greek philosophers noticed that emotions did not depend on the mind and in their essence were "irrational."

Some Criteria of Differentiation—This alleged "irrationality" of human affectivity has perhaps been the cause of the one-sided and oversimplified tendency to identify it with sensuousness. We stress once again the specific difference between the stirring of emotion and excitement, a difference in natures and not just in intensity or degree. We refer to this difference of level when we discriminate between man's excitability and his affectiveness. Psychologists also distinguish between lower and higher emotions, of emotions of different "depth," or of "peripheral" or more "central" emotions. These distinctions presuppose an innerness to the man-person, something like an immaterial space, where we can make such distinctions according to the particular feelings in question. From another point of view, the different "levels of depth" point to a certain integration in the man-subject of his emotional stirrings (with the ensuing emotions) and project on the efficacy of the person.

7. EMOTIVITY OF THE SUBJECT AND THE EFFICACY OF THE PERSON

Emotions Differentiate According to their Emotive Content—Every emotion has its own emotive core as an original and unique psychic event. It is vested with a content which is neither cognitive nor appetitive but solely emotive. Each is also a manifestation of man's psychical potentialities and in a special manner his subjectivity. Since in the sphere of emotions a certain tension arises between efficacy and subjectivity, this domain deserves special analysis concerning the integration of efficacy and subjectivity.

Spontaneity and Self-Determination—Emotional experiences only happen in man as subject. Their happening is *spontaneous,* i.e., independent from the *proper efficacy* of the person, his self-determination. While experiencing feelings man has the most vivid awareness that it is not he who is acting but that something is happening in him, indeed happening *with him,* just as if he had lost control of himself. This presents a special task for man (with the power of self-governance and self-possession) to cope with.

Affectivity is not the Source of Disintegration—The fact that with the emergence of an emotion or passion man is prompted to seek some sort of integration and this becomes a special task for him, does not signify in any way that they are themselves a cause of disintegration. The view about their disintegration role appeared in the philosophy of the Stoic school (criticized by Aristotle) and in modern times was to some extent revived by Kant (criticized by Scheler). Such views disregard the evidence of experience.

The Creative Role of Tensions between Emotivity and Efficacy—There is a clearly marked tension between the spontaneous efficacy of the human psyche (in emotivity) and the efficacy of the human person. This is crucial for human personality and morality. Traditionally this has been seen as a tension between the rational appetite (will) and the sensitive appetite. However, we examine it first as a tension between the subjectivity and the efficacy of the person, requiring a specific kind of effort appropriate to man's inwardness. This relating of sensitivity and truthfulness in cognition, between emotivity and efficacy is specifically creative.

Emotions Tend to be Rooted in the Subjective Ego—We are speaking of the relation between the will and emotion. Emotive happenings may be short-lived but they also have a tendency to be rooted in the subjective ego, to become long-standing inner attitudes. Thus, repeated anger can become lasting resentment. It is here that we come to the point where "what happens in man" is nearest to his self-determination. The influence of emotions on the will may be such that instead of determining man's attitudes, the will tends to adopt the attitude presented by emotion, thus, leading to what we call "the emotional attitude." Such attitudes are subjectivistic; efficacy is dominated by subjectivity. There is a preponderance of psychical immanence over personal transcendence.

The Role of Emotion with Respect to the Will Stresses Personal Efficacy—All these considerations do not, however, justify the conclusion that emotion leads to disintegration. Despite the emotionalization of consciousness, the limitations of responsibility in actions performed under emotional stress, the way in which emotivity may to some extent thrust its values on the will, it is by any standards no more than an obstacle to the integration of the person in action. Indeed this integration is possible, and then emotion adds special vividness to efficacy and with it to the whole personal structure of self-governance and self-possession.

8. THE EMOTIVITY OF THE SUBJECT AND THE EXPERIENCE OF VALUE

Emotivity and Conscious Efficacy—In a way the emotionalization of consciousness is a limiting phenomenon when excessive emotion damages consciousness and the ability to have a normal experience. Man then lives engrossed in his emotions, his excitement, or his passion, and though the condition is undoubtedly subjective, his "subjectivity" brings only negative results so far as efficacy, self-determination, and transcendence of the acting person are concerned. There are many degrees of such an effect however and this is not to be reduced to just the effect of the "intensity of emotions." That would be too simplistic for the force of emotion derives mainly from the experience of value. Thus, in this domain there are special opportunities for creative integration.

The Expressiveness of Human Experience is Emotional—Asserting that the intensity of emotion "mainly derives from the experience of value" we touch on what appears to be the most remarkable in human emotivity and what distinguishes it from the purely somatic reactivity. Emotions are intrinsically accessible to consciousness and have a special vividness in our experience.

The Content of Emotions Refers to Values—Both the emotional stirrings and the emotions of the human being always relate to a value and are born out of this relation. This is true when we are angry and it is equally true when we love, mourn, rejoice, or hate. The reference in all these cases is to a value, and the whole emotion may be said to consist of this reference. Nevertheless, it is neither cognitive nor appetitive. Emotions are an indication of values that exist apart from emotions. If parallel to this indication of values there is some cognition of them, then it results from sensations and feelings which constitute an "emotive condition" or "emotive reflex." The more fully consciousness is penetrated by this reflex, the fuller and more complete becomes the experience of value. The emotionalization of consciousness, however, hinders this experience and sometimes may even prevent it.

The Source of the Spontaneous Experience of Value—An emotion, when stirred, spreads out and, becoming rooted in the subject, spontaneously sets off a reference to value which in its own way has a specific "psychical value" because it brings about an emotional fulfillment. It generates a feeling of being entirely contained within oneself and at the same time in an intimate nearness to the object, that is, to the value with which the contact is spontaneously established.

Relieving of Tensions between Spontaneity and Self-Determination—A tension between emotivity and efficacy occurs in man because of a two-fold reference to value. Efficacy and with it self-determination through choice and decision presuppose a dynamic relation to truth in the will itself. This factor directs the person toward his fulfillment in action not through emotional spontaneity alone but by means of the transcendent relation to truth, obligation, and responsibility. The intellect has precedence over emotion, over emotional spontaneity in man, and denotes the power and ability to be guided in choice and decision by the truth itself about good. This power presupposes a certain detachment from spontaneously experienced values but is never manifested by a denial of these values (as we find in the Stoics and in Kant). On the contrary, the authentic subordination to truth as the principle controlling the choices and decisions made by the free human will demands an intimate interrelation between transcendence and integration in the domain of emotions, reflecting the two complementary aspects of the complexity of man's acting.

9. ACTION AND EMOTION—THE INTEGRATING FUNCTION OF SKILL

Attraction and Repulsion in the Spontaneous Reference to Values—The whole emotive dynamism brings with it a spontaneous orientation "toward" a positive value (attraction) or "away" from a counter-value, something negative (repulsion). Attraction and repulsion are not at first defined as to their objects, nor are they a function of emotional stirring, but originally follow the orientation of nature expressed by instincts. To define them as to their objects is the task and function of the person and, thus, of the intellect, which cognitively forms man's attitude to truth, in this case the truth about "good" and "evil."

Moral Decision and Spontaneous Attraction and Repulsion—Different emotions introduce into man's attitude toward truth their own spontaneous reference of an emotional and emotive character. The distinction between attractive (love, joy, desire, courage) and repulsive (fear, dislike, sorrow, anger) emotional experiences or responses seems to have a special significance for the spontaneous orientation of the psychical subjectivity of man to the good and against the evil. Here lies the main tension between the spontaneous emotivity of nature and the efficacy and self-determination of the person. At this point we see the integrating function of proficiency expounded by the great masters of classical philosophy in their comprehensive teaching on virtues or moral proficiency. The integration of the person and action on the basis of emotivity of the human psyche is accomplished through proficiency, which from the point of view of ethics deserves to be called "virtue." An essential element in the idea of "virtue" is that of moral value and this entails a reference to a norm. Here we face the personalistic problem of integration.

The Function of Moral Proficiency or Virtue—The personal structure of self-governance and self-possession is realized by means of different proficiencies and skills. These aim at subordinating the spontaneous emotivity of the subjective ego to its self-determination. Their way to achieve this end, however, is to make the best use of the emotive energy and not to suppress it. When properly assimilated, spontaneous emotive energy adds considerably to the energy of the will itself and this is precisely the task of proficiency. But another purpose must also be gradually achieved. The proficiencies or skills acquired in different domains allow the will to secure—and without any risk to itself to adopt as its own—the spontaneity of emotions. In a way, spontaneity is also a trait of proficiency, though not in its primitive state but after transformation in the course of a persevering process of character formation. So far as the reference to truth is concerned, the result is that the will—guided by the light of reason—learns how by spontaneous reference to emotion, by a spontaneous move of attraction or repulsion, to choose and to adopt the real good; it also learns how to reject the real bad. This task, this integration, lasts until the end of a man's life. It is a level of skill far beyond that of somato-reactive integration and involves character formation or the molding of one's psycho-moral personality.

10. CONDUCT AND BEHAVIOR

The Meaning of Terms—The word "conduct" (implying guidance along a road) denotes the acting of the human being so far as it is an outcome or a resultant of his efficacy, actions that the man-person performs and that he fulfills himself in. "Behavior" however only describes the way of acting or comportment of a person that is easily noticeable to an observer. It may, thus, refer to elements not necessarily or entirely controlled by man, defining the outward expression or simply the "appearance" of acting. The stress is on how a man behaves in his acting and not on how he actually acts.

Conduct and Behavior in the Person's Integration in Action—Thus, the "appearance" (the speech, gesture, and pose) of a spirited speaker sound and looks different from that of one who is slow and phlegmatic. Even when they do the same thing each does it somewhat differently, each precisely *behaves* differently. This throws additional light on the problem of integration.

11. THE PERSON'S INTEGRATION IN ACTION AND THE SOUL-BODY RELATION

Human Complexity Revealed in Transcendence and Integration—Integration is the manifestation and realization of unity on the basis of the multifarious complexity of man. It is a complementary aspect of the dynamism of the person, an aspect that is complementary to transcendence. Man's complexity appears to be most clearly revealed by the reality of integration, but to show psychosomatic complexity in man is not equivalent to revealing the proper relation of soul and body, and inversely.

The Relation of Soul and Body to Integration and Transcendence—An insight into the relation between the soul and the body may be reached only through the total experience of man. They are not directly intuited (not given directly in human experience, not a content of intuition alone). Both the reality of the soul and that of the soul's relation to the body are in this sense trans-phenomenal and extra-experiential. Nevertheless, the total and comprehensive experience of man shows the soul as real and as staying in relation to the body. They both have been discovered and are continuously being discovered in the philosophical reflection resulting from human experience. In this respect, the relation and subordination of integration to the transcendence of the person is highly significant, the significance being contained in their complementarity. Highly significant also is the fact that man as person is simultaneously the one who governs and possesses himself, and who is subordinate to and possessed by himself.

The Current and Hylomorphic Meaning of the Body-Soul Relation—All these categories as given in experience appear to pave the way for and lead us near to an understanding of the body-soul relation, though we cannot grasp this relation directly. We must approach it in terms of metaphysical categories. Still, the current sense of the "soul" and of its relation to the "body" is a fruit of commonsense experience, with firmly grounded essentially metaphysical content. Important for us are first that on the evidence of experience and intuition we may unravel the complexity of man, and second that we are able to define the limits of this intuition.

The Soul as the Principle of Transcendence and Integration—While the body itself is the source of the reactive dynamism, specific to the human soma, and indirectly also to the emotive dynamism of the human psyche, the integration of these two dynamisms has to have a common origin with the person's transcendence. Can we infer that it is the soul which is the ultimate source or, to put it differently, the transcending principle and also the principle of the integration of the person in his acting? At any rate, it seems that this line of reasoning has brought us much closer to the soul. Our analyses have divulged something like a boundary in man which sets a limit to the scope of the dynamism and, thus, also of the potentiality of the body, or of what is called "matter." They also reveal a capacity of a spiritual nature that seems to lie at the root of the person's transcendence, but also indirectly of the integration of the person in action. This however is not equivalent to a boundary *between* the body and the soul. The experience of integration intervenes against any such unwarranted oversimplification. Integration—precisely because it is the complementary aspect of the transcendence of the person in action—tells us that the soul-body relation cuts across all the boundaries we find in experience and that it goes deeper and is more fundamental than they are. We have, thus, confirmed, even if indirectly, our earlier assertion that the complete reality of the soul itself and of the soul's relation to the body can be completely expressed only in metaphysical terms.

PART FOUR

PARTICIPATION

CHAPTER SEVEN

INTERSUBJECTIVITY BY PARTICIPATION

1. AN INTRODUCTION TO PARTICIPATION

Man's Acting "Together With Others"—The current chapter adds one more element to the previously outlined whole: that aspect of the dynamic correlation of the action with the person which issues from the fact that actions can be performed by people together with other people. The mark of this communal—or social—trait is firmly imprinted on the human life and human existence itself.

An Appreciation of Cooperation Involves an Understanding of Human Acting—"To cooperate" is not the same thing as "to act together with others." We will use the latter expression, which appears to be more amenable to further differentiation. We know that human activities may be performed in various interhuman relations and also in various social situations. We have logically first considered the nature of human acting and may now consider acting "together with others" in its full human significance.

The Participatory Aspect in the Person's Acting "Together With Others"—To explain the personal nature of human actions it is absolutely necessary to understand the consequences of the fact that they may be performed "together with others" in a participatory aspect. How does this effect the dynamic correlation of action with person? Our answer will gradually emerge.

2. THE PERSONALISTIC VALUE OF ACTION

The Performance of Action Is a Value—The performance itself of an action by the person is a fundamental value, which we may call the personalistic—or personal—value of action. Such a value always differs from those moral values which belong to the performed action and issue from their reference to norms. The personalistic value, on the other hand, inheres in the performance itself of the action by the person, in the very fact that man acts in a manner appropriate to himself, that self-determination (together with integration on various levels) Thus, authentically in the nature of his acting—the transcendence of the person being realized through his acting. Though being is prior to action, and, thus, the person and his value is prior to and more fundamental than the value of action, it is in actions that the person manifests himself—a fact we have been stressing from the first.

The Personalistic Value of Action Conditions Its Ethical Value—Any moral value good or bad presupposes the performance of the action. If there are any defects in the authentic self-determination of the action, then the moral value in it would lose its foundations, partly if not completely. The performance of action by the person has not only an ontological but an axiological significance. The value is "personalistic" because the person performing an action also fulfils himself in it. Self-fulfillment in action is strictly related to ethical value, so much so that moral evil may be regarded as the non-fulfillment of the self in acting.

The Relation of "Communal Action" to the Personalistic Value of Action—The traditional teaching on human action *(de actibus humanus),* with its distinction between perfect and imperfect volitions of the will, must be supplemented and rethought to the end. To reduce the content of volition to will seen solely as a power may to some extent impoverish the reality contained in action: in this approach the action appears to have but an instrumental significance relatively to the whole ethical order. We have been stressing the authenticity of personalistic value revealing and confirming ethical values in strict correspondence with the person. Now we ask what relation acting "together with others" has to the personalistic value of the action.

3. A MORE DETAILED DEFINITION OF PARTICIPATION

The Person in the Philosophy of Man—The traditional philosophy of man—as contrasted with the doubt permeating the thinking of contemporary man—tended to underline the role of nature; the nature of man is rational and, thus, he is a person, but at the same time he has a "social" nature. We have to ask, however, what this means from the point of view of the dynamic correlation of action with person and from the point of view of existing, living, and acting "together with others."

Participation as Trait of Acting "Together With Others"—In current usage, "participation" means having a share or a part in something. Philosophically considered, the trait of participation, thus, indicates that man, when he acts together with other men, retains in this acting the personalistic value of his own action and at the same time shares in the realization and results of the communal acting. *In this very manner* (communal acting), he realizes the personalistic value of his own acting.

Participation as a Trait of the Person Acting "Together with Others"—Participation implies that the personalistic value of the action with its transcendence and integration is not only maintained but is realized because of acting with others. If genuine participation is limited then so is the personalistic value. This may sometimes go so far that we can hardly speak any more of "acting together with others" in the sense of "authentic" actions of the person, rather we should speak only of something that "happens" to a particular man under the influence of other men, e.g. mass psychology affecting people in an uncontrolled way.

Participation as the Ability to Form Interpersonal Relations—In the diverse relations of acting together with others, participation presents itself as an adaptation to these relations and hence as a multifarious reference of the person to other persons. Participation corresponds to the person's transcendence and integration in action when man chooses what is chosen by others or even *because* it is chosen by others—he then identifies the object of his choice with a value that seen as in some way homogeneous and his own.

4. INDIVIDUALISM AND ANTI-INDIVIDUALISM

The Theoretical and Normative Significance of Participation—"Participation" has a theoretical significance in explaining the social nature of man on the ground of the dynamic correlation of action with person. It also has an indirectly normative significance, pointing to certain obligations that are the consequence of the principle of participation. For if man can fulfill himself through participation, then everyone ought to strive for this personalistic type of acting with others, and every society ought to allow the person remaining within its orbit to realize himself through such participation.

Individualism and Totalism as the Two Limits of Participation—The personalistic value of participation may be limited in two ways. First, there may be a lack of participation caused by the person as the subject-agent of acting. "Individualism" sees in the individual the supreme good to which all interests of the community must be subordinated. Second, participation may become impossible for reasons external to the person and resulting from defects in the system according to which the community operates. "Objective totalism" or "anti-individualism" unconditionally subordinates the individual to the community or society (collectivism).

Individualism Implies a Denial of Participation—Individualism limits participation inasmuch as it isolates the person who is then conceived of solely as an individual concentrated on himself and on his own good, which is also regarded in isolation from the good of others and of the community. "Others" are seen only as a source of limitation and if community is formed its purpose is to protect the good of the individual from the "others." There is an implied denial and rejection any genuine participation.

Totalism as Reversed Individualism—The dominant trait of totalism (anti-individualism, "reversed individualism") is the need to find protection *from* the individual seen as the chief enemy of society and the common good. It assumes the same view of the individual that individualism does, i.e., seeking only his own good and incapable of genuine participation; thus, the "common good" can only be attained by limiting the individual, frequently presupposing the use of coercion.

The Conception of the Human Being Underlying Both Systems—The way of thinking about man underlying both systems may be defined as "impersonalistic" or "antipersonalistic," inasmuch as the distinctive trait of the personalistic approach is the conviction that to be a person means to be capable of participation. The personalistic value of human action and of acting together with others for his own development and fulfillment grounds the right to man's total freedom of acting, which conditions the ethical order and simultaneously determines it. On the other hand, the moral order instills into human actions—in particular those within the orbit of acting "together with others"—those determinants, and, thus, also those limitations, which are the consequence of purely ethical values and norms. These however are not opposed to the personalistic value, for it is only in the "moral good" that the person can fulfill himself, inasmuch as "evil" is always a "nonfulfillment." There can be no doubt that man has the freedom to act, he has the right to action, but he has not the right to do wrong.

5. PARTICIPATION AND MEMBERSHIP OF THE COMMUNITY

Participation as a Constitutive Factor of the Community—In the thinking about man which distinguishes these two tendencies of individualism and totalism, there seems to be no sufficient ground for any authentic human community. The reality of participation is that property of the person which enables him to exist and to act "together with others" and, thus, to reach his own fulfillment. Simultaneously, participation as a property of the person is a constitutive factor of any human community. Person and community are, thus, neither alien nor mutually opposed to each another.

The Community Is not the Substantial Subject of Acting—The notion of "community" corresponds to the phrase "together with others" while simultaneously introducing a new plane or a new "subjectivity"—a quasi-subjectivity which is constituted by all the people existing and acting together. It is only a "quasi-subjectivity" because even when the being and acting is realized together with others it is the *man-person who is always its proper substantial subject.*

Associational Relationship and Community Membership—Within the framework of a community we see man, with all his appropriate dynamism, as one of its members. This membership can be differently regarded. There are words such as "society" which objectivize the community from without as a group working together. There are other words like "community" which seek to disclose the bases or foundations of community membership rather than the mere associational relationship of the society. For instance, "brother" and "sister" stress the family bonds—the communal existence, the community of being—rather than mere membership in a family group denoted by the term "kinship."

Associational Relationship Differs from Participation—The community of being always conditions the community of acting and so the latter cannot be considered apart from the former. However, objective membership in these communities is not to be identified with participation, which always involves a subjective moment and not just being "objectively" a member of a community. In participation, a man makes choices and undertakes a way of acting "together with others" by choosing what others choose and indeed often because others choose it, but even then he chooses it as his own good in the sense that he as the person can fulfill himself in it. Perhaps it is only then that such acting deserves to be called "cooperation," inasmuch as acting "together with others" does not by itself necessarily result in cooperation (just as it does not necessarily initiate the moment of participation). Within the sphere of acting, just like within the sphere of existing, a community may remain at the objective level and never pass to the subjective level.

6. PARTICIPATION AND THE COMMON GOOD

The Common Good and the Problem of Community and Participation—We now see that the solution to the problem of the community and participation lies not in the reality itself of acting and existing "together with others," but is to be looked for in the "common good"—though this term also must not be understood in a one-sided sense. The common good may be seen as the immediate goal of a community (laborers excavating a ditch, students studying a lecture) or these common goods may be seen as links in a teleological chain (excavation is for the foundation of the building, study is for learning in that particular field).

Teleological and Personalistic Conceptions of the Common Good—It is inadequate however to simply identify the "common good" with the goal of common acting by a group of people. It is impossible to define the common good without simultaneously taking into account the subjective moment, that is, the moment of acting in relation to others. Thus, the common good does not consist solely in the goal of common acting (objective sense of common good), but also, or even primarily, consists in that which conditions or initiates in the persons acting together their participation and thereby develops and shapes in them a subjective community of acting (subjective sense of common good). Its subjective sense is strictly related to participation as a property of the acting person; it is in this sense that it is possible to say that the common good corresponds to the social nature of man.

The Common Good as the Foundation of Authentic Human Communities—Everybody expects that natural communities (family, nation, religious community, state: those inherently corresponding to the social nature of man) will allow one to choose what others choose and because they choose it, and that his choice will be *his own good* that serves the fulfillment of *his own* person.

At the same time, owing to the same ability of participation, man expects that in communities founded on the common good his own actions will serve the community and help to maintain and enrich it. Under conditions established according to this axiological pattern he will readily relinquish his individual good and sacrifice it to the welfare of the community. Since such a sacrifice corresponds to the ability of participation inherent in man, and because this ability allows him to fulfill himself, it is not "contrary to nature." Thus, the priority of the common good over partial or individual goods does not rest solely on quantity. It is not the numbers or even the generality in the quantitative sense but the intrinsic character that determines the proper nature of the common good. We can see how, from the reality constituted be "common acting" and "common being," participation emerges as a property of the person and action and also as the basis of every human community.

7. AUTHENTIC ATTITUDES

The Preethical Significance of this Analysis—We will now proceed to analyze the attitudes of "solidarity" and "opposition" in connection with community and the common good. Though we border on ethics here, our analysis concentrates on the personalistic significance of each of these attitudes and, thus, is really preethical. Our aim continues to be an outline of the structures of human acting and in this connection to underline the value of the fulfillment itself of an action rather than that value of a performed action which issues from its relation to ethical norms.

The Attitude of Solidarity—Solidarity is the attitude of a community in which the common good properly conditions and initiates participation and participation in turn properly serves the common good, fosters it, and furthers its realization. Solidarity signifies the constant readiness to accept and to realize one's share in the community—because of one's membership in that community. In solidarity, man does what he is supposed to do not only because of his membership in the group, but because he has the "benefit of the whole" in view: he does it for the common good. The attitude of solidarity pays due regard to the parts that are the share of every member of the community. To take over a part of the duties and obligations that are not mine is intrinsically contrary to participation and the essence of the community. Nevertheless, there are situations that make even this necessary, when to keep strictly to one's own share would signify and confirm a lack of solidarity. The acute sense of the needs of the community, which distinguishes the attitude of solidarity, brings out over and above any particularism or divisions its trait of complementarity; this consists in the readiness of every other member of a community to "complement" by his action what is done by other members of the community. Complementarity helps explain why we see in the attitude of solidarity an intrinsic manifestation of participation as a property of the person. It is this attitude that allows man to find the fulfillment of himself in complementing others.

The Attitude of Opposition—It is important to note that opposition is not contradictory to or intrinsically inconsistent with solidarity. The one who voices his opposition does not thereby reject his membership in the community; he does not withdraw his readiness to act and work for the common good. Rather those who stand up in opposition seek their own place within the community, seek for that participation and that attitude to the common good which would allow them a better, a fuller, and a more effective share in the community (i.e., loyal opposition). This is essentially constructive and a condition of the correct functioning of communities and of their inner system. The structure of a human community is correct only if it admits not just the presence of justified opposition but also that effectiveness of opposition which is required by the common good and the right of participation.

The Sense of Dialogue—Thus, the common good must be conceived of dynamically and not statically. In fact, it must liberate and support the attitude of solidarity but never so as to stifle and shut itself off from opposition. The principle of dialogue is aptly suited to these needs. By "dialogue" we mean here the formation and the strengthening of interhuman solidarity through the attitude of opposition. Admittedly dialogue may make the coexistence and cooperation of men more difficult, but it should never damage or prevent them. It is meant to select and bring out what is right and true in controversial situations, and to eliminate any partial, preconceived, or subjective views and attitudes.

8. NONAUTHENTIC ATTITUDES

Authentic and Nonauthentic Attitudes—Both the attitude of solidarity and that of opposition appear to be intrinsically authentic, i.e., each allows the realization not only of participation but also of the transcendence of the person in action. However, these attitudes may become distorted and inauthentic. The touchstone in each case is the dynamic subordination to truth that is so essential to the person's transcendence in action. Inauthentic attitudes would be on the one hand a servile conformism and on the other avoidance or non-involvement. Either may be reached by deviating from the authentic attitudes of solidarity and opposition when they are deprived of those inherent elements which are the condition of participation and personalistic value.

Conformism as a Nonauthentic Attitude—Constructive and creative assimilation in the community is a confirmation and also a manifestation of human solidarity. But when it begins to sway toward servility, it becomes highly negative. It is this negative tendency that we call "conformism," which evidences an inherent lack of solidarity and simultaneously an attitude of evading opposition. Thus, conformism consists primarily in an attitude of compliance or resignation, in a specific form of passiveness that makes the man-person to be but the subject of what happens instead of being the actor or agent responsible for building his own attitudes and his own commitment in the community. He then fails to accept his share in constructing the community and allows himself to be carried with and by the multitude. This involves a definite resignation from seeking the fulfillment of oneself in and through acting "together with others." At the same time, he withdraws himself from the community in a mere semblance of genuine participation. We may also look at it as a specific form of individualism: it then becomes an evasion from the community. The individual dissimulates himself from the community behind a mask of external appearances. Hence comformism brings uniformity rather than unity.

Avoidance as a Nonauthentic Attitude—Avoidance or non-involvement is nothing but withdrawal, sometimes to manifest a protest, but even then it still lacks the active concern for the common good and participation: it consists in a lack of participation and in being absent from the community. The absent, so the saying goes, are always in the wrong. This is often true with avoidance, though sometimes it is adopted in the hope that even absence can be telling, that it may in certain situations become an argument. If the members of a community see the only solution to their problems in withdrawal, then this is a sure sign that the common good in this community is erroneously conceived. Nevertheless, for all that may in a way justify avoidance as a kind of compensatory attitude, it is impossible to ascribe to it the traits of authenticity within the frame of being and acting "together with others." At many points it borders on conformism, not to mention the instances when both attitudes merge into what can be called "conformist avoidance." Both attitudes deprive man of that dynamic trait of participation appropriate to the person which allows him to perform actions and thereby to fulfill himself authentically in the community of being and acting together with others.

9. FELLOW MEMBER AND NEIGHBOR

Two Interrelated Systems of Reference—Man belongs to different communities (family, nation, religious community, state). His membership in any one of them is like a specific reference system. As a "member of a community" he may be closer or more distant to others: we are closer to our family than to our compatriots. However, there is another reference system closely related to that of being a "member of a community" and which also plays a very important role in participation: it is best designated by the word "neighbor." The notion of neighbor has, however, a deeper application than closeness or alienation in interhuman relationships and it is, thus, more fundamental that the notion of membership in a community. Membership of any community presupposes the fact that men are neighbors, but it neither constitutes nor abolishes this fact. People are, or become, members of different communities: in these communities they either establish close and even friendly relations or they remain strangers—the latter reflects a lack of the communal spirit—but they are all neighbors and never cease to be neighbors.

The Interrelation of All Men in Humanity—The notion of "neighbor" forces us not only to recognize but also to appreciate that which in man is independent of his membership in any community whatever; it forces us to observe and appreciate in him something that is for more absolute. The notion of neighbor is strictly related to man as such and to the value itself of the person regardless of any of his relations to one or another community or to the society. It, thus, provides the broadest basis for the community, a basis that extends beyond any strangeness or foreignness, as well as beyond the strangeness that results from membership of different human communities. Thus, from the point of view of participation, the man-person is capable not only of partaking in the life of a community, of being and acting together with others, but he is also capable of participating in the humanity of others. It is on this ability to participate in the humanity of every human being that all participation in a community is based and it is there that is receives its personal meaning. This is what is ultimately contained in the notion of neighbor.

Participation Consists in Sharing in the Humanity of Every Man—Any suggestions tending to mutually oppose the notions of "neighbor" and "member of a community" are wholly unwarranted. Rather there is a concurrence of these notions, evidenced by the societal nature of man. The objective order shows every neighbor as belonging to a community and every member of a community as a neighbor. More important than the objective order is, however, the interpenetration in the subjective order of participation. Participation is closely associated with both the community and the personalistic value. This is precisely why it cannot be manifested solely by membership in some community but through membership must reach to the humanity of every man. The ability to share in the humanity itself of every man is the very core of all participation and the condition of the personalistic value of all acting and existing "together with others."

10. THE COMMANDMENT OF LOVE

The Neighbor as the Fundamental System of Reference—In view of what we have just said concerning each man's ability to share in the humanity of all, it seems appropriate to dedicate the last pages of this book to the evangelical commandment to love. Our aim is not to analyze its objective ethical content but to note that it very strongly and very consistently confirms that the reference system centered on "the neighbor" has a crucial significance in any acting and existing "together with others." This is achieved by the juxtaposition of the neighbor with one's own ego: "the neighbor as thyself." The significance of the system referring to the neighbor is fundamental because this system surpasses any other reference system existing in a human community and surpasses it by its scope, simplicity, and depth. The relation to the neighbor brings to its ultimate consequences any system of reference resulting from the membership in a community. The former is essentially superior to the latter. Such is the correct hierarchy of values, because the system of reference to the neighbor shows the mutual relation and subordination of all men according to the principle of humanity itself while the system of reference based on membership in a community is insufficient to reveal this relation and this subordination. This is not to depreciate the communal. The commandment, "Thou shalt love," has a thoroughly communal character: it is an expression of what is necessary for a community to be formed, but more than anything else it brings into prominence what is necessary for a community to be really human.

The Commandment of Love Discloses the Roots of Alienation—The reference systems of "neighbor" and "membership of a community" have to interpenetrate each other and become mutually complementary. Any separation between them is inadmissible and dangerous because it leads to downright alienation: the separation of man from his humanity, his deprivation of the value we have defined here as personalistic. This danger becomes most imminent when participation in the community itself limits and overshadows participation in the humanity of others, when that fundamental relation and subordination which imparts the human quality to any community of men becomes defective. This is why we must assume that the alienation for which man himself is responsible is the prime cause of any alienation resulting from the reference systems based on things (systems of production, etc.). The real essence of alienation appears to be revealed by the commandment, "Thou shalt love." Man's alienation from other men stems from a disregard for, or a neglect of, that real depth of participation which is indicated in the word *neighbor.*

The Commandment of Love as the Rule of Being and Acting "Together With Others"—Considering the hierarchy of the systems outlined here and keeping to the personalistic implications of the evangelical commandment of love, we must protect the fundamental and privileged position of the reference system to the neighbor compared to that of different communities. This will protect us from the dangers of alienation. Any human community that allows this system of reference to become defective condemns itself to a deficiency of participation and fixes an unbridgeable gap between the person and the community. Such disintegration is an ominous threat first to the person and then through him to the whole community. This ominous aspect, however, is not the most significant. The commandment "Thou shalt love" gives prominence first of all to the brighter aspects in the reality of man's existing and acting "together with others." But the commandment of love is also the measure of the tasks and demands that have to be faced by all men—all persons and all communities—if the whole good contained in the acting and being "together with others" is to become a reality.

POSTSCRIPT

The question may arise whether the experience of acting "together with others" was not the fundamental experience, and if so, whether the conception of the community and intersubjective relations should not be presupposed in any discussion of the acting person. The author is convinced, however, that no interpenetration of the community and interpersonal relations is correct if it does not rest on some already existing conception of the acting person, indeed, on the conception that in the experience of "man acts" is adequately disclosed the transcendence of the person in action. Thus, from the point of view of method as well as of substance the correct solution seems to be the one that would recognize the priority of the conception of person and action, and at the same time on the basis of this conception would search for an adequate interpretation of the community and of interpersonal relations with all their richness and differentiations.

—adapted from *The Acting Person*, ANALECTA HUSSERIANA, The Yearbook of Phenomenological Research, Volume X, ed. Anna-Teresa Tymieniecka, *The World Institute for Advanced Phenomenological Research and Learning*

LOVE AND RESPONSIBILITY

Introduction to the Present Edition—This work is open to every echo of experience from whatever quarter it comes, and it is at the same time a standing appeal to all to let experience, their own experience, make itself heard, to its full extent: in all its breadth, in all its depth. When we speak here of depth we have in mind all those things which do not always show themselves directly as part of the content of experience, but are nonetheless a component, a hidden dimension of it, so much so that it is impossible to omit them, if we want to identify fully the contents of experience. If we do omit them, we shall be detracting from and impoverishing experience, and so robbing it of its validity, though it is the sole source of information and the basis of all reliable knowledge on whatever subject. *Love and Responsibility,* with this sort of methodological basis, fears nothing and need fear nothing which can be legitimized by experience. We do not have to be afraid of experience. Truth can only gain from such a confrontation.

Introduction to the First Edition—The present book was born principally of the need to put the norms of Catholic sexual morality on a firm basis, a basis as definitive as possible, relying on the most elementary and incontrovertible moral truths and the most fundamental values or goods. Such a good is the person, and the moral truth most closely bound up with the world of persons is 'the commandment to love'—for love is a good peculiar to the world of persons. And therefore the most fundamental way of looking at sexual morality is in the context of 'love and responsibility'—which is why the whole book bears that title.

The subject of analysis is in the first place the person as affected by the sexual urge, then the love which grows up on this basis between man and woman, next the virtue of purity as an essential factor in that love, and finally the question of marriage and vocation. In the context of relations between persons of different sexes, when we speak of 'sexual morality' we are really thinking of 'love and responsibility'. There exists, especially if we start from the Christian ethics born of the New Testament, a problem which can be described as that of 'introducing love into love'. The word as first used in that phrase signifies the love which is the subject of the greatest commandment, while in its second use it means all that takes shape between a man and a woman on the basis of the sexual urge.

The fundamental perspective of this book is that sexual morality is within the domain of the person. It is impossible to understand anything about it without understanding what the person is, its mode of existence, its functioning, its powers. The personal order is the only proper plane for all debate on matters of sexual morality. Physiology and medicine can only supplement discussion at this level. They do not in themselves provide a complete foundation for the understanding of love and responsibility, but this is just what matters most in the relations between persons of different sex.

CHAPTER I

THE PERSON AND THE SEXUAL URGE

ANALYSIS OF THE VERB 'TO USE'

The Person as the Subject and Object of Action—Every subject also exists as an object, an objective 'something' or 'somebody'. As an object, a man is 'somebody'—and this sets him apart from every other entity in the visible world, which as an object is only 'something'. It is not enough to define man as an individual of the species (Homo sapiens). The term 'person' has been coined to signify that a man cannot be wholly contained within the concept 'individual member of the species', but that there is something more to him. Compared to inanimate objects, plants (with a rich sensual life), and even animals (with their strivings related to cognition and desire at a certain level), man (an individual being of a rational nature) is a personal subject distinguished from even the most advanced animals by a specific inner self, an inner life, characteristic only of persons. Inner life means spiritual life. It revolves around truth and goodness.

A human person, as a distinctly defined subject, establishes contact with all other entities precisely through the inner self and neither the 'natural' contacts which are also its prerogative (since it has a body and in a certain sense 'is a body') nor the sensual contacts in which it resembles the animals constitute its characteristic way of communication with the world. Moreover, man's nature differs fundamentally from that of the animals in that it includes the power of self-determination, based on reflection, and manifested in the fact that a man acts from choice. This power is called free will.

Because a human being—a person—possesses free will, he is his own master (*sui juris*). This characteristic goes with another distinctive attribute, that personality is not capable of transmission, not transferable (*alteri incommunicabilis*). This means not only that the person is unique and unrepeatable (which is true of every entity), but also that the incommunicable, the *inalienable*, in a person is intrinsic to that person's inner self, to the power of self-determination, free will. *No one else can want for me.* I am, and I must be, independent in my actions. In human relationships, in dealings between persons of different sexes, and especially in the sexual relationship, persons are alike the subjects and the objects of action. It is now necessary to consider carefully the principles to which a human being's actions must conform when the object is another human person.

The First Meaning of the Verb 'to Use'—To use means to employ some object of action as a means to an end, thus, subordinating that object both to the end and to the agent. Man in his various activities makes use of the whole created universe, takes advantage of all its resources for ends which he sets himself (with ethical limits as to squandering or destroying resources or causing suffering in the higher animals), for he alone understands them. But how does this apply to persons (employer-employee, officer-foot soldier, parent-child [even unborn])? Ethically, a person must not be merely the means to an end for another person. This is precluded by the very nature of personhood, by what a person is. For a person is a thinking subject, and capable of making decisions: these, most notably, are the attributes we find in the inner self or a person. This being so, every person is by nature capable of determining his or her aims. Anyone who treats a person as the mere means to an end does violence to the very essence of the other, to what constitutes its natural right. Obviously, the ends of the person should be genuinely good, since the pursuit of evil ends is contrary to the rational nature of the person, but a person may never be treated as just the means to an end. This principle has universal validity. Nobody can use a person as a means toward an end, no human being, nor yet God the Creator. On the part of God, indeed, it is totally out of the question, since, by giving man an intelligent and free nature, he has thereby ordained that each man alone will decide for himself the ends of his activity, and not be a blind tool of someone else's ends. God allows man to learn His supernatural ends, but the decision to strive towards an end, the choice of course, is left to man's free will. God does not redeem man against his will.

Kant already formulated this elementary principle of the moral order in the following imperative: act always in such a way that the other person is the end and not merely the instrument of your action. It can be restated as follows: whenever a person is the object of your activity, remember that you may not treat that person as only the means to an end, as an instrument, but must allow for the fact that he or she, too, has, or at least should have, distinct ends.

'Love' as the Opposite of 'Using'—If we seek a positive statement of this moral dictum, we begin to discern love as the only clear alternative to using a person as the means to an end, or the instrument of one's own action. Man's capacity for love depends on his willingness consciously to seek a good together with others, and to subordinate himself to that good for the sake of others, or to others for the sake of that good. Compared to any mere need, striving, drive or instinct as we might find in the animal world, love is exclusively the portion of human persons. To love means to free oneself from the mere utilitarian or 'consumer' attitude towards other persons (including employees, foot soldiers, etc.); it means to be united in a common good and in love of some form. For example, in a common love of and defense of the fatherland even a foot soldier is not merely used by an officer as a blind tool, as a means to an end.

Concerning 'woman and man'—the background to sexual ethics—here, and even especially here, only love can preclude the use of one person by another. How is it possible to ensure that one person does not become for the other—the man for the woman or the woman for the man—nothing more than the means to an end, i.e., an object used exclusively for the attainment of a selfish end? To exclude this possibility, they must share the same end. Where marriage is concerned, this end is procreation (the future generation, a family) and, at the same time, the continual ripening of the relationship between two people in all the areas of activity which conjugal life includes. But this statement of the objective purpose of marriage does not yet solve the problem, for the sexual relationship presents more opportunities than most other activities for treating a person—sometimes even without realizing it—as an object of use. Indeed, if we take this basic relationship 'woman-man' in the broadest sense, and not merely within the limits of marriage, then the love of which we speak is identified with a particular readiness to subordinate oneself to that good which 'humanity'—or more precisely *the value of the person*—suggests.

The Second Meaning of the Verb 'to Use'—Our thinking and our acts of will—and it is these which determine the objective structure of human activity—are accompanied by various emotional overtones or states, carrying a positive (ranging from sensual satisfaction to emotional contentment to a profound, total joy) or a negative (sensual disgust, emotional discontent, or a deep sadness) charge. These emotional-affective experiences are especially vivid in relation to a person of the opposite sex and to the sexual relationship proper. This is why the second meaning of the verb 'to use' looms particularly large in this area of activity. 'To use' (=to enjoy) means to experience pleasure, the pleasure which in slightly different senses is associated both with the activity itself and with the object of the activity. In any association between a man and a woman, and in the sexual relationship itself, the object of the activity is of course always a person. And it is a person who becomes the proper source of various forms of pleasure, or even of delight. But the sexuality of man is on the personal and moral level, not merely on the natural and instinctive level as in animals. Sexual morality comes into being not only because persons are aware of the purpose of sexual life, but also because they are aware that they are persons. The whole moral problem of 'using' as the antithesis of love is connected with this knowledge of theirs. For man, precisely because he has the power to reason, can, in his actions, not only clearly distinguish pleasure from its opposite, but can also isolate it, so to speak, and treat is as a distinct aim of his activity. His actions are then shaped only with a view to the pleasure he wishes to obtain, or the pain he wishes to avoid. If actions involving a person of the opposite sex are shaped exclusively or primarily with this in view, then that person will become only the means to an end—and 'use' in its second meaning (=enjoy) represents, as we see, a particular variant of 'use' in its first meaning. But a person of the opposite sex cannot be for another person only the means to an end—in this case sexual pleasure or delight. The belief that a human being is a person leads to the acceptance of the postulate that enjoyment must be subordinated to love. 'Use', not only in the first, broader and more objective meaning, but also in its second, narrower, more subjective meaning can be raised to the level appropriate to an interpersonal relationship only by love. Only 'caring' precludes 'using' in the second sense as well as in the first. Thus, ethics must distinguish very carefully between whatever shows 'loving kindness', and whatever shows not that but the intention to 'use' a person even when it disguises itself as love and seeks to legitimate itself under that name.

Critique of Utilitarianism—True to its etymology ('to use', 'to take advantage of'), 'utilitarianism' puts the emphasis on the usefulness (or otherwise) of any and every human activity. Utilitarians regard the principle of the maximization of pleasure accompanied by the minimalization of pain as the primary rule of human morality, with the rider that it must be observed not only by individuals, egotistically, but also collectively, by society. But pleasure and pain are always connected with a concrete action, so that it is not possible to anticipate them precisely, let alone to plan for them or—as the utilitarians would have us do—even compute them in advance. However, the real mistake here is the recognition of pleasure in itself as the sole or at any rate the greatest good, to which everything else in the activity of an individual or a society should be subordinated—whereas pleasure in itself is not the sole good, nor is it the proper aim of a man's activity, as we shall have the opportunity to see later. Pleasure is essentially incidental, contingent, something which may occur in the course of an action. Naturally, then, to organize your actions with pleasure itself as the exclusive or primary aim is in contradiction with the proper structure of human action. Quite obviously, that which is truly good, that which morality and conscience bid me do, often involves some measure of pain and requires the renunciation of some pleasure. In this connection, Kant with his moral imperative that a person should never be the means to an end, but always an end, in our activities, reveals one of the weakest points of utilitarianism. That is, if the only or the main good, the only or the main aim, of man is pleasure, if it is also the whole basis of moral norms in human behavior, then everything we do must perforce be looked at as a means towards this one good, this single end. Hence the human person, myself or another, must be looked at from the same point of view, as a possible means of obtaining the maximum pleasure.

This makes for great difficulties in the various areas of human coexistence but would seem to be a particular threat in the sphere of sexual relations. The great danger lies in the fact that starting from utilitarian premises it is not clear how the cohabitation or association of people of different sex can be put on a plane of real love, and so freed from the dangers of 'using' a person (whether in the first or in the second meaning of that word) and of treating a person as the means to an end. Utilitarianism seems to be a programme of thoroughgoing egoism quite incapable of evolving into authentic altruism. *Pleasure is, of its nature, a good for the moment and only for a particular subject, it is not a super-subjective or trans-subjective good.* It is crystal clear that if utilitarian principles are followed, a subjective understanding of the good (equating the good with the pleasurable) leads directly, though there may be no conscious intention of this, to egoism. The only escape from this otherwise inevitable egoism is by recognizing beyond any purely subjective good (i.e., beyond pleasure) an objective good, which can also unite persons—and thereby acquire the characteristics of a common good. Such an objective common good is the foundation of love, and individual persons, who jointly choose a common good, in doing so subject themselves to it. Thanks to it they are united by a true, objective bond of love which enables them to liberate themselves from subjectivism and from the egoism which it inevitable conceals. *Love is the unification of persons.*

Moreover, love cannot be reduced to a mere harmonization of egoisms—which could never deliver one from egoism and which would leave love without objective reality. 'Love' in such a utilitarian conception is a union of egoisms, which can hold together only on condition that they confront each other with nothing unpleasant, nothing to conflict with their mutual pleasure. Therefore, love so understood is self-evidently merely a pretence which has to be carefully cultivated to keep the underlying reality hidden: the reality of egoism, and the greediest kind of egoism at that, exploiting another person to obtain for itself its own 'maximum pleasure'. Each of the persons is mainly concerned with gratifying his or her own egoism, but at the same time consents to serve someone else's egoism, because this can provide the opportunity for such gratification—and just as long as it does so. There is an ineluctable, an overwhelming necessity in this pattern (the only possible pattern when utilitarian thinking and attitudes are acted upon): if I treat someone else as a means and a tool in relation to myself I cannot help regarding myself in the same light. We have here something like the opposite of the commandment to love.

The Commandment to Love and the Personalistic Norm—The commandment formulated in the New Testament, demanding love toward persons, is implicitly opposed to the principle of utilitarianism, which as we have seen is unable to guarantee the love of one human being, one person, for another. If the commandment to love, and the love which is the object of this commandment, are to have any meaning, we must find a basis for them other than the utilitarian premise and the utilitarian system of values. This can only be the personalistic principle and the personalistic norm, i.e., that the person is the kind of good that does not admit of mere use, of being approached as a mere means to an end. In its positive form, the personalistic norm confirms this: the person is a good towards which the only proper and adequate response is love. The foundation for the commandment to love must also be found not in a utilitarian system of values but in a personalist axiology, within whose framework the value of the person is always greater than the value of pleasure. This is why a person cannot be subordinated to this lesser end, cannot be the means to an end, in this case to pleasure.

This personalistic norm, this commandment, defines a certain way of relating to God and to people. This way of relating, this attitude, is in agreement with what the person is, with the value which the person represents, and therefore it is fair. Fairness takes precedence over mere utility—although it does not cancel it but only subordinates it—in dealings with another person everything that is at once of use to oneself and fair to that person falls within the limits set by the commandment of love. The personalistic norm in the form of the commandment to love also assumes that this relation, this attitude, will be not only fair but just. For to be just always means giving others what is rightly due to them. A person's rightful due is to be treated as an object of love, not as an object for use. Although we can correctly say that whoever loves a person is for that very reason just to that person, it would be quite untrue to assert that love for a person consists merely in being just. Still, there can be no doubt that the one who loves will, *ipso facto,* be just toward the other person as a person.

This interpenetration of love and justice in the personalistic norm is very important for sexual morality. For in the sexual context what is sometimes characterized as love may very easily be quite unjust to a person. This occurs not because sensuality and sentimentality play a special part in forming this love between persons of different sex, but rather because love in the sexual context lends itself to interpretation (sometimes conscious, sometimes unconscious) along utilitarian lines. In a sense this kind of love is wide open to such an interpretation, which turns to account the natural gravitation of its sensual and sentimental ingredients in the direction of pleasure. It is easy to go from the experience of pleasure not merely to the quest for pleasure, but to the quest for pleasure for its own sake, to accepting it as a superlative value and the proper basis for behavior. This is the very essence of the distortions which occur in the love between man and woman. It is also the basis for the distinction which St. Augustine makes between *uti* (intent upon pleasure for its own sake with no concern for the object of pleasure) and *frui* (finding joy in a totally committed relationship with the object precisely because this is what the nature of the object demands). The commandment to love shows the way to enjoyment in this sense—*frui*—in the association of persons of different sex both within and outside marriage.

INTERPRETATION OF THE SEXUAL URGE

Instinct or Urge?—'Instinct' means a certain mode of action which automatically declares its origin. This is the reflex mode of action, which is not dependent on conscious thought. But man is by nature capable of rising above instinct in his actions. There is in man a principle which makes him capable of considered behavior, of self-determination. Now 'urge' suggests the action of urging, or instigation, always felt to be to some extent in conflict with freedom. However, it can be given another meaning more suitable to man's real nature. When we speak of the sexual urge in man we have in mind not an interior source of specific actions 'imposed in advance', but a certain orientation, a certain direction in man's life implicit in his very nature: a natural drive born in all human beings, a vector of aspiration along which their whole existence develops and perfects itself from within. This is something which 'happens in man' (begins to take place without any initiative on his part) and this internal happening creates as it were a base for definite actions, for considered actions, in which man exercises self-determination, decides for himself about his own actions and takes responsibility for them. This is the point at which human freedom and the sex urge meet. Man is not responsible for what *happens* in him in the sphere of sex since he is obviously not himself the cause of it, but he is entirely responsible for what he *does* in this sphere.

***The Sexual Urge as an Attribute of the Individual*—** Every human being is by nature a sexual being and belongs to one of two sexes (hermaphroditism and other sickness or deformity does not militate against the fact that there is a human nature and that it is divided into two sexes). This fact is manifested internally but also turns outwards and manifests itself in a certain natural predilection for, a tendency to seek, the other sex. Sexual attraction makes obvious the fact that the attributes of the two sexes are complementary, so that a man and a woman can complete each other. Ultimately, through the prism of this need, one might be led to a deeper understanding of one's own limitation and inadequacy, and even, indirectly, of the contingent character of existence. In any case, each sex possesses some specific value for the other based on the existence of the sexual urge. But the sexual urge is not merely towards attributes of the other sex as such. It is always directed towards another human being—this is the normal form which it takes. If it is directed towards the sexual attributes as such this must be recognized as an impoverishment or even a perversion of the urge. The natural direction of the sexual urge is towards a human being of the other sex and not merely towards 'the other sex' as such. It is just because of this that the sexual urge can provide a framework within which, and the basis on which, the possibility of love arises—because the objects affected are both people. Nonetheless, love is not merely a biological or psycho-physiological crystallization of the sexual urge, though love may grow out of it and develop on that basis; love is given its definitive shape by *acts of the will at the level of the person.* The sexual urge only furnishes, so to speak, in the form of all that 'happens' in man's inner being under its influence, what might be called the 'stuff' from which action is made. Since there is nothing in all this to deprive man of the power of self-determination, the sexual urge (despite its great force) is by its nature dependent on the person and is in the control of the person; in the person, as opposed to animals, it is naturally subordinate to the will and to the specific dynamics of freedom. Thus, the sexual urge can transcend the determinism of the natural order by an act of love and its manifestations must be evaluated on the plane of love, forming a link in the chain of responsibility, responsibility for love. Hence the sexual urge is an attribute and a force common to humanity at large, at work in every human being. Living in society we are continually concerned with the various forms of coexistence of the two sexes and for this reason ethics must put these relationships on a level consonant both with the dignity of human persons and with the common good of society.

The Sexual Urge and Existence—Independent of love and of the personal level and though it furnishes what we may call 'material' for love between persons (man and woman), the sexual urge shows its proper end in the existence of the species *Homo*, the constant prolongation of its existence. Now existence—of the human species and of each individual person within it—is the first and basic good of every creature. Thus, we have here a fact which is of existential, and not merely biological character, and therefore is the prerogative of philosophy. This is very important when we are trying to determine the true importance of the sexual urge, which has obvious implications in the realm of sexual morality. If the sexual urge has a merely biological significance it can be regarded as something to be used. We can agree that it is an object for man to enjoy just like any other object of nature, animate or inanimate. But if the sexual urge has an existential character, if it is bound up with the very existence of the human person—that first and most basic good—then it must be subject to the principles which are binding in respect of the person. Hence, although the sexual urge is there for man to use, it must never be used in the absence of, or worse still, in a way which contradicts, love for the person. Therefore, the type of love between man and woman which incorporates the sexual urge (with its proper purpose of existence of the species *Homo*, the procreation of new human persons) can take its correct shape only in so far as it develops close harmony with that proper purpose. An outright conflict with that purpose will also undermine love between persons. The importance of the existential significance of the sexual urge only emerges into consciousness when man is moved by love to take on himself the natural purpose of that urge. This is in fact the character of true conjugal love between two persons, a man and a woman, who have consciously taken the decision to participate in the whole natural order of existence, to further the existence of the species *Homo*. Looked at more closely and concretely, these two persons, the man and the woman, facilitate the existence of another concrete person, their own child, blood of their blood and flesh of their flesh. This person is at once an affirmation and a continuation of their own love. The natural order of human existence is not in conflict with love between persons but in strict harmony with it.

The Religious Interpretation—A man and a woman by means of procreation (bringing a new human being into the world), participate in their own fashion in the work of creation. They are the rational co-creators of a new human being, a person. The parents take part in the genesis of a person, not merely an organism. A human body is the body of a person because it forms a unity of substance with the human spirit. The human spirit is not born merely in consequence of the physical union of man and woman in itself.

The spirit can never originate from the body, nor be born and come into being in the same way as the body. The sexual relationship between man and woman is fundamentally a physical relationship, though it should also be the result of spiritual love. A relationship between spirits which beget a new embodied spirit is something unknown to the natural order. Therefore, the essence of the human person is the work of God himself. It is He who creates the spiritual and immortal soul of that being, the organism of which begins to exist as a consequence of physical relations between man and woman. Furthermore, while love owes its fertility in the biological sense to the sexual urge, it must also possess a fertility of its own in the spiritual, moral and personal sphere. It is here that the full productive power of love between two persons, man and woman, is concentrated, in the work of rearing new persons. This is its proper end, its natural orientation. Education is a creative activity with persons as its only possible object—only a person can be educated, an animal can only be trained. This work of education may in a certain sense be called the continuous creation of a personality and is not left wholly and entirely to the parents. Rather, God himself takes part in it, in His own person, by His grace. The parents, though, if they are not to fail in their proper role, that of co-creators, must make their contribution here too. Note that when it comes to the sexual urge and all that it implies, the expressions 'the order of nature' and 'the biological order' must not be confused or regarded as identical. The 'biological order' does indeed mean the same as the order of nature but *only insofar as this is accessible to the methods of empirical and descriptive natural science,* and not as a specific order of existence with an obvious relationship to the First Cause, to God the Creator.

The Rigorist Interpretation—This is a puritanical view (with paradoxical links to sensualist empiricism) which can easily lapse into a utilitarianism as well. It holds that, in using man and woman and their sexual intercourse to assure the existence of the species *Homo*, the Creator Himself uses persons as the means to his end. It follows that conjugal life and sexual intercourse are good only because they serve the purpose of procreation. Man and woman use—and do well to use—one another and marriage as mere means for procreation (first sense of 'use') while descrying the seeking of pleasure and enjoyment in intercourse (second sense of 'use') as wrong and impure, but a necessary evil that must be tolerated.

But the Creator, in giving men and women a rational nature and the capacity consciously to decide upon their own actions, thereby made it possible for them to choose freely the end to which sexual intercourse naturally leads. And where two persons can join in choosing a certain good as their end there also exists the possibility of love. The Creator, then, does not utilize persons merely as the means or instruments of His creative power but offers them the possibility of a special realization of love. It is for them to put their sexual relations on the plane of love, the appropriate plane for human persons, or on a lower plane. The Creator's will is not only the preservation of the species by way of sexual intercourse but also its preservation on the basis of a love worthy of human persons, according to the commandment of love. The problem for ethics is how to use sex without treating the person as an object for use. Puritanical rigorists with their one-sided spiritualism so intent on overcoming the *uti* in sex, unavoidably leave sexual enjoyment as merely an evil but necessary by-product of the sexual act. The only way to overcome this is through St. Augustine's fundamentally different attitude of *frui*. There exists a joy which is consonant both with the nature of the sexual urge and with the dignity of human persons. This joy, this *frui* may be bestowed either by the great variety of pleasures connected with differences of sex, or by the sexual enjoyment which conjugal relations can bring. The Creator designed this joy, and linked it with love between man and woman insofar as that love develops on the basis of the sexual urge in a normal manner, in other words in a manner worthy of human persons.

The 'Libidinistic' Interpretation—Linked with Freud, this approach sees the pursuit of pleasure, in a narrow and subjective sense, as the primary aim or drive in human life and the sexual urge as the most intense and strongly felt experience of it. The transmission of life, procreation, is in this conception only a secondary end, an end *per accidens*. This almost totally negates the inner life of the person (capable of knowing the truth, comprehending the true ends, and participating in the common good of the work of creation) and reduces the person to a subject 'externally' sensitized to enjoyable sensory stimuli of a sexual nature. This puts human psychology on the same level as animal psychology. But a subject endowed with an 'inner self' as man is, a subject who is a person, cannot abandon to instinct the whole responsibility for the use of the sexual urge and make enjoyment his sole aim—but must assume full responsibility for the way in which the sexual urge is used. The libidinistic distortion is a frank form of utilitarianism. Those like Freud who have eyes merely for the subjective purpose of the urge will also logically aim at preserving in full that subjective purpose (sexual pleasure) while at the same time curbing or even suppressing the objective purpose (procreation). Utilitarians think of this as purely *technical* problem, but Catholic moral teaching regards it from first to last as an *ethical* problem on personalist grounds. No one must take the 'calculus of pleasure' as his sole guide where a relationship with another person is concerned—a person can never be an object of use. That is the nub of the conflict.

Furthermore, however correct or incorrect the demographic difficulties raised by economists may be, the general problem of sexual relationships between a man and a woman cannot be solved in such a way as to contradict the personalist norm. We have to do here with the value of the person, which is for all humanity the most precious of goods—more immediate and greater than any economic good.

Note that in the objective purpose of the sexual urge, in the very nature of it, there is—and this is where it differs from the instinct of self-preservation—something that may be called 'altero-centrism' (other-centeredness). This it is that creates the basis for love. Now, the 'libidinistic' interpretation of the sexual urge utterly confuses these two concepts. It endows the sexual urge with a purely egocentric significance, of the sort which naturally belongs to the instinct of self-preservation. For the same reason, the utilitarianism in sexual morality (which goes with this interpretation) involves a danger perhaps greater than is generally realized, that of confusing the basic and fundamental human tendencies, the main paths of human existence. Such confusion must, clearly, affect the whole spiritual position of man. After all, the human spirit here on earth forms a unity of substance with the body, so that spiritual life cannot develop correctly if the elementary lines of human existence are hopelessly tangled in contexts where the body is immediately involved.

Final Observations—The Church has always taught that the primary end of marriage is procreation (providing the means of continuing existence), but that it has a secondary end of mutual help (a conjugal life for man and woman), and a tertiary aim of being a remedy for concupiscence (giving a legitimate orientation for desire). It must be stated, however, that in marriage the ends mentioned above are to be realized on the basis of the personalistic norm. Sexual morality, and therefore conjugal morality, consists of a stable and mature synthesis of nature's purpose with the personalistic norm. The latter is a principle on which the proper realization of each of the aims mentioned, and of all of them together, depends—and by proper I mean in a manner befitting man as a person. The same principle also guarantees that the ends will be achieved in the order of importance accorded them here, for any deviation from this is incompatible with the objective dignity of the human person. The practical realization of all the purposes of marriage must then also mean the successful practice of love as a virtue—for only as a virtue does love satisfy the commandment of the Gospel and the demands of the personalistic norm embodied in that commandment. The idea that the purposes of marriage could be realized on some basis other than the personalistic norm would be utterly un-Christian, because it would not conform to the fundamental ethical postulate of the Gospels. For this reason too we must be very much on guard against trivialization of the teaching of the purposes of marriage.

With this in mind, it seems equally clear that the term 'mutual help' cannot be interpreted simply as 'mutual love' as if the other ends (procreation and giving a legitimate orientation to desire) were somehow distinct from 'love' and only 'mutual help' were grounded in love. Rather, all three ends in their proper order (procreation/continuing existence, mutual help/conjugal life, and remedy for concupiscence/legitimate orientation for desire) are grounded in the virtue of love and so must fit with the personalistic norm. But there is no question of opposing love to procreation nor yet of suggesting that procreation takes precedence over love.

These aims can, moreover, only be realized in practice as a single complex aim. To rule out, totally and positively, the possibility of procreation undoubtedly reduces or even destroys the possibility of an enduring marital relationship of mutual education. If there is an intimate cooperation between the man and the woman in a marriage, and if they are able to educate and complement each other, their love matures to the point at which it is the proper basis for a family. However, marriage is not identical with the family, and always remains above all an intimate bond between two people. The third purpose, a remedy for concupiscence, in its turn depends upon the two others for its practical realization by human beings. We must recognize once again that those who cut themselves off absolutely from the natural results of conjugal intercourse ruin the spontaneity and depth of their experiences, especially if artificial means are used to this end. Lack of mutual understanding, and of rational concern for the full well-being of a partner, leads if anything still more certainly to the same result.

CHAPTER II

THE PERSON AND LOVE

METAPHYSICAL ANALYSIS OF LOVE

The Word 'Love'—The word 'love' has more than one meaning. In this book we narrow down the range of its meanings to love between two persons who differ with respect to sex. Even here it has various meanings. But love is always a mutual relationship between persons, based on particular attitudes toward the good, individually and jointly. We will do a general metaphysical analysis (love as attraction, as desire, as goodwill). Then we will do a psychological analysis (love of man and women takes shape deep down in the psyche of two persons, and is bound up with the high sexual vitality of human beings, requiring a psycho-physiological analysis). Finally, these will culminate in an ethical analysis (love between man and woman possesses a personal character with profound ethical significance: love as a virtue).

Love as Attraction—Love as attraction is a basic component of the love between man and woman. This is based in a concrete sense impression of the other as well as an intellectual knowledge of the other, but these are also influenced by the emotions and the will. To be attracted does not mean just thinking about some person as a good, but involves a commitment in the will to think of that person as a good. This is based in one's knowledge of the other but with an interpenetration of reason and will. The emotions too are present at the birth of love favoring the development of the attraction between a man and a woman with a positive emotional-affective reaction.

The kind of good or person which an individual finds attractive will depend on many factors: heredity, environment, and one's own free choices in developing the self. But love will always go beyond just attractive qualities to the person. Nonetheless the depth and quality of the love will be affected by the kinds of qualities through which the attraction comes. *Attraction is of the essence of love and in some sense is indeed love, although love is not merely attraction.* Emotional-affective reactions have the power to guide and orient cognitive acts but must not overwhelm or eliminate the role of knowledge in love. Love must be anchored in the truth about the human person in general and the truth about this particular person. Our emotional life can color things either positively or negatively, but this must be balanced by a knowledge of the truth. Our response to the other can not be based only in partial truths about the other, such as just his/her sexual attractiveness, charm, or emotional "fit" with our needs at the moment. In responding to others as persons, we must see their inner as well as outer beauty and be attracted to and respectful of their *full beauty and dignity as persons* and not just as *pleasing in various respects.*

Love as Desire—Love as desire of also of the very essence of the love between man and woman, though love is not only desire. Desire is rooted in the fact that the human person is limited, is not self-sufficient, and therefore needs other beings (other persons, ultimately God) to complete his own being. Particularly, on the natural level, man and woman need one another to complete their own being. The sexual urge or sexual desire is an indication of this objective need. But *love as desire* is altogether different from just *desire* by itself in which the other is just used as a means of satisfaction. A man may, for instance, desire a woman in this way: a human person then becomes a means for the satisfaction of desire, just as a nutriment serves to satisfy hunger. But this utilitarian attitude does violence to the dignity of the human person and to the whole truth about the human person. Love-as-desire then is not merely desire. Love is apprehended as *a longing for the person*, and not as mere sensual desire. It is felt as a longing for some good for its own sake: 'I want you because you are a good for me'. If desire alone is predominant it can deform love between man and woman and rob them both of it. Therefore, the true lover will strive to see that desire alone does not dominate and overwhelm all else that love comprises.

Love as Goodwill—Genuine love brings with it the fullest realization of man's possibilities and of his existence, but of course only if it is directed toward a genuine good in a true way. A "false" love will have opposite consequences of destruction, constriction and evil. Love between man and woman would be evil in this way if it went no further than love-as-desire, for love as desire is not the whole essence of love between persons. It is not enough to long for a person as a true good for oneself, one must also, and above all, long for that person's good. This is love as goodwill or as benevolence and it must be at the heart of one's response to the other person or the love will not be genuine but will devolve back into an egoism. Thus, what is primary is not 'I long for you as a good' but 'I long for your good, I long for that which is good for you.' This is the deepest point of love and must finally inform love-as-desire and love-as-attraction, though the latter two are also essential to love between man and woman. Genuine love as goodwill can keep company with love as desire, and even with desire itself, provided that desire does not overwhelm all else in the love of man and woman, does not become its entire content and meaning.

The Problem of Reciprocity—Love also exists *between* two individuals as a single entity in which they are joined. The route from one 'I' (possessing its own inner self, 'a little world' created by God) to another leads through the free will. If this love is a one-way street (unrequited love) it will be fraught with pain and suffering. But love by its very nature is not unilateral but bilateral, something shared: it involves not just two 'I's but a single 'we'. This is reciprocity. This illuminates the previous discussion. The fact is that a person who desires another as a good desires above all that person's love in return for his or her own love, desires that is to say another person above all as co-creator of love and not merely as object of appetite. The desire for reciprocity does not cancel out the disinterested character of love. Reciprocity brings with it a synthesis, as it were, of love as desire and love as goodwill.

Of course, the quality and the permanence of the love depend upon the character of the good on which reciprocity or friendship is based, as Aristotle says. If it is a genuine good (an honest good) reciprocity is something deep, mature and virtually indestructible. On the other hand, if reciprocity is created only by self-interest, utility (a utilitarian good), or pleasure then it is superficial and impermanent. It depends on what both persons contribute to it. If each person contributes genuine personal love—a love of the highest ethical value, virtuous love—then reciprocity assumes the characteristics of durability and reliability (a friend who will never prove false) and becomes a source of peace and joy. But if utility or pleasure is the main reason for a relationship on the part of one or both of the partners, then trust, peace and joy will not be the result, but suspicions and jealousies. Their 'mutual love' will only last as long as they are a source of pleasure or profit to one another; once this is gone, the illusion of 'reciprocity' will burst like a bubble. Genuine reciprocity inevitably presupposes altruism in both persons; it cannot arise from two egoisms. Two conclusions follow: 1) love must always be analyzed from an ethical point of view and 2) people should always carefully 'verify' their love before exchanging declarations and trying to build their lives on it.

From Sympathy to Friendship—Sympathy means above all that which 'happens' between people in the realm of their emotions—that by means of which emotional and affective experiences unite people. This is love at a purely emotional stage, at which no decision of the will, no act of choice, as yet plays its proper role. *Only sympathy has the power to make people feel very close to one another*, but there is a hint here of subjectivism and passivity.

Friendship, as has been said, consists in a full commitment of the will to another person with a view to that person's good. There is, therefore, a need for sympathy to ripen into friendship and this process normally demands time and reflection. What is necessary is to supplement the sympathetic emotion toward another person with an objective knowledge of and belief in the value of that person. Only on this basis can the will actively commit itself. Friendship demands a sincere commitment of the will with the fullest possible justification. However, it is also necessary to supplement friendship with sympathy, without which it will remain cold and incommunicable.

It is a mistake to leave love at the level of sympathy and to think that when sympathy breaks down love is also at an end. What lies behind this mistake is an incongruity between the feelings of the subject and objective reality: the subjective and objective shapes of love do not exactly fit. It is part of the 'education of love' to overcome such gaps. Love cannot be merely a matter of 'consuming' sympathy, or of finding an outlet for one's feelings in it (frequently accompanied by sexual relief). No, love consists in the thoroughgoing transformation of sympathy into friendship. It is of its very nature creative and constructive, and not merely bent on enjoyment. Sympathy is always only a signal, and decidedly not a fully formed personal relationship. It must first establish itself on a firm foundation of friendship, just as friendship must be reinforced by the climate and temperature of sympathy. Sympathy and friendship are two processes which must interpenetrate without hindering each other. This is where the 'art' of education in love comes into its own.

Comradeship is distinct from both sympathy and friendship. It differs from sympathy in that it is not confined mainly to the emotional-affective sphere of life, but rests on objective foundations as joint work, common, goals, shared concerns, etc. It differs from friendship in that it is not an expression of the principle 'I want your good as much as I want my own'. Sharing brought about by particular objective factors is, then, the distinctive feature of comradeship. It favors the development of love's objective side, without which it is always incomplete. The 'we' of comradeship lacks the cohesion and depth of friendship, but being able to live as comrades in a distinct circle develops characteristics and abilities helpful in founding and maintaining a family community and in creating of a good atmosphere for family life.

Betrothed Love—Betrothed love is something different from and more than all the forms of love so far analyzed, though they are also a dimension of it. When betrothed love enters into an interpersonal relationship something more than friendship results: two people give themselves each to the other. The essence of this love, its decisive character, is this self-giving, the giving of one's own person to another, the surrender of one's 'I'. But how is this possible if the person is untransferable, incommunicable, his own master, etc. Of its very nature, no person can be transferred or ceded to another. Yet what is impossible and illegitimate in the natural order and in a physical sense, can come about in the order of love and in a moral sense. In this sense, one person can give himself or herself, can surrender entirely to another (whether to a human person or to God), and such a giving of the self creates a special form of love which we define as betrothed love. This fact goes to prove that the person has a dynamism of its own and that specific laws govern its existence and evolution. The fullest and most uncompromising form of love consists precisely in self-giving, in making one's inalienable and non-transferable 'I' someone else's property. This is doubly paradoxical: firstly in that it is possible to step outside one's own 'I' in this way, and secondly in that the 'I' far from being destroyed or impaired as a result is enlarged and enriched—of course in a super-physical, a moral sense. Such self-surrender presupposes a mature vision of values and a will ready and able to commit itself in this particular way. Betrothed love can never be a fortuitous or imperfect event in the life of the person. It always constitutes a special crystallization of the whole human 'I', determined because of its love to dispose of itself in this particular way. In giving ourselves we find clear proof that we possess ourselves.

'Self-giving', in the sense in which we are discussing it, should not be identified (or confused) with 'giving oneself' in a merely psychological sense, still less with 'surrender' in a merely physical sense. Further, on the psychological level, it must not only be the woman who experiences 'giving herself' while the man experiences only the correlative of 'conquest' or 'possession'. The acts of reciprocal self-giving, of mutual self-surrender, of mutual betrothed love must reciprocate each other in order to live up to the personalistic norm. Hence a special duty devolves upon the man: he must give to 'conquest' or 'possession' its appropriate form and content—which means that he too must give himself, no less than she does. Giving oneself only sexually, without the full gift of the person to validate it, must lead to those forms of utilitarianism which we have previously analyzed. A personalistic interpretation is absolutely necessary in this context. Thus, the moral code which has the commandment to love at its center finds itself in perfect agreement with the identification of marriage with betrothed love, or rather—looking at it from an educational point of view—with the treatment of marriage as the result of this form of love.

When a woman gives herself to a man as she does in matrimony, this—morally speaking—precludes a simultaneous gift of herself to other persons in the same way, and similarly with a man. Sexual intercourse has the effect of limiting betrothed love to a single pair of persons, though at the same time it gains in intensity. Moreover, only when it is so limited can that love open itself fully to the new persons who are the natural result of marital love between man and woman. There can be no question of a sexual giving of oneself which does not mean a giving of the person—and does not come in one way or another within the orbit of those demands which we have a right to make of betrothed love. These demands are derived from the personalistic norm. Betrothed love, though of its nature it differs from all the forms of love previously analyzed, can nevertheless not develop in isolation from them, in particular *goodwill* and *friendship*. Without these allies it may find itself in a very dangerous void, and the persons involved in it may feel helpless in face of conditions, internal and external, which they have inadvertently permitted to arise within themselves or between themselves.

PSYCHOLOGICAL ANALYSIS OF LOVE

Sense Impression and Emotion—'Sense impression' is our general term for the content of any sensory reaction to objective stimuli. Sense impressions are very closely connected with that specific property and power of the senses which is called cognition. The object is reflected or mirrored, the senses seize and retain its image. But a sensory image is often connected with a particular feeling or reaction. When someone says that a certain thing or person has 'made an impression' on him, he means that together with the reflection of a certain sense content he has experienced a palpable stimulus thanks to which the impression has impinged heavily on his consciousness. This is where we move on to the sphere of emotions. An emotion is also a sensory reaction to some object, but in an emotion we are reacting to a value which we find in the object. Emotion is in itself sensory, and what is more even has its corporeal coefficient—but this does not at all mean that only material values can evoke it. We know very well that emotions can be equally well evoked by non-material, by spiritual values. It makes no difference that the value in question must somehow be 'materialized' in order to cause an emotion. We have to observe or hear or imagine or remember the value for the emotions to arise. But such an emotion possesses greater depth. When its object is a material value the emotion is shallower, more superficial. When however the object of an emotion is a supra-material, or spiritual value, it reaches more deeply in a man's psyche. The ability to experience emotions which are at once profound and powerful seems to constitute a particularly important factor in the interior life. But if human love begins with an impression, if everything in it (even its spiritual content) depends upon that impression, this is because the impression is accompanied by an emotion—which makes it possible to experience another person as a value (or each to experience the other as a value). For this reason, we must in our further psychological analysis of love constantly refer to values.

Analysis of Sensuality—Sensuality expresses itself mainly in an appetitive form: a person of the other sex is seen as an 'object of desire' specifically because of the sexual value inherent in the body itself. This value reaches the consciousness by way of an impression, accompanied by an emotion experienced not only mentally but bodily. Sensuality is connected with the stirrings of the body, especially in its so-called erogenous zones. This shows its close connection with the inner sexual vitality of the organism itself (revealing its natural orientation toward procreation or continued existence). For a body possessing male characteristics needs a body possessing female characteristics for the objective ends served by the sexual urge. The promptings of sensuality would give man all the guidance he needs in his sexual life if, in the first place, his sexual reactions were infallibly guided by instinct, and if in the second place the object of those reactions—a person of the other sex—did not demand a different attitude from that which is proper to sensuality.

However, a human person, as we know, cannot be an object for use. Now, the body is an integral part of the person, and so must not be treated as though it were detached from the whole person: both the value of the body and the sexual value which finds expression in the body depend upon the value of the person. Given, then, interdependence, a sensual reaction in which the body and sex are a possible object for use threatens to devalue the person. To react in this way to the body of a person means to see using that body as a possibility. It is, therefore, easy to understand the reaction of conscience to the stirrings of sensuality. For it reacts either to an attempt artificially to divorce body and sex from the person, so that they are left alone as a 'possible object of use' or else to a valuation of the person exclusively as 'body and sex', as an object for use. In either case, we have something completely incompatible with the value of the person as such. Let us add that in man there can be no such thing as 'pure' sensuality, such as exists in animals, nor of the infallible regulation of sensual reactions by instinct. What then is completely natural in animals becomes sub-natural in man. Pure, natural sensuality, governed in its reactions by instinct (toward procreation and continued existence), is not oriented towards enjoyment divorced from the end of sexual life, whereas sensuality in man is so oriented.

This further means that sensuality by itself is not love, and may very easily become its opposite. At the same time, we must recognize that when man and woman come together, sensuality (as the natural reaction to a person of the opposite sex) is a sort of raw material for true conjugal love. But sensuality must be integrated into a fully formed and mature attitude toward the person, or else it certainly is not love. Sensuality must then be open to the other, nobler aspects of love. Further, though sensuality may insinuate itself into male-female relationships 'uninvited' so to speak and may be a constant possibility lurking just below the surface (to see the person as only 'the body and sex'), nonetheless sensual excitability is not in itself morally wrong. An exuberant and readily roused sensuality is the stuff from which a rich—if difficult—personal life may be made. It may help the individual to respond more readily and completely to the decisive elements in personal love.

Sentiment and Love—However, a sexual value which is the object of emotion is by no means necessarily connected with the 'body' itself as a 'possible means of enjoyment'. It may be connected with the 'whole person of the other sex', with 'femininity' or 'masculinity', and may be called *sentiment.* It does not have that drive for enjoyment, or the urge to consume, which is so characteristic of sensuality. It involves more contemplative moods, openness to beauty and to aesthetic values, and a strong feeling of admiration for the other. But a different sort of desire or need makes itself felt here: the desire for nearness, for proximity, and simultaneously for exclusivity or intimacy, a longing to be always alone together. It does not, however, so much arouse the will, but charms and disarms it. It can be mistaken for full spiritual love. However, there are dangers for this 'sentimental' love and tenderness. It can easily slip back onto the territory of sensuality and this can cause deep misunderstandings between the man and the woman. It is pretty generally recognized that woman is 'by nature' more sentimental, man more sensual. For this reason, the woman may be more inclined to go on seeing as a manifestation of affection what a man already clearly realizes to be the effect of sensuality and the desire for enjoyment. There is a further danger, arising from the fact that sentimental love influences memory and imagination and is influenced by them in return: a variety of values may be bestowed on the beloved which he or she does not necessarily possess in reality, but which the lover longs with all his or her heart to find in the beloved so as to fulfill the lover's own wishes, dreams, and desires. The other is then less an object of affection than an *occasion* for affection (a subtle form of using the other). This is why sentimental love (particularly characteristic of young love) is very often an occasion of disillusionment. The discrepancy between the ideal and the reality often results in such love fading or indeed changing into a feeling of hatred (which of course is *intrinsically* unable to discern the values which really exist in the other person).

Thus, it is clear that sentimental love by itself, as a form of reciprocal relationship between man and woman, is insufficient. It too needs to be integrated, as does sensual desire. If 'love' remains just sensuality, just a matter of 'sex-appeal', it will not be love at all, but only the utilization of one person by another, or of two persons by each other. While if love remains mere sentiment, it will equally be unlike love in the complete sense of the word. For both persons will remain in spite of everything divided from each other, though it may appear that they are very close just because they so eagerly seek proximity. Sentiment itself suffers from subjectivism, so that although objective love can begin to take shape on this ground, in order to ripen it must draw sustenance from other sources—sentiment alone will not mould such a love.

We must now turn to those forces which have the capacity to fashion an objective love, the forces of the human spirit. It is they which make the integration of love possible.

The Problem of Integrating Love—Psychology, the science of the soul, endeavors to lay bare the structure and foundation of man's inner life. Its investigations serve to confirm that the most significant characteristics of that inner life are the sense of truth and the sense of freedom. This involves not a mere 'reflecting' of objects (which one might suspect was 'material' in character), but an awareness of truth and falsehood which lies altogether outside the boundaries of that which matter can furnish. Truth is a condition of freedom. Without this faculty, man would inevitably be determined by the goods he experiences—they would possess him and determine the character of his actions and the whole direction of his activity. His ability to discover the truth gives man the possibility of self-determination (according to that truth), of deciding for himself the character and direction of his own actions, and that is what freedom means.

But a salient feature of sexual love (whether focused on the sensual, the sentimental, or both) is its great intensity. This intense concentration of vital and psychic forces so powerfully absorbs the consciousness that other experiences sometimes seem to pale and to lose their importance in comparison with sexual love. You only have to look closely at people under the spell of sexual love to convince yourself of this. Plato's thinking on the power of Eros is forever being confirmed. Each love is unique and unrepeatable in its elements and in relation to its object, but each involves this intensely pleasurable situation, a concentration of energies which a person did not know he possessed before this experience, associated with the joy of existing, of living and of acting—even if discomfort, sadness, or depression may from time to time break in upon it. Nonetheless, *the process of integrating love* (of genuine 'integration', 'wholeness', or 'completeness'—whether 'within' the person or 'between' persons) *relies upon the primary elements of the human spirit, freedom and truth.* These latter determine the spiritual imprint which marks the various manifestations of human life and human activity. They penetrate the remotest recesses of human action and experience, filling them with a content of which we never meet the slightest trace in the lives of animals. It is to this content that love between persons of different sexes owes its special consistency. Love is always an interior matter, a matter of the spirit. To the extent to which it ceases to be an interior matter and a matter of the spirit (i.e., grounded in freedom and truth), it also ceases to be love. What remains of it, in the senses and in the sexual vitality of the human body, does not constitute its essential nature. The will is, so to say, the final authority in ourselves, without whose participation no experience has full personal value, or the gravity appropriate to the experiences of the human person. It is love, especially, that 'demands' freedom—the commitment of freedom is, in a sense, its psychological essence. Therefore, the process of psychological integration which accompanies sexual love with a person involves not only commitment of the will, but unconditional commitment of the will—demands that the will should commit itself in the fullest possible way and in a way proper to itself. But a really free commitment of the will is possible only on the basis of truth, and not only the 'subjective' truth involving the genuine and powerful experience of sensual desire or of emotional commitment. These are aspects of true love. But genuine love also insists on the objective truth. Only thanks to this, only on this basis, can the integration of love take place. As long as we see only its subjective truth, we can obtain no full picture of love and can say nothing of its objective value. But this last is, after all, what matters most. It is this that we shall try to bring out by means of the ethical analysis of love.

THE ETHICAL ANALYSIS OF LOVE

Experience and Virtue—Where love between man and woman is concerned we must admit two meanings of the word: love can be understood as a certain situation with a psychological significance, but it also has an ethical significance—and so is connected with a norm. The norm in question here is the personalistic norm: it finds its expression in the commandment to love. Situationism, which recognizes no norm, falls into vulgar psychologism in its understanding of love. For love in the psychological sense must be subordinated in man to love in the ethical sense—otherwise there is no question of integration so called. As a result, *there is no possibility of psychological completeness in* *love unless ethical completeness is attained.* Whether we look at love as a concrete situation or as a whole series (a continuum) of such situations, all of them separately and together are psychologically complete and 'integrated' to the extent that the ethical value of love is present in them. In other words, *love as experience should be subordinated to love as virtue*—so much so that without love as virtue there can be no fullness in the experience of love. It will then be well for us to take a look at love as a virtue in the relationship between man and woman.

Affirmation of the Value of the Person—A person differs from a thing in structure and in degree of perfection. A person must not be put on the same level as a thing (or for that matter as an individual animal): the person possesses spiritual perfectibility, and is—by way of being—an (embodied) spirit, not merely a 'body' magnificently endowed with life. Between the psyche of an animal and the spirituality of a man there is an enormous distance, an uncrossable gulf. Now, the value of the person as such must be clearly distinguished from the particular values present in a person, including their sexual value (as a basis for sensuality or sentimentality). The sexual value is given in an immediate impression, while the knowledge of the person is of an intellectual, conceptual kind. Nonetheless, the truth that 'a human being of the other sex' is a person, 'some-one', as distinct from any other thing, is ever present in consciousness. This it is that awakens the need for the integration of sexual love and demands that the *sensual and emotional reaction* to a 'human being of the other sex' be somehow adjusted to the knowledge that the human being concerned is a person. Love demands integration: it is an affirmation of the person or else not love at all. Conversely, unintegrated love, not formed by affirmation of the value of the person, is not properly speaking love at all, although it may have the most 'amorous' (erotic) character possible. Love in the full sense of the word is a virtue, not just an emotion, still less mere excitement of the senses. It is a virtue oriented by the will towards the value of the person.

The will then is the source of that affirmation of the person which permeates all the reactions, all the feelings, the whole behavior of the subject. It is not really love when it directs itself merely to the 'body' of the other person, involving a desire to use the other in ways fundamentally incompatible with love. Nor yet is it really love when it is merely an emotional attitude to a human being of the other sex. Such a feeling may easily fade and shift if it is not firmly tied to affirmation of the person. Emotional love while bringing the 'human being' (if it carries an adequate charge of 'femininity' or 'masculinity') closer can easily miss the 'person'. Such love does not in itself have the mature interior cohesion which knowledge of the full truth about the human person, the object of love, necessarily brings. Affirmation of the value of the person generally leads in two directions: 1) it may point the way to control over those experiences whose immediate source is man's sensuality and emotionalism and 2) it may lead toward the choice of one's principal vocation in life. When a man chooses a woman to be the companion of his whole life, he designates the person who will play a bigger part in his life than any other and indicates the direction which his life vocation will take. There is the closest possible link between the two choices, so that the direction in which he feels himself called can only be an affirmation of that person's value.

Membership of One Another—Love forcibly detaches the person, so to speak, from its own natural inviolability and inalienability. It makes the person want to do just that—surrender itself to another, to the one it loves. The person no longer wishes to be its own exclusive property, but instead to become the property of that other. This means the renunciation of its autonomy and its inalienability, guided by the conviction that this does not diminish and impoverish but on the contrary enlarges and enriches the existence of the person. The law of *ekstasis* seems to operate here: the lover 'goes outside' the self to find a fuller existence in another. In no other form of love does this law operate so conspicuously as it does in betrothed love. Furthermore, the intensity of this love is explained not merely from the biological force of the sexual instinct, but also by the nature of that form of love which here shows itself. The sensual and emotional experiences are only the outward expression and gauge of what is happening (or should be happening) deep inside the persons involved. Self-giving can have its full value only when it involves and is the work of the will: it means disposing of one's whole self, 'giving one's soul'. Only then can we speak of the mutual surrender of both persons, of their belonging equally to each other. This is quite different from merely surrendering one's body—love cannot take the form of mere use, even if enjoyment is mutual and simultaneous. The unification of the two persons must first be achieved by way of love, and sexual relations between them can only be the expression of a unification already complete. The result of unification is that each belongs to the other, a reality expressed in various ways, among them full sexual intercourse, which we shall call marital intercourse since, as we shall see, marriage is the only proper place for it. Love makes for unification through the reciprocal gift of self. Sensual and emotional experiences are not to be identified with it, though they create the set of conditions in which it is realized in practice. Betrothed love, which carries within itself an inner need to make a gift of one's own person to another human being (a need realized between man and woman in surrender of the body and in a full sexual relationship, as well as in other ways) has a natural grandeur of its own. But take away from love the fullness of self-surrender, the completeness of personal commitment, and what remains will be a total denial and negation of it. This subtraction, taken to its conclusion, leads to what we call prostitution.

Betrothed love comprises not only the gift of the person but also the acceptance of that gift. Implicit in all this is the 'mystery' of reciprocity: acceptance must also be giving, and giving receiving. Love is of its nature reciprocal: *he who knows how to receive knows also how to give.* The skill in giving and receiving which is typical of love is exhibited by the man whose attitude to a woman is informed by total affirmation of her value as a person, and equally by the woman whose attitude to a man is informed by affirmation of his value as a person. This skill creates the specific climate of betrothed love—the climate of surrender of the inmost self. A woman is capable of truly making a gift of herself only if she fully believes in the value of her person and in the value as a person of the man to whom she gives herself. And a man is capable of fully accepting a woman's gift of herself only if he is fully conscious of the magnitude of the gift—which he cannot be unless he affirms the value of her person. This leads to gratitude and reciprocity, and contains an inner structure of friendship essential to betrothed love.

Choice and Responsibility—There exists in love a particular responsibility—the responsibility for a person who is drawn into the closest possible partnership in the life and activity of another, and becomes in a sense the property of whoever benefits from this gift of self. It follows that one also has a responsibility for one's own love: is it mature and responsible enough to justify the enormous trust of another person? The true 'relish' of love goes with a sense of responsibility for the person, a concern for the good of the person and not just with the sexual values of the person (sensual or sentimental). *The greater the feeling of responsibility for the person the more true love there is.* This truth throws a great deal of light on the problem of choice—whom do you choose to give yourself to? Naturally this depends on many factors (somatic and constitutional factors, temperament, character, etc.) and ultimately remains one of the secrets of human individuality. Sexual values play a role here but if they were dominant (even as a 'human being of the opposite sex', much less as a 'body as a possible means of enjoyment') we could not speak of 'choosing a person'. Clearly, if we are to speak of choosing a person, the value of the person must itself be the primary reason for choice. Primary reason does not mean sole reason—this would be to fall back into a Kantian formalistic personalism. Thus, if we consider the whole process by which a man chooses a woman or a woman a man, we can say that it is set in motion by recognition of and reaction to sexual values, but that in the last analysis each chooses the sexual values because they belong to a person, and not the person because of his or her sexual values. Only such an act of choice can be fully valid—when the truth about the person is fully apprehended. The essential reason for choosing a person must be personal, not merely sexual. Such a choice is tested over time most severely when the sensual and emotional reactions grow weaker, and sexual values as such lose their effect. But we must never forget that only when love between human beings is put to the test can its true value be seen. When a person's choice is a mature and valid act, and love is integrated as it should be in the inner life of the person, it is transformed both in its psychological and emotional aspect. It becomes simpler and soberer, less given to idealization. The love of a person which results from a valid act of choice is concentrated on the value of the person as such and makes us feel emotional love for the person as he or she really is, not for the person of our imagination, but for the real person.

The Commitment of Freedom—Only true knowledge of a person makes it possible to commit one's freedom to him or her. Love consists of a commitment which limits one's freedom—it is a giving of self, and to give oneself means just that: to limit one's freedom on behalf of another. This might seem negative and unpleasant, but love makes it a positive, joyful, and creative thing. *Freedom exists for the sake of love.* If freedom is not used, is not taken advantage of by love, it becomes a negative thing and gives human beings a feeling of emptiness and unfulfillment. Love commits freedom and imbues it with that to which the will is naturally attracted—goodness. The will aspires to the good, and freedom belongs to the will, hence freedom exists for the sake of love, because it is by way of love that human beings share most fully in the good. The will, however, cannot allow an object to be imposed upon it as a good; yet, this is precisely what the 'sexual instinct' attempts to do if it becomes unhinged from its proper role. It then attempts to take possession of an individual's senses and emotions (in light of sexual values) and, so to speak, to lay siege to his will. However, if the will capitulates to this assault, it cannot make its proper creative contribution to love. The sexual instinct wants above all to take over, to make use of another person, whereas love wants to give, to create a good, to bring happiness. From the desire for the 'unlimited good' of another 'I' springs the whole creative drive of true love—the drive to endow beloved persons with the good, to make them happy. This is, so to speak, the divine aspect of love—for to desire 'unlimited' good for another person is really to desire God for that person (whether this is clearly seen by the lover or not). The great moral force of true love lies precisely in this desire for happiness, for the true good, of another person. True love compels me to believe in my own spiritual powers. Even when I am 'bad', if true love awakens in me it bids me seek the true good where the object of love is concerned. In this way, affirmation of the worth of another person is echoed in affirmation of the worth of one's own person. When love attains its full dimensions, it introduces into a relationship not only a 'climate' of honesty between persons but a certain awareness of the 'absolute', a sense of contact with the unconditional and the ultimate.

The Education of Love—Love is never something just ready made, something merely 'given' to man and woman; it is always at the same time a 'task' which they are set. Love should be seen as something which in a sense never 'is' but is always 'becoming', and what it becomes depends upon the contribution of both persons and the depth of their commitment. Man is condemned, so to speak, to create. Creativity is a duty in the sphere of love too. We find that what develops from 'promising' raw material in the form of emotions and desires is often not true love, and often indeed sharply opposed to it, whereas a truly great love sometimes develops from modest material. But such a great love can only be the work of persons and —let us add here to complete the picture—the work of Divine Grace, who is Himself love and has the power to fashion any love. Grace has the power to make straight the sometimes tortuous paths of human love.

CHAPTER III
THE PERSON AND CHASTITY

THE REHABILITATION OF CHASTITY

Chastity and Resentment—'Resentment' distorts and devalues the features of a good that rightly deserves respect, stopping not only at *acedia* (sloth—sadness over the fact that the good is difficult of attainment) but going on to belittle the good in question (in this case chastity) in favor of what is convenient, comfortable, and pleasurable. Thus, chastity, continence, and sexual self-control are sometimes presented even as the enemies of true love between man and woman, as harmful to the health, as causing sexual and psychological frustration, etc., and therefore as objects of resentment. And yet a genuine love, one that is properly integrated, must be based on a certain selflessness or altruism, a whole-hearted desire for the beloved person's good—a good worthy of the person. This it is which makes love genuinely a 'bringer of happiness'. But none of this will happen if the love between man and woman is dominated by an ambition to possess, or by concupiscence born of sensual reactions, even if these are accompanied by intense emotion. The very exuberance of the emotions born of sensuality may conceal an absence of true love, or indeed an outright egoism. Sensual or emotional reactions to a person of the opposite sex which arise before and develop more quickly than virtue are something less than love. They are however more often than not taken for love and given that name—and it is to love, thus, understood that chastity is hostile, and an obstacle. Only the correct concentration of particular sensual and emotional elements *around the value of the person* entitles us to speak of love. We cannot give the name to that which is only a particular element or 'part' of it, for these components, if they are not held together by the correct gravitational pull, may add up not to love, but to its direct opposite. The special virtue which tries to preserve the truth of the love between man and woman, which wants to eliminate anything unworthy of love, anything which sullies or 'makes dirty', anything which would deprive love of it crystal clarity, is chastity. This virtue must be analyzed, and the resentment against it addressed.

Carnal Concupiscence—Both our internal and our external attitudes toward other persons need to be governed by the personalistic norm: love is the only adequate response to persons. But between man and woman, interest can immediately be aroused sensually (the other 'as a body to be enjoyed'). An arousal of interest on this level can quickly lead to sensual concupiscence (desire: the *concupiscible* appetite) and then to carnal desire (the urge to act and satisfy one's desire: the *irascible* appetite). When this carnal desire imposes itself on the will, it orients the subject first towards 'the body and sex' and secondly toward 'enjoyment'. As soon as it achieves its ends, its attitude to the object changes completely, all 'interest' in it disappears until desire is aroused again. Sensuality is 'expended' in concupiscence. In the animal world, this serves its purpose (procreation, preservation of the species) and nothing is lost when a carnal reaction ends in this way. But in the world of persons a serious danger of a moral nature arises when this happens. 'Carnal love' (born of carnal concupiscence alone) lacks the value which love for the person must contain. The sexual value as such usurps the place of the personal value which is essential to love, and becomes the core around which the whole experience crystallizes. Carnal concupiscence impels people very powerfully towards physical intimacy (sexual intercourse), but *if this grows out of nothing more than concupiscence it does not unite a man and a woman as persons*, it is not love in the true sense, it does not have the value of *personal* union. On the contrary, it is even a negation of the love of persons, for it rests on the impulse to 'enjoy' which is a characteristic of pure sensuality. There is here a serious possibility not only that love will be deformed, but also that its natural raw material will be squandered. For sensuality furnishes love with 'material', but material which can only be shaped by the appropriate creative activity on the part of the will. Without this there can be no love, there is only the raw material which is used up by carnal concupiscence as it seeks an 'outlet'.

Emotion serves to some extent as natural safeguard against carnal concupiscence. Sentiment reacts not just to 'the body as an object of enjoyment' but to a 'human being of the other sex'. Indeed, sentimental love rejoices in the emotion for its own sake (being 'in love' with someone or being the object of someone else's emotion, 'being loved'). Such emotional love seems so pure that any comparison of it with sensual passion is thought of as degrading and brutalizing it. Sentimental love is not, however, a full and positive solution to the problem of concupiscence, and if not reinforced by virtue but left to its own resources, can often be pulled back down to the level of concupiscence by the mighty force of the latter, even if enriched by a 'lyricism' deriving from sentiment. Furthermore, sentiment introduces a new problem: the tendency to idealize the other which can lead away from a contact with reality and toward bitter disappointments later on. Thus, what emotion brings into the relationship between man and woman is also only part of the 'raw material' of love. Emotion, and the 'idealization' of man by woman and woman by man to which it gives rise, may help greatly in the formation of the virtue of chastity; however, complete security against carnal concupiscence is something we find only in the profound realism of virtue, and specifically the virtue of chastity.

Subjectivism and Egoism—The integration of love requires the individual consciously and by acts of will to impose a shape on all the material that sensual and emotional reactions provide. The danger is that the latter will tip love in the direction of a false subjectivism, a distortion of the true nature of love in which there is a hypertrophy of the subjective element such that the objective value of love is partially or wholly swallowed up and lost in it. Emotions, of course, play an enormous part in the development of the legitimate subjective aspect of love—it is impossible to imagine the subjective aspect of love without emotion. It would be absurd to want love to be 'free of emotion', as the Stoics and Kant did. On the other hand, we must not overlook the possibility that emotion may be excessively subjective. We can indeed say that emotion has its dangers, and that they may be a threat to love. Emotion may affect our apprehension of the truth—the objective truth about our actions which is the core of human morality. This provokes 1) a certain 'dis-integration', since the immediate emotion overshadows and detaches itself from the totality of other objective factors in the situation and the principles which govern them; and 2) a replacement of these objective principles (as guide for action) with the emotion itself as the determining criterion by which an act is evaluated (does it feel authentic, sincere, genuine, 'true'?). Yet, sincere feelings may inform an act which is objectively not good.

The road from this form of subjectivism (subjectivism of the emotions) to subjectivism of values is a straight and easy one—so easy that once a man has set foot on the inclined plane of subjectivism it is hard to see how he can stop halfway. Ultimately, *subjectivism of values means fixation on pleasure alone:* pleasure is the end, and all else—the 'person', that person's 'body', 'femininity' or 'masculinity'—is only a means to it. Yet love itself is oriented towards *objective values,* first among them *the value of the person (which both partners in love affirm),* and the true union of persons to which love leads. This form of subjectivism, then, destroys the very essence of love, and finds the whole value of erotic experiences (and indeed of love in general) in pleasure (whether of the senses or of the emotions). Hedonism, in theory and in practice, is the end result of subjectivism in love. Thus, subjectivism is the soil in which egoism grows.

But both subjectivism and egoism are inimical to love—in the first place because love has an objective orientation (towards the person and the good of the person), and in the second place because love is altruistic (it is directed towards another human being). Subjectivism, on the contrary, is exclusively concerned with the subject and the 'authenticity' of the subject's feelings, the affirmation of love through those feelings alone. Further, *the egoist is preoccupied to the exclusion of all else with his own 'I', his ego, and so seeks the good of that 'I' alone, caring nothing for others.* Egoism precludes love, as it precludes any shared good, and hence also the possibility of reciprocity (which always presupposes the pursuit of a common good). Egoism excludes love and reciprocity, but permits calculation and compromise in a 'bilateral' fashion— mutual pleasuring. In these circumstances there cannot, however, be any question of a 'common I', of the sort which comes into being when one of the persons *desires the good of the other as his own and finds his own good in that of the other person.* It is not possible to desire pleasure itself in this way, because it is a purely subjective good, not trans-subjective, nor even inter-subjective. At most we can want another's pleasure 'besides' and always 'on condition of' our own pleasure. So, then, the subjectivism of values (the fixation on pleasure for its own sake) as the exclusive end of the association and cohabitation of man and woman, is necessarily egoistic. This results from the very nature of pleasure. But this does not mean that we must see pleasure itself as evil—pleasure itself is a specific good—but only points to the moral evil involved in fixing the will on pleasure alone. Such fixation is not only subjective but egoistic.

There can be a subtle 'egoism of the emotions' as well as the more obvious 'egoism of the senses' (using the other as an object for sexual pleasure). When an emotion becomes an end in itself, merely for the sake of the pleasure it gives, then the person who causes the emotion (or to whom it is directed) is once again a mere 'object' providing an opportunity to satisfy the emotional needs of one's own ego. This is no less drastic a distortion of love than the egoism of the senses, yet it can more easily disguise itself as love and, thus, can be more difficult to recognize or overcome.

Love is always a uniquely subjective and inter-subjective fact; yet, it must be protected from subjectivist distortions, and consequent disintegration and egoism. Consequently, both persons involved, while cultivating as intensively as they can the subjective aspect of their love, must also endeavor to achieve objectivity. Combining the one with the other requires a special effort, but this is the unavoidable labor and creative call of love.

The Structure of Sin—The analyses of concupiscence, subjectivism, and egoism enable us to understand the concept of 'sinful love', which embodies a profound paradox—for love is a synonym of the good, while sin means moral evil. This can occur when sensuality or emotionalism, which furnish so to speak the 'raw material' for love, are mistakenly or prematurely given the title of 'love'. In fact, they only become love as a result of integration, or in other words by being raised to the personal level, by reciprocal affirmation of the value of the person. Without this, sensuality alone (or emotion alone) may easily become the raw material for sin. We must examine this structure of sin.

'Sensuality' implies the capacity to react to the sexual values connected with the body and 'carnal desire' implies the wish to enjoy the promise of those values. Both of these are part of the natural endowment of human beings and a human being would be defective if he or she did not possess these capacities. Integrated into a genuine love, involving a true affirmation of the person, they are a dimension of the good which is the love between man and woman. However, 'concupiscence' further implies a consistent tendency (theologically we might say as a result of original sin) to see persons of the other sex through the prism of sexuality alone, as 'objects of potential enjoyment', thereby revealing a latent inclination of human beings to invert the order of objective values. Concupiscence is then in every man the terrain on which two attitudes to a person of the other sex contend for mastery: love or use. Concupiscence itself means a constant tendency merely to 'enjoy', whereas man's duty is to 'love'. Thus, when we say that sensuality and emotion furnish the 'raw material' for love, we must add that this happens only to the extent they are not swallowed up by concupiscence but absorbed in true love. Otherwise, sensuality and emotion can become the 'germ for sin'. Thus, it is not altogether safe to put one's trust in the reactions of the senses or the emotions—they cannot be acknowledged as love, but only as something from which love must be obtained. There is in this a certain hardship, since any human being would like simply to follow his spontaneous inclinations, to find love fully present in all his reactions which have another human being as their object.

Still, neither sensuality nor even concupiscence is a sin in itself, since only that which derives from the will can be a sin—an act of a voluntary and conscious nature, not merely a 'tendency'. Yet the problem is that concupiscence tends to become active 'wanting', which is an act of the will. Here we stand on the threshold of sin. The concupiscent tendency continually seeks to induce the will to consent to the attitude of using the other as an object for enjoyment, to make what is merely 'happening' in the senses into an active doing by conscious consent of the will in interior acts (which might then have exterior manifestations). Though sometimes it is difficult to discern the dividing line, it is important to discriminate between an act of the will and the mere prompting of the senses and of carnal desire. No one can demand of himself either that he should experience no sensual reactions at all, or that they should immediately yield just because the will does not consent, or even because it declares itself definitely 'against'. A sensual reaction follows its own course for a time. It only becomes sin if the will leads the way—because it is wrongly *oriented* (i.e., this is not just 'wrong thinking') and is guided by a false conception of love. Temptation presupposes an *awareness that 'A is bad'* which is somehow falsified so as to suggest that 'A is good after all'. Subjectivism in all its guises creates opportunities for such chicanery between the sexes.

Emotional subjectivism makes us susceptible to the suggestion that whatever is connected with 'genuine emotion' is good. Hence the temptation to reduce love to nothing more than subjective emotional states. Here sin arises from the fact that a human being does not wish to subordinate emotion to the person and love, but on the contrary to subordinate the person and love to emotion. 'Sinful love' is not wrong in such a case because it is saturated with emotion but because the will puts emotion before the person, allowing it to annul all the objective laws and principles which must govern the unification of two persons, a man and a woman.

Subjectivism in values insinuates yet another false suggestion: that what is pleasant must be good. Once again the evil here lies not merely in an 'error in thinking' but results from a disposition of the will, which wants unconditionally the enjoyment of the senses or the emotions. The suggestion that 'what is pleasant is good', if it comes to govern the whole activity of the will, completely perverts it. It results in an habitual incapacity for 'loving kindness' towards a person—the will to love is lacking. Love as a virtue is ousted from the will and is replaced by a preoccupation with the sensual or emotional enjoyment connected with sexual experiences, attraction, and desire between man and woman. Yet a special danger lies in the fact that, while making true love unrealizable, such an attitude (the subjective state of being saturated in emotion) often, at least initially, wants to present itself as love in its fullest and most perfect sense, as 'everything' that love has to offer. This is the particular danger of a 'sinful love' (grounded in subjectivism and tending toward egoism), and it consists in a fiction: immediately, and before reflection, it is not felt to be 'sinful', but is above all felt to be 'love'. Yet, though this presence of powerful emotion may mitigate the gravity of the sin, it does not in the least alter the fact that the personalistic norm exists and is also binding in relations between persons. Sin always flaunts this principle and sin remains a violation of the true good. For the true good in the love of man and woman is first of all the person, and not emotion for its own sake, still less pleasure as such. The person must never be sacrificed to them, for this is to introduce the 'germ of sin' into love. The will can and must be guided by objective truth. It can, and therefore must, demand of the reason a correct vision of love and of the true happiness which love can bring to a woman and a man. It must guard both the self and the other from the destructive tendencies of subjectivism and egoism which result in the disintegration of love.

The True Meaning of Chastity—A negative attitude about 'chastity', and even resentment of it, arises when people are unwilling to acknowledge the enormous value of chastity to human love because they reject the full objective truth about the love of man and woman, and put a subjectivist fiction in its place. Thus, it is necessary to emphasize strongly the principle of integration: *love* in a world of persons must possess its peculiar ethical wholeness and fullness, its psychological manifestations are not sufficient in themselves. Indeed, *love is only psychologically complete when it possesses an ethical value,* when it is a virtue. Only in love as a virtue is it possible to satisfy the objective demands of the personalistic norm, which requires 'loving kindness' towards a person and rejects any form of 'utilization' of the person.

But how should we understand chastity in the true sense? In traditional philosophy, it is rightly presented as a species or type of one of the four cardinal virtues: 'moderation' or temperance, having for its immediate subject man's concupiscence. 'Moderation' retrains or orders man's instinctive appetites according to reason. The fully formed virtue of chastity would then involve an efficiently functioning control which permanently keeps the appetites in equilibrium by means of its habitual attitude to the true good determined by reason, and thereby is able to properly moderate and regulate.

But is it enough to say that chastity lies in moderation? Is this the best way to bring out the real value and significance of chastity in human life? I think, rather, we must endeavor to bring out and emphasize much more forcefully the kinship between chastity and love. *Chastity can only be thought of in association with the virtue of love.* Its function is to free love from the utilitarian attitude. Thus, it must control not only sensuality and carnal concupiscence, but—perhaps more important—those centers deep within the human being in which the utilitarian attitude is hatched and grows. All varieties of subjectivism and egoism must be overcome; but, *the more successfully the utilitarian attitude is camouflaged in the will the more dangerous it is*—especially in a 'sinful love' which calls itself simply love, since those who experience it try to convince themselves and others that love is just this and cannot be otherwise. To be chaste means to have a 'transparent' attitude to a person of the other sex—*chastity means just that, the interior 'transparency'* without which love is not itself, for it cannot be itself until the desire to 'enjoy' is subordinated to a readiness to show loving kindness in every situation.

The essence of chastity consists in quickness to affirm the value of the person in every situation, and in raising to the personal level all reactions to the value of 'the body and sex'. This requires a special interior, spiritual effort, for affirmation of the value of the person can only be the product of the spirit, but this effort is above all positive and creative 'from within', not negative and destructive (chastity is not just one long 'no'). It is not a matter of summarily 'annihilating' the value 'body and sex' in the conscious mind by pushing reactions to them down into the subconscious (creating the danger of 'explosions'), but is a matter of sustained long-term integration. The value 'body and sex' must be grounded and implanted in the value of the person. Thus, the objection that chastity is merely negative is incorrect. For by 'moderating' the feelings and actions connected with the sexual values we serve the values of the person and of love. True chastity does not lead to disdain for the body or to disparagement of matrimony and the sexual life—this is 'false' chastity, tinged with hypocrisy. Rather only the chaste man and the chaste woman are capable of true love. For chastity frees their association, including their marital intercourse, from that tendency to use a person which is objectively incompatible with 'loving kindness', and by so freeing it introduces into their life together *and their sexual relationship* a special disposition to 'loving kindness'. It requires maturity for a man and a woman (each in their own way) to become capable of and learn to 'savor' this dimension of 'loving kindness' informing sexual love, since every human being is by nature burdened with concupiscence and apt to find the 'savor' of love above all in the satisfaction of carnal desire. Thus, chastity is a difficult long term matter; one must wait patiently for it to bear fruit, for the happiness of loving kindness which it must bring. But at the same time, chastity is the sure way to happiness.

It does not lead to disdain of the body, but it does involve a certain humility of the body before three great facts. The human body must be 'humble' in face of the greatness represented by the person: for in the person resides the true and definitive greatness of man. Furthermore, the body must 'humble itself' in face of the magnitude represented by love—and here 'humble itself' means subordinate itself. Finally, 'the body' must also show humility in face of human happiness. How often does it insinuate that it alone possesses the key to the secret of happiness! But this superficial view of happiness for one thing obscures the truth that man and woman can and must seek their temporal, earthly happiness in a lasting union which has an interpersonal character, since it is based in each of them on unreserved affirmation of the value of the person. Still more certainly does the 'body'—if it is not 'humble' and subordinate to the full truth about the happiness of man—obscure the vision of the ultimate happiness: that of the human person in union with a personal God.

THE METAPHYSICS OF SHAME

The Phenomenon of Sexual Shame and its Interpretation—The phenomenon of shame (which can relate to either something good or to something bad) arises when something which of its very nature (or in view of its purpose) ought to be private passes the bounds of the person's privacy and somehow becomes public. Thus, we see that shame is a uniquely personal response, requiring an inner self (or inner life of the person) capable of such a motive of concealment. Animals can fear, but they cannot feel shame. Particular objects of shame are those parts and organs of the body which determine its sex. Human beings show an almost universal tendency to conceal them from the gaze of others, and particularly of persons of the other sex. Here there can be considerable variations due to the effect of habit, collective custom, prevailing climate, etc., and dress may at times serve not to conceal but in one way or another to draw attention to these parts of the body. Sexual modesty cannot then in any simplistic way be identified with use of clothing, nor shamelessness with the absence of clothing and total or partial nakedness. A tendency to cover the body and those parts of it which declare it male or female goes together with sexual shame, but is not an essential feature of it.

What is essential is the tendency to conceal sexual values themselves, particularly insofar as they constitute in the mind of a particular person 'a potential object of enjoyment' for persons of the other sex. This awareness develops only gradually (children do not feel 'shame' for their awareness of sexual values is not yet awake) and follows one course in girls and women and another in boys and men. The man is very keenly aware of his own sensuality, and for him this is a source of shame. He is, then, ashamed above all of the way in which he reacts (as potential objects for use and enjoyment) to the sexual value of persons of the other sex. As a consequence, he is equally ashamed of the sexual values of his own body. We feel shame when we feel reactions which are incompatible with the value of the person. Since this sensual reaction is more importunate in man than in woman (in whom the emotional response is generally more pronounced—though this tells us nothing about the *virtue of chastity*), modesty and shame (concealing the sexual values of the body) must be more pronounced in girls and women. For a woman to feel this need, however, requires some insight into male psychology.

Shame serves three positive functions in the relations between man and woman. First, it reveals deeply and intimately the truth that the person cannot be approached merely or primarily as an object of use or enjoyment. Only the person can feel shame, because only the person of its very nature cannot be the object of use. However, it is not just a matter of hiding anything that might produce a sexual reaction in another person, nor yet of internally hiding from one's own reaction to a person of the other sex. For, secondly, this 'shrinking back' from 'use' goes together with the longing to inspire love, to inspire a 'reaction' to the value of the person and with the longing to experience love in the same sense. Sexual modesty is not a flight from love, but on the contrary the opening of a way towards it. *The spontaneous need to conceal mere sexual values bound up with the person is the natural way to the discovery of the value of the person as such.* But there is more to it than that. Thirdly, it is not just a matter of protecting or defending *but of revealing the value of the person*, and doing so in the context of sexual values simultaneously present in a particular person but subordinate to the value of the person. Hence the feeling of 'inviolability': 1) expressed in the woman, 'You must not touch me, not even in your secret carnal thoughts'; 2) expressed in the man, 'I must not touch her, not even with the deeply hidden wish to enjoy her, for she cannot be an object for use'. This 'fear of contact' (so characteristic of persons who truly love one another) is an indirect way of affirming the value of the person as such. Finally let us note that there is also a certain natural shame associated with love in its physical aspect, because the experiences which go with it are specifically 'intimate'. Men and women avoid other people, avoid being seen, when they make love, and any morally sound human being would consider it extremely indecent not to do so. This is because only the couple are aware of the inner justification of personal love and self-donation behind the physical intimacy, only for them is that love an 'interior' matter of the soul, not just a physical matter. Anyone else would find himself confronted simply by the external manifestations (shared sexual values) while the union of persons itself (the objective reality of love) remains inaccessible to outsiders. This is what 'privacy' guards against.

Law of the Absorption of Shame by Love—Between man and woman, a natural phenomenon occurs (dependent upon grasping the relative importance of the value of the person and of sexual values) which we shall call here 'the absorption of shame by love'. To say that shame is 'absorbed' by love does not mean that it is eliminated or destroyed, only that love now realizes (makes real) the characteristic effects of shame. Shame is a natural form of self-defense for the person against the danger of descending or being pushed into the position of an object for sexual use. But love and the tendency to regard a person as an object of use, are mutually exclusive. Thus, where there is genuine love, shame (as the way to avoid such 'use') loses its *raison d'etre* and gives ground. But this can only be true to the extent that a person loved in this way—and this is most important—is equally ready to give himself or herself in this way in love. Thus, sexual intercourse between spouses is not a form of shamelessness legalized by outside authority, but is *felt to be* in conformity with the demands of shame (unless the spouses themselves make it 'shameless' by performing it for mere use and enjoyment). Only love is capable of absorbing shame—true love in which sexual values are subordinate to the value of the person, the latter pervading all sensuality and sentiment. Thus, even in the midst of sexual attraction and desire, even in the midst of emotional closeness and enjoyment, it becomes impossible for the will to regard the other as a mere object for use. This is where the real strength of love lies—mere theoretical affirmation of the value of the person is not enough. Given such an attitude there is no longer any reason for shame over the body or the emotions. This is the point at which love is psychologically complete and sexual shame can be thoroughly absorbed. The two can become 'one flesh' and this will not be a form of shamelessness, but only the full realization of the union of persons resulting from reciprocal conjugal love. This has a very direct relevance to the problem of procreation, but this will be discussed in Chapter IV.

But there is a danger connected with the phenomenon of the absorption of sexual shame—that it may be treated too superficially. This can occur when the growing emotional-affective dimension of love begins to swallow up the feeling of shame as a part of the natural growth of love. This emotional-affective process explains the view, so very often expressed or implied, that 'the emotion (love) itself gives men and women the right to physical intimacy and to sexual intercourse'. This is a mistaken view, for love as an emotion (even if reciprocated) is very far from being the same as love completed by commitment of the will. This last requires that each of the two persons chooses the other, on the basis of an unqualified affirmation of the value of the other person, with a view to a lasting union in matrimony, and with a clearly defined attitude to parenthood. Love between persons possesses—and must possess—a clear-cut objective purpose. Love as an emotional-affective experience often has a purely subjective character, and is from the ethical point of view immature. Thus, the mere elimination of the feeling of shame by an amorous feeling is not enough to open the door to physical intimacy and sexual intercourse. Indeed, we have here a form of shamelessness taking advantage of transitory emotions to legitimate itself.

The Problem of Shamelessness—Though there is some relativity in the definition of what is shameless, depending on differences of individuals and of cultures, this does not mean that shamelessness itself is relative and without common elements. *Shame is a tendency, uniquely characteristic of the human person, to conceal sexual values sufficiently to prevent them from obscuring the value of the person as such*—but to conceal them only to a certain extent, so that in combination with the value of the person they can still be a point of origin for love. 'Physical shame' concerns the sexual values externally connected to the body; shamelessness here involves any mode of being or behavior (e.g. provocative dress) which gives such prominence to the sexual values that they obscure the essential value of the person.

'Emotional shame' endeavors to conceal one's own reactions and feelings if they tend toward mere use of the other; shamelessness here consists in the rejection of that healthy tendency to be ashamed of the urge toward sensual and sexual exploitation of another person. Such a 'shame over one's feelings of wanting to use another' has nothing in common with prudery, hypocrisy, or the condemnation of sexual feelings as inherently bad or selfish. It is a healthy reaction within a person against any attitude which would degrade the person's essential value. To combat either type of shamelessness, whether originating in man or in woman, it is important to develop healthy customs in the context of sexual relations and in the different sectors of the life of men and women together. 'Healthy customs', however, have nothing in common with puritanism in sexual matters, for exaggeration easily results in prudery (which involves concealing one's real intentions with regard to sex).

Concerning the problem of dress, what is truly immodest is that which frankly contributes to the deliberate displacement of the true value of the person by sexual values. This principle is simple and obvious, but its application in specific cases depends upon the individual, the milieu, and the society. Further, it is not always clear where the line is to be drawn between a woman 'dressing shamelessly' and a man 'looking shamelessly' (or vice versa, though this is perhaps less common). Dress is a function of (healthy or unhealthy) social custom and questions of aesthetics may seem decisive here (i.e., men can strive to look handsome and women beautiful), but they cannot be the only considerations given. Ethical considerations must also be acknowledged. *Man, alas, is not such a perfect being that the sight of the body of another person, especially a person of the other sex, can arouse in him merely a disinterested liking which develops into an innocent affection.* In practice it also arouses concupiscence and this must be taken into account. This does not, however, mean that physical shamelessness is to be simply and exclusively identified with complete or partial nakedness. There are circumstances in which nakedness is not immodest. The human body is not in itself shameful (nor, for the same reasons, are sensual reactions or human sensuality in general). Nonetheless, it requires a real internal effort to refrain from reacting to the naked body in an immodest way. While on the subject of dress, it is also important to note functional differences in what is modest or immodest: what is modest at the beach may not be modest while strolling on a city street.

Finally, we must refer here at least cursorily to the problem of shamelessness in art or pornography. An artist's work is meant to serve the truth and the human body, with its beauty, is certainly part of the truth about man, just as its sensual and sexual aspects are an authentic part of the truth about human love. But it would be wrong to let this part obscure the whole—and this is what often happens in art. Pornography is a marked tendency to accentuate the sexual element when reproducing the human body or human love in a work of art, with the object of inducing the reader or viewer to believe that sexual values are the only real values of the person, and that love is nothing more than the experience (individual or shared) of those values alone. In this sense, pornography does not reveal too much about the human person but too little. For the truth about human love consists always in reproducing the interpersonal relationship, however large sexual values may loom in that relationship. Just as the truth about man is that he is a person, however conspicuous sexual values are in his or her physical appearance. A work of art must get at this truth, no matter how deeply it has to go into sexual matters; otherwise, it can only give a distorted picture of reality. But this distorted image, coupled with the power and prestige of artistic beauty, yields a greater likelihood that it will take root and establish itself in the mind and the will of the person contemplating it.

THE PROBLEMS OF CONTINENCE

Self Control and Objectivization—Control of concupiscence has as its objective not only the perfection of the person who attempts to achieve it (through 'moderation' or 'self-control'), but also the realization of love in the world of persons. By moderation we mean the ability to find that 'mean' in the control of sensual excitability and sentimental impressionability which in each concrete case, in every interpersonal configuration or situation, will best facilitate the realization of love and avoid the danger of exploitation. Moderation does not mean mediocrity or having only a 'medium' capacity for sensual or sentimental reactions (such capacities will vary with each person). The word 'continence'—having to do with containing— gives us the perfect image of those well-known interior crises in which the person undergoes something like an invasion of the forces of sensuality or sentiment. The person feels the need, natural to a reasonable being, to defend itself against these forces: above all their invasion threatens the person's natural power of self-determination. The person cannot allow things to 'happen' to it which it has not willed, since the person (in the true order of values) *is his own master.* But chastity cannot consist merely in blind self-restraint; continence cannot be an end in itself (self-control for the sake of self-control).

Rather, *virtue can come only from spiritual strength,* and ultimately this strength comes from the reason which 'sees' the real truth about the values and puts the values of the person and love *above* the values of sex and enjoyment associated with them. 'Blind' self-restraint is not enough. There is no valid continence without recognition of the objective order of values: the value of the person is higher than the values of sex. This is the first step on the road to chastity: self-control subordinated to the process of objectivization (i.e., recognition of the objective order of values). Thereafter, the value of the person must 'take command' so to speak, of all that happens in a man; then continence is no longer 'blind' but permits the mind and will to 'open up' to genuine and superior values. Here 'objectivization' is closely linked with 'sublimation' (i.e., the elevation of sensual and emotional attachments and enjoyments to a higher level as an expression of love). But a mere knowledge of the value of the person does not dispense with self-control: the latter must be effectively practiced. But such practice is again based on knowledge, for man is so constructed internally that the promptings of carnal desire do not disappear merely because they are 'contained' by will power, although superficially they may appear to do so. For them to disappear completely, a man must know 'why' he is containing them, and to simply answer 'you must' does not solve the problem sufficiently—for a sufficient answer must be given to the natural and characteristic '*sense of loss' of the lower values of sensual or emotional enjoyment.* Why should I restrain myself? I do not acquiesce in such a loss just to prove my self-control. Furthermore, it is not only in view of my own perfectibility in virtue (though this is a legitimate and necessary motive), but also *for the love of the other person and out of respect for the truth of our love.* This becomes the sufficient reason for restraint. However, sentiment, while it has the danger relapsing into sensuality without the participation of reflection and virtue, nonetheless can play an important role in the process of sublimation or elevation of our motives. *For the value of the person must not be merely understood by the cold light of reason but deeply felt.* An abstract understanding of the person does not necessarily beget a feeling for the value of the person: but there are elements in sentiment which provide this feeling (its orientation is quite distinct from that which prevails in sensuality) and help us towards this fuller realization. In this way the intellectual and moral virtue of chastity finds some support in the emotional sphere.

Aristotle and St. Thomas Aquinas both emphasize that in relation to the sensual and emotional sphere of his inner life a man must employ appropriate tactics and even a certain 'diplomacy'. The use of the imperative is of little avail here, and it may even produce results the very opposite of what was intended. Every man must effectively deploy the energies latent in his sensuality and his sentiments, so that they become allies in his striving for authentic love—for they may, as we know, become his foes. This ability to make allies of potential foes is perhaps an even more decisive characteristic of self-mastery and the virtue of chastity than is 'pure' continence.

Tenderness and Sensuality—We feel tenderness for a person (or even for an animal or plant) when we become conscious of the ties which unite us. It is especially between two human beings that one of them is able to (and feels the need to) enter into the feelings, the inner state, the whole spiritual life of the other—and is able (and needs) to make the other aware of this. These are precisely the functions of tenderness, which can 'elevate' the sensual and emotional relations between man and woman. Tenderness includes the capacity for compassion and sensitive awareness of another's feelings or state of mind, but goes on to *make one's own* the feelings and mental states of the other. *Tenderness, then, springs from awareness of the inner state of another person and whoever feels it actively seeks to communicate his feeling of close involvement with the other person and his situation.* It is the result of emotional commitment (and sentiment enables us to feel close to another 'I') and this is often expressed in a touch, an embrace, a hug, certain forms of kissing, etc. But tenderness resides in an inner emotional attitude (personal, interior, and private), not in its outward manifestations, for they can equally well be purely conventional and social. Tenderness must not be confused with sensuality, which aims at satisfying a need for enjoyment. It is not an expression of concupiscence but of benevolence and devotion; its immediate aim is not 'enjoyment' but the 'feeling of nearness'. Unlike sensuality and sensual enjoyment, tenderness may be entirely disinterested—when it exhibits above all concern for the other person and his situation.

However, since we can be 'disinterested' only within limits, tender moments may also be 'turned' toward a need to gratify one's own feelings. Indeed, tenderness demands vigilance against the danger that its manifestations may acquire a different significance and become merely forms of sensual and sexual gratification. There exists then a problem of 'educating' tenderness within the general problem of educating love 'in' man and woman, and consequently 'between' them. Tenderness, therefore, cannot do without a perfected inner self-control, which becomes the index of the inner refinement and delicacy of one's attitude toward a person of the other sex. Whereas mere sensuality pushes us on to enjoyment and the man exclusively under its sway cannot even see that the association between man and woman may have some other significance, that its 'style' can be quite different, tenderness reveals so to speak this other 'style' and takes care that it is not subsequently destroyed.

Tenderness is the 'right' of all those who have a special need for it—the weak, the sick, the afflicted. It would seem that children, to whom it is the natural way of showing love, have a special right to tenderness. We must, however, apply to all (and particularly the outward) manifestations of tenderness one single criterion: that of love and love of the person. For there also exists the danger of inflaming egoism by an exaggerated and self-absorbed tenderness without regard to the objective good of the other. Thus, genuine love must combine two elements: tenderness and a certain firmness and strength of will. The latter will prevent tenderness from sinking into sickly sentimentality, which does not inspire profound confidence but rather the suspicion that for this human being tender moments are only a way of trying to satisfy his own emotional (or even sensual) needs. Clearly, then, tenderness has no *raison d'etre* outside love. Save in love, we have no 'right' to show or receive tenderness—its exterior manifestations are empty gestures.

These observations apply particularly to relations between man and woman. Here more than anywhere the various forms of tenderness must be fully warranted by true love of the person. Since this type of love receives great force from the senses and sentiments, various forms of tenderness have the danger of easily 'diverging' from love of the person and straying in the direction of sensual, or at any rate emotional, egoism. Apart from this, exterior manifestations of tenderness may create the illusion of love, which in reality does not exist. The seducer's methods usually include a display of tenderness, just as the coquette tries to play on the senses, though in both cases genuine love of the person is absent. Furthermore, even in cases of genuine love, the emotional side (especially in young people or those of especially 'ardent' temperament) often develops more quickly (sometimes explosively) compared to its objective and ethical dimensions. Accordingly, if we are to grant to a man or a woman the 'right to tenderness'—whether to show it or to receive it—we must also demand an even greater sense of responsibility (responsibility for the person). Besides the danger of excessive familiarity of the senses in the direction of sexual enjoyment, there also exists the danger of an immoderate 'tenderness' that wishes to stop at purely subjective manifestations of the 'feeling of closeness', deriving only a fleeting pleasure from them. Then this 'raw material' which should be a part of the order of love is squandered. Without chastity and self-control, it is impossible so to educate and develop tenderness that it does not harm love but serves it.

Yet we must stress again that tenderness is an important factor in love. The love between man and woman is based to a very great extent on sentiment (as the 'raw material' to be genuinely knit into love). This refers not so much to the first emotional transports (sometimes artificially heightened) over the value of the beloved person but is much more a matter of the steady participation of emotion, of a durable commitment of love—for it is this which brings a man and a woman close together, creates an interior climate of 'communicativeness'. Tenderness, when it has a base of this kind, is natural and authentic, and a great deal of this kind of tenderness is needed in marriage. Organically combined with genuine love of the person and 'disinterested', it has the power to deliver love from the various dangers implicit in the egoism of the senses and the hedonistic attitude. *Tenderness is the ability to feel with and for the whole person,* to feel even the most deeply hidden spiritual powers, and always to have in mind the true good of that person. This is the sort of tenderness which a woman expects from a man, and she has a special right to it in marriage, in which she gives herself to a man and goes through such extremely important periods in her live (pregnancy, childbirth, etc.). Moreover, her emotional life is richer than man's, and so her need for tenderness is greater. A man also has need of it, but to a different degree and in a different form. Both in the woman and in the man tenderness creates a feeling of not being alone, a feeling that her or his whole life is equally the content of another and very dear person's life. This conviction very greatly facilitates and reinforces their sense of unity. But there can be no genuine tenderness without a perfected habit of continence, which has its origin in a will always ready to show loving kindness and so overcome the temptation 'merely to enjoy' which is put in its way by sensuality and carnal concupiscence.

Without such continence, the natural energies of sensuality, and the energies of sentiment drawn into their orbit, will become merely the 'raw material' of sensual or at best emotional egoism. Life teaches us this lesson at every step. For believers, we see here something of the mystery of original sin, the consequences of which are particularly grave in the sphere of sex and are a threat to the person—the greatest good in the created universe. Continence plays an important role here in that it liberates us from that attitude and from egoism, and so indirectly creates love. Love between man and woman cannot be built without sacrifices and self-denial.

CHAPTER IV

JUSTICE TOWARDS THE CREATOR

MARRIAGE

Monogamy and the Indissolubility of Marriage—The whole course of the discussion in previous chapters logically and inevitably leads to recognition of the principle of monogamy and the indissolubility of the marriage tie. The personalistic norm is the foundation and the source of this principle. If the person can never be a mere object of enjoyment but can only be an object (or co-subject) of love, then the union of man and woman needs a suitable framework, permitting full development of the sexual relationship while ensuring durability of the union. This is marriage, compatible with the personalistic norm (requiring 'loving kindness' and treating a person in a manner appropriate to his or her essential nature) insofar as it implies monogamy and indissolubility. Thus, it is fundamentally opposed to all forms or polygamy and is opposed in principle to the dissolution of marriage ('divorce'). In effect, in these latter cases, a person is put in the position of an object for use by another person. Marriage is then only (or mainly) an institutional framework within which a man and a woman obtain sexual pleasure, not a durable union of persons based on the mutual affirmation of the value of the person. However, since marriage is strictly a feature of man's physical and terrestrial existence, it is naturally dissolved by the death of one of the spouses. The other person is then free to marry another person, though to remain a widow or widower is nonetheless praiseworthy since (among other things) it emphasizes more fully the reality of the continuing spiritual union with the person now deceased. But both outright polygamy and the dissolution of lawful marriages (divorce) which in practice leads to polygamy, are incompatible with the personalistic norm. There is sufficient evidence that they are in practice conducive to the treatment of women by men as objects of enjoyment and so at once degrade women and lower the level of morality among men. We need only remember the story of King Solomon.

However, if we adhere consistently to the personalistic norm, we must admit that where there are serious reasons why husband and wife cannot go on living together there is one possibility—separation, but without dissolution of the marriage itself. Separation is certainly an evil ('a necessary evil'), but it does not negate the personalistic norm: neither of the persons (and it is the woman who is more at risk) is put in the position of an object of use for the other. This would be the case if a person could abandon the person *to whom he or she had legally belonged in marriage* and marry again during the lifetime of this former spouse.

We must accept the fact that in their conjugal life a man and a woman *unite as persons* and that their union therefore lasts as long as they live. We cannot accept that their union lasts only as long as the persons themselves wish it to last, for that would be a contradiction of the personalistic norm, which is based on the concept of the person as a primary being. Thus, a man and a woman who have lived as husband and wife within the framework of a valid marriage are joined in a union which only the death of one of them can dissolve. The fact that one or even both of them may cease in course of time to want this does nothing to alter the situation: *their change of mind cannot alter the fact that they are objectively united as man and wife.* One or another may cease to feel any subjective justification for the union, but this cannot annul the fact that they are objectively united, and united in wedlock. The objective order of love is preserved in the principle of monogamy and indissolubility. Of course, we are concerned here with love in its full objective sense, love as a virtue—and not only in its subjective, psychological sense. Difficulty arises because 'love' is so often understood and practiced only in the second rather than the first sense. Monogamy and indissolubility make necessary the full *integration* of love in marriage. Without integration, marriage is an enormous risk. A man and a woman whose love has not begun to mature, has not established itself as a genuine union of persons, should not marry, for they are not ready to undergo the test to which married life will subject them. This does not, however, mean that their love must have reached full maturity at the moment of marriage, but only that it must be ripe enough for its continued ripening in and through marriage to be ensured. Concerning monogamy and indissolubility, what is at stake is the superiority of the value of the person to the value of sex as such, and the application of the norm in a context in which it can easily be ousted by the utilitarian principle. Strict monogamy is a function of the personal order.

The Value of the Institution—These considerations make it easier for us to understand the value of marriage as an institution. Marriage is both an inter-personal (having an intimate character between the two) and a social (having a relation to others) concern. The normal consequence of a sexual relationship between man and woman is progeny. A child is new member of society. The birth of a child turns the union of a man and a woman based on the sexual relationship into a family. The family is in itself a small society, and the existence of all large societies—nation, state, Church—depends on it. The family is an institution based on marriage, though marriage itself is not as a result absorbed by and lost in the family, but retains its own interpersonal structure as a union and community of two persons. The inner and essential *raison d'etre* of marriage is not simply eventual transformation into a family but above all the creation of a lasting personal union between a man and a woman based on love. Thus, a marriage which, through no fault of the spouses, is childless retains its full value as an institution. The social structure of the family is sound to the extent that it makes possible and maintains the interpersonal character of marriage. This is why a family originating in polygamy (though it may serve the end of procreation and be a large and strong society materially) will nonetheless necessarily have a lower moral value than a family originating in a monogamous marriage. In the latter, the value of the persons and the personal value of their love as a lasting union (which in itself has great educational value) are much more conspicuous.

The importance of the institution of marriage lies in the fact that it provides a justification for the sexual relationship between a particular couple within the whole complex of society. This is important not only because of the consequences of such a relationship—children and family as spoken of above—but also for the sake of the partners themselves. Without this acceptance by other people in the whole context of society, their love lacks something very important. They will begin to feel that it must ripen sufficiently to be revealed to society. On the one hand there is a need to keep private the sexual relations deriving from love, and on the other a need for social recognition of this love as a union of persons. Love demands this recognition, without which it does not feel fully itself. There is more than merely a conventional difference of meaning between such words as 'mistress', 'concubine', and 'kept woman' on the one hand and 'wife' or 'fiancée' on the other. These words all refer to woman, but whenever we use them we also say something about a man. This then is the meaning of marriage as an institution. In a society which accepts sound ethical principles and lives in accord with them (without hypocrisy or prudery), this institution is necessary to signify the maturity of the union between a man and a woman, to testify that theirs is a love on which a lasting union and community can be based. An actual sexual relationship between a man and a woman demands the institution of marriage as its natural setting, for the institution legitimates the actuality above all in the minds of the partners to the sexual relationship itself.

Sexual relations outside marriage automatically put one person in the position of an object to be used by another. Which is the user, which the used? It is not excluded that the man may also be an object to be enjoyed, but the woman is always in that position in relation to the man. A 'marital' sexual relationship outside the framework of marriage is always objectively a wrong done to the woman—even when she consents, desires, and seeks it. Thus, 'adultery' in the broadest sense of the word (either with another's spouse or with another who is not 'one's own') is always morally wrong. The boundary is illegally crossed not only by those who aspire to what expressly belongs to another, but just as surely by anyone who seeks what is not his own. It is the institution of marriage—*in which two people belong each to the other*— which decides in such cases the question of 'ownership'. Marriage as an institution is essential to justify the existence of 'conjugal' relations between a man and a woman—in their own eyes above all, but also in the eyes of society. The use of the word 'justification' clearly implies that the institution of marriage derives from the objective order of justice.

There is also a need to justify sexual relations between a man and a woman in the eyes of God the Creator, according to the objective order of justice, whether 'internally' in relation to the couple or 'externally' in relation to society. Admittedly, only a religious person can carry out such an analysis and accept its results. Thanks to his reasoning power man realizes that he is at once his own property (*sui juris*) and as a creature, the property of the Creator: he feels the effects of the Creator's proprietorial rights over himself. He also recognizes that every other person is also *sui juris,* and at the same time, as a creature, the property of the Creator. Hence the dual necessity to justify sexual relations between a man and a woman by means of the institution of marriage, for the effect of such a relationship is to make each person in some way the property of the other. If then there is a need to justify this fact *in the relationship between them*, there is also an objective need to justify it *in the eyes of the Creator,* for the religious man is above all one who is just to God the Creator. It is not enough for a woman and a man to give themselves to each other in marriage. If each of these persons is simultaneously the property of the Creator,

He also must give the man to the woman and the woman to the man, or at any rate approve the reciprocal gift of self implicit in the institution of marriage. Here we find the coming together of marriage as a 'sacrament' (or 'mystery') of nature and marriage as a 'sacrament' of grace.

Procreation and Parenthood—Marriage justifies sexual relations between a man and a woman not just as an isolated act but as a regular succession of acts, as a part of the 'married state'. However, every such act must have its own internal justification—for, unless justice is done, there can be no question of a union of persons. Sexual relations must be adapted to the demands of the personalistic norm and the persons must show responsibility for their love.

A man and a woman who, as husband and wife, unite in a full sexual relationship thereby enter into the realm of what can properly be called the order of nature, involving the fundamental good of existence and procreation. This is not merely a 'biological order' involving reproduction of a 'member of a species'. Indeed, the marital act is not even just a 'union of persons', but a union of persons *affected by the possibility of beginning of a new person's existence* (procreation). Thus, in the sexual relationship between a man and a woman two orders meet: *the order of nature* which has as its object reproduction or procreation, and *the personal order* which finds its expression in the love of persons and aims at the fullest realization of that love. We cannot separate the two orders, for each depends on the other. In particular, the correct attitude to procreation is a condition of the realization of love as a personal act. In the animal world, there is only instinctual reproduction—no persons and no personalistic norm of love. But in the world of persons, the sexual urge passes, so to speak, through the gates of consciousness and will, thus, furnishing not merely the conditions of fertility but also the raw material of love. At a truly human, truly personal level, the problems of procreation and of love cannot be resolved separately. Both procreation and love are based on the conscious choice of persons. When a man and a woman consciously and of their own free will choose to marry and have sexual relations they choose at the same time the possibility of procreation, *choose to participate in creation.* And only when they do so do they put their sexual relationship within marriage on a truly personal level. Here the problem of parenthood arises. Since a human being is a person, the simple natural fact of becoming a father or mother has a deeper significance—not merely a biological but a personal significance. Inevitably, 'parenthood' has profound effects on the 'interior' of a person. Since marital intercourse is and must be a manifestation of love *at the personal level*, we must find the proper place for parenthood too within the limits of love. Sexual relations between a man and a woman in marriage have their full value as a union of persons only when they go with conscious acceptance of the possibility of parenthood. This is a direct result of the synthesis of the natural and the personal order. Marital relations between two persons 'may' give life to a new person. Hence, when a man and a woman capable of procreation have intercourse their union must be accompanied by awareness and willing acceptance of the possibility that 'I might become a father' or 'I might become a mother'. Without this the marital relationship will not be 'internally' justified—quite the contrary. If the possibility of parenthood is deliberately excluded from marital relations, the character of the relationship changes—away from unification in love and in the direction of mere bilateral 'enjoyment' incompatible with the personalistic norm. Sexual (marital) relations have the character of a true union of persons as long as a general disposition towards parenthood is not excluded from them. This implies a conscious attitude to the sexual instinct: to master the sexual urge means just this, to accept its purpose in marital relations. Some people might say that this ruling subordinates man (who is a person) to 'nature', whereas in so many fields he triumphs over nature and dominates it. This however is a specious argument, for wherever man dominates 'nature' it is by adapting himself to its immanent dynamic. *Nature cannot be conquered by violating its laws.*

In the order of love a man can remain true to the person only insofar as he is true to nature. If he does violence to 'nature' he also 'violates' the person by making it an object of enjoyment rather than an object of love. Acceptance of the possibility of procreation in the marital relationship safeguards love and is an indispensable condition of a truly personal union. It is of course much easier to understand the 'power' of the natural order here (and its significance to both morality and to the development of the human personality) if we see behind it the personal authority of the Creator. Again, the 'order of nature' here is not to be confused with the mere 'biological order' and, thus, deprived of all significance. We are dealing with love between persons expressed in such a way (marital relations) that a new human person may come to be: the couple as co-creators with God. Erotic experiences (ever in danger of subjectivization and the 'claim' that they are the fullness of 'love') favor the true union of love *only insofar as* they do not negate the value of the person. But the value of the person is fully brought out only by fully conscious activity which is completely in harmony with the objective purposes of the world ('the order of nature'), and by excluding all possibility of exploitation or 'use' of the person.

Marital relations in fact become, and can be experienced as, 'shameful' if the possibility of parenthood ('I may become a father', 'I may become a mother') is artificially precluded by the persons involved. True, this feeling does not always show itself in the same way. It may seem at times that it is more easily awakened in women than in men. It must, however, be emphasized that this conjugal shame (which is at the base of conjugal chastity) meets with powerful resistance in the consciousness of men and women alike. This resistance originates in the fear of maternity and paternity. A man and a woman may 'be afraid of a child'; often a child is not only a joy but also—there is no denying it—a burden. But when fear of having a child goes too far it paralyzes love and deadens the feeling of shame. There is a solution to this problem, which conforms to the laws of which we know and is worthy of human persons: continence, which demands however control over erotic experiences. It also demands a profound culture of the person and love. This is not only part of Christian teaching, but also an elementary component of natural morality—as Gandhi's testimony bears witness.

However, conscious and willing acceptance of the possibility of parenthood is all that is called for here. We cannot demand of spouses that they must *positively desire* to procreate on every occasion when they have intercourse. Nature is not set up in this way (procreation is not an inevitable consequence of sexual relations) and we must not instrumentalize sexual intercourse as if only justified for procreation (this is a disguised utilitarianism in conflict with the personalist norm). Thus, 'planned maternity' making use of the fertile and infertile times while respecting nature is justified. It is certainly not necessary then that the couple always resolve 'we are performing this act in order to become parents'. It is sufficient to say that 'in performing this act we know that we may become parents and we are willing for that to happen'. This approach alone is compatible with love and makes it possible to share the experience of love. *A man and a woman become father and mother only in consequence of the marital act; but it must be an act of love, an act of unification of persons, and not merely the 'instrument' or 'means' of procreation.*

If, however, excessive emphasis on the intention to beget a child seems incompatible with the true character of conjugal relations, the express exclusion of procreation (or to be more exact *the possibility* of procreation) is even more so. The latter deprives marital intercourse of its true character (*as potentially an act of procreation*), which is what fully justifies the act, especially in the eyes of the persons taking part in it, since it enables them to see it as modest and chaste. When a man and a woman who have marital intercourse decisively preclude (i.e., by artificial means) the possibility of maternity and paternity, their intentions are thereby diverted from the person and directed to mere enjoyment: 'the person as the co-creator of love' disappears and there remains only the 'partner in an erotic experience'. Nothing could be more incompatible with the proper ends of the act of love. The true good and the specific value of the other person must be affirmed in intention and attention, in will and heart. The very fact of deliberately excluding the possibility of procreation from marital intercourse makes 'enjoyment' the intention of the act. However, if the couple adapt themselves to the fertility cycle, then procreation may be excluded in the natural way. Then they are merely adapting themselves to the laws of nature, to the order which reigns in nature. 'Artificial means' deprive conjugal relations of their 'naturalness', which cannot be said when procreation is avoided by adaptation to the fertility cycle. The latter is fundamentally 'in accordance with nature'. Since sexual intercourse implies the possibility of procreation, conjugal love demands that the possibility of paternity and maternity shall not be completely excluded when intercourse takes place. However, infertility in itself is not incompatible with the inner willingness to accept procreation, should it occur. It is only the *deliberate exclusion* of God's co-creative power with the couple which makes the situation unjust between the couple and before God.

The true greatness of the human person is manifested in the fact that sexual activity is felt to require such a profound justification. It cannot be otherwise. *Man must reconcile himself to his natural greatness.* It is especially when he enters so deeply into the natural order, immerses himself so to speak in its elemental processes, the *he must not forget that he is a person.* Responsibility for love, to which we are giving particular attention, is very closely bound up with responsibility for procreation. Love and parenthood must not therefore be separated one from the other. Willingness for parenthood is an indispensable condition for love.

Periodic Continence: Method and Interpretation—From all of the above, it follows that the man and the woman should refrain from intercourse when they are 'unwilling to' or 'must not' become father and mother. This requires the virtue of continence. But marital continence is so much more difficult than continence outside marriage because the spouses grow accustomed to intercourse, as befits the state they have both consciously chosen. This need is a normal manifestation of love, for in matrimony the man and the woman belong to each other in this special way. On the other hand, a couple who do not sometimes refrain from sexual intercourse may see their family grow excessively. Nevertheless, they cannot revert to a mere utilitarian mode, seeking the greatest pleasure and the least pain. This will lead to the conclusion that *some means must be found to spare them the need to refrain* from the intense pleasure of sexual relations even when they do not want offspring or 'cannot' become father and mother. But when the idea 'I may become a father' and 'I may become a mother' is totally rejected in the mind and will of husband and wife nothing is left of the marital relationship, objectively speaking, except mere sexual enjoyment. This is incompatible with the personalistic norm. Man is endowed with reason not primarily to 'calculate' the maximum of pleasure attainable in his life, but above all to seek knowledge of objective truth, as a basis for absolute principles (norms) to live by. This he must do if he is to live in a manner worthy of what he is, to live justly. In sexual matters in particular it is not enough to affirm that a particular mode of behavior is expedient. We must be able to say that it is 'just'. Now if we wish to take our stand firmly on the dictates of justice and the personalistic norm which goes with it, the only acceptable 'method' of regulating conception in marital relations is continence. Those who do not desire or are not open to the consequence (conception) must avoid the cause (intercourse). However, one may ask, if the purpose is the same (avoidance of conception), why should the natural method be morally superior to the artificial method? However, the equation of these two approaches as mere alternative 'utilitarian methods', seeing the natural method as just another means to ensure the maximum pleasure, is where the fundamental error resides. We must interpret 'method' correctly here. Periodic continence as a means of regulating conception is, then, (1) permissible because it does not conflict with the personalistic norm and (2) permissible only with certain qualifications.

It does not conflict with the demands of the personalistic norm because it is in agreement with the demands of the natural order. With periodic continence, lack of conception results from taking advantage of the circumstances of the natural operation of the laws of fertility, whereas with artificial contraception it is imposed in defiance of the laws of nature. This is closely bound up with the *justice to the Creator*, in its personalistic significance. Besides preserving the 'naturalness' of intercourse, the personalistic value of periodic continence is evident even more in the fact that in the wills of the persons concerned it must be grounded in a sufficiently mature virtue—very closely connected with love of the person.

Continence must, like all other virtues, be disinterested and wholly concerned with 'justice', not with 'expediency'. Otherwise, there will be no place for it in genuine love of persons. Continence, unless it is a virtue, is alien to love. *Thus, continence as a virtue cannot be regarded merely as a contraceptive measure.* The love between man and woman must ripen to the point where continence is possible and acquires constructive significance for them, becomes one of the factors which gives shape to their love. Only then is the 'natural method' congruent with the nature of the person. Its secret lies in the practice of virtue—technique alone is no solution here.

We have noted above (point 2) that the natural method is permissible only with certain reservations. We cannot speak of continence as a virtue where the spouses take advantage of the natural cycle exclusively for the purpose of avoiding parenthood altogether. This would be contrary to nature—both the objective order of nature and the essential character of love are hostile to such a policy. Thus, if it is to be regarded as a 'method' at all, it can only be a method of regulating conception and not of avoiding it, avoiding a family. The parents create the community of the family as a complement to and extension of their love—and to form a 'community' it must have a certain size (not necessarily just one or two children). Thus, parents themselves must be careful, when they limit conception, not to harm their families or society at large, which has an interest of its own in the optimum size of the family. A determination on the part of husband and wife to have as few children as possible, to make their own lives easy, is bound to inflict moral damage both on the family and on society at large. *Periodic continence as a method of regulating conception is permissible insofar as it does not conflict with a sincere disposition to procreate.* Acceptance of parenthood also expresses itself in not endeavoring to avoid pregnancy *at all costs,* in readiness to accept it if it should unexpectedly occur (even when they do not want it or deliberately choose to have intercourse at a period when it may be expected not to occur). This acceptance, in the context of any particular occasion of intercourse, together with the general disposition to parenthood in the broader context of marriage as a whole, determines the moral validity of periodic continence. There can be no question here of hypocrisy, of disguising one's true intentions—it cannot be said that the couple, in defiance of the Creator, are unwilling to become father and mother, since they themselves do nothing definitively to preclude this possibility (though of course they obviously could). Thus, they do not deprive marital intercourse of the value of love and leave it only the value of 'enjoyment'.

VOCATION

The Concept of 'Justice Towards the Creator'—'Horizontal justice' between spouses according to the personalistic norm has been our main theme. However, we must now investigate more thoroughly 'vertical justice': the justification of the whole sexual behavior of man in the eyes of God. When we speak of justice towards God we are saying the He too is a Personal Being, with whom man must have some sort of relationship. This involves a knowledge of the rights of God as Creator and the duties of man as creature. In the world of human beings the dictates of the natural order are realized not just by instinct and (in the animal world) with the help of sensory cognition, but by understanding and rational acceptance—*and this is at the same time recognition of the rights of the Creator.* Elementary justice on the part of man towards God is founded on it. Man is just towards God the Creator when he recognizes the order of nature and conforms to it in his actions. But it is not just a matter of respecting the objective order of nature. Man, by understanding the order of nature and conforming to it in his actions, participates in the thought of God, becomes *particeps Creatoris,* has a share in the law which God bestowed on the world when he created it at the beginning of time. The value of man as a reasonable being is nowhere more obvious that in the fact that he is called to strive in all his activities to achieve this specifically human value, by behaving as a *particeps Creatoris.* Man is not his own lawgiver (Kant)—this would require that he be his own first cause, instead of a creature. Rather, man's reason must assist him to read aright the laws of the Creator and, above all else, his conscience (his immediate guide in all his doings) must be in harmony with nature. Then man is just to his Creator. Justice towards the Creator then comprises two elements: obedience to the order of nature and emphasis on the value of the person. This attitude is a specific form of love and not merely love of the world, but also love of the Creator (at least implicitly). In any case, there can be no justice towards the Creator where a correct attitude to his creatures, in particular to other human beings, is lacking.

This brings us back to the personalistic norm. *Man can only be just to God the Creator if his loves his fellows.* This principle has a special relevance to the conjugal and sexual life of men and women. It is impossible for a man and a woman to behave justly towards God the Creator if their treatment of each other falls short of the personalistic norm. The conjugal relationship makes a man and a woman intermediaries in the transmission of life to a new human being. Because they are persons, they take part consciously in the work of creation *(procreatio)* and from this point of view are *particeps Creatoris.* It is therefore impossible to compare their marital life with the sexual life of animals, which is governed completely by instinct. Hence the question of justice towards the Creator arises, for marital relations are inseparable from responsibility for love. This makes necessary the institution of marriage and a morally correct single solution (periodic continence) to the problems of reproduction and parenthood within the framework of marriage. Man does not fully discharge his duties to the Creator simply be successfully reproducing his kind. A man and a woman who have marital relations fulfil their obligations to God the Creator only when they raise their relationship to the level of love, to the level of truly personal union. Only then are they *particepes Creatoris* in the true sense of those words. It further follows that marital intercourse itself must be informed by a willingness for parenthood. Love itself, and not merely reproduction, demands this.

Mystical and Physical Virginity—To be just means rendering to another person all that rightly belongs to that person. This being so, the rights of the Creator over the creature are very extensive: it is in its entirety the property of the Creator. Thus, if I want to be completely just to God the Creator, I must offer him all that is in me, my whole being, for he has first claim on all of it. Yet a creature can never really 'contract' with God as if an equal partner, nor ever 'cancel his debt'. Here we see that man's relations with God are not based on justice alone. *Self-giving has other roots—not justice, but love.* Justice is not at all concerned with the unification of persons, whereas love aims precisely at this. When the relationship of man to God is understood in this way the idea of virginity acquires its full significance. Applied to a man or a woman, 'virgin' means untouched, intact from the sexual point of view. Physical virginity is an external expression of the fact that the person belongs only to itself *(sui juris)* and to the Creator. When a person gives himself or herself to another person in marital intercourse, this gift must have the full value of betrothed love. Marriage rests on mutual betrothed love: without that the reciprocal physical surrender of man and woman would not be fully warranted by an interpersonal relationship.

Within man's relationship with God, understood as a relationship of love, man's posture can and must be one of surrender to God. We see then the possibility of betrothed and requited love between God and man: the human soul, which is betrothed of God, gives itself to Him alone. This is the essence of mystical virginity—*conjugal love pledged to God Himself.* Such spiritual virginity emphasizes still more than physical virginity that the person belongs to God: what was a natural condition becomes an object of will, of conscious choice and decision. Renunciation of marriage, however, is only a negative solution. Man has an inborn need of betrothed love, a need to give himself to another. The man who chooses virginity (whether as his 'primary choice' together with physical virginity or as a 'secondary choice'—secondary virginity—when no longer physically virgin) chooses God. This does not, however, mean that in choosing marriage he renounces God for a human being. But marriage and the betrothed love for a human being which goes with it, the dedication of oneself to another person, is not a final and completely satisfying solution to the need for betrothed love—the need to give oneself to and unite with another person. This need is deeper; it is connected with the spiritual existence of the person and can be satisfied perfectly only through union with God in eternity. Spiritual virginity, the self-giving of a human person wedded to God Himself, expressly anticipates this eternal union with God and points the way towards it. The value of virginity, and indeed its superiority to marriage, is to be found in the exceptionally important part which it plays in 'realizing' the kingdom of God on earth—in that particular people gradually prepare and perfect themselves for eternal union with God. In this union, the objective development of the human person reaches its highest point.

The Problem of Vocation—The concept of vocation is confined to the world of persons and the order of love—in the world of things it is meaningless. It implies choice and self-determination, being 'summoned' or 'called', and a personal commitment to a purpose such as only a rational being can make. This takes us into a very interesting and profound area of man's interior life. The deepest meaning of the word 'vocation' indicates that *there is a proper course for every person's development to follow,* a specific way in which he commits his whole life to the service of certain values.

But it is not enough merely to plot the course—active commitment of one's whole life to it is essential. That a particular person has a particular vocation always, then, means that his or her love is fixed on some particular goal. A person who has a vocation must not only love someone but be prepared to give himself or herself for love. We have already said in our analysis of love that this self-giving may have a very great creative effect on the person: the person fulfills itself most effectively when it gives itself most fully. The process of self-giving is an essential part of wedded or betrothed love. *Hence both virginity and marriage, understood in an uncompromisingly personalistic way, are vocations* and as such are only meaningful within a personalistic vision of human existence, in which conscious choice determines the direction which a person's life and actions will take. But here an inner need to determine the main direction of one's development by love encounters an objective call from God: *a call to self-perfection through love.* This is a summons addressed to everyone, and each must give it concrete meaning in application to himself by deciding what is the main direction of his life. He must consider his own personality, what he has to offer, and what others—other people and God—expect of him. Yet beyond that, every man must learn to integrate himself into the activity of God and respond to His love. A fully valid solution to the problem of vocation depends on this. Every man solves the problem of his vocation in practice above all by adopting a conscious personal attitude towards the supreme demand made on us by the commandment to love. This attitude is primarily a function of the person: the condition of the person (married, celibate, or ever virgin) is here of secondary importance.

Paternity and Maternity—Parenthood is something more than the external fact of bringing a child into the world and possessing it. More particularly it implies an internal attitude, which should characterize the love of a man and a woman living a conjugal life. Parenthood, considered on the personal and not merely the biological level, is so to say a new crystallization of the love between persons, the result of their perfect union. However, the physical implications of paternity have a smaller place in the life of a man, and especially the life of his organism, than those of maternity in the life and organism of the woman. For this reason, paternal feelings must be specially cultivated and trained, so that they may become as important in the inner life of the man as is maternity in that of the woman, for whom the biological facts alone suffice to make it important. A certain natural perfection of man's being finds expression in the fact of giving life and transmitting existence to a being in his own likeness—and this makes plain his intrinsic value, for *the good is diffusive of itself.* This makes the desire for a child perfectly comprehensible in a man as well as a woman. Both find in parenthood a confirmation of their physical and spiritual maturity, and the promise of a prolongation of their own existence—in the child who is 'flesh of their flesh', and above all a human person whose inner self they have both helped to form, in whom they have fashioned that which above all determines personhood. For the person is much more an 'interior' than a 'body'.

Thus, paternity and maternity in the world of persons are the mark of a certain spiritual perfection, the capacity for 'procreation' in the spiritual sense, the forming of souls—so that spiritual paternity and maternity have a much wider significance than physical parenthood. A father and mother who have given their children life in the merely biological sense must then supplement physical parenthood by spiritual parenthood, taking whatever pains are necessary for their education. *Spiritual paternity and maternity are characteristics indicative of mature parenthood in man and woman.*

Furthermore, 'spiritual paternity', since it is not limited to being a follow-up and completion of physical paternity, may have various manifestations—such as a priest's love of souls, a teacher's love for his pupils, etc. Spiritual kinship based on the union of souls is often stronger than the kinship created by the blood tie. Spiritual paternity and maternity involve a certain transmission of personality. 'Father' and 'mother' in the world of persons are, so to speak, embodied ideals, models for others, and specifically for those whose personality must take shape and evolve within their sphere of influence. Here the 'Father' is the supreme model, and human beings will come particularly close to God when the *spiritual parenthood of which God is the prototype* takes shape in them.

CHAPTER V

SEXOLOGY AND ETHICS

A SUPPLEMENTAL SURVEY

Introductory Remarks—Given that the love between man and woman is above all inter-personal, then the proper concerns of sexual morality are not 'the body and sex' but the personal relationships and the interpersonal love between man and woman inseparable from them. Questions of 'the body and sex' play a part in it in that they are subject to the principles which determine the order which should prevail in the world of persons. *This means too that sexual morality cannot be the same thing as sexology,* i.e. a view of man and woman and of love which approaches the whole problem solely or mainly from the point of view of 'the body and sex'. This is only part of the truth (e.g. in the 'clinical sexology' dimension of medicine), but if we do not recognize the primary importance of the person, if we do not make the necessary connection between love and the person, we deny ourselves the necessary basis for judgments in this difficult sphere of human morality. Fundamentally, the proper concern of medicine ('take care of your health, avoid sickness') is only marginally connected with sexual ethics, in which the personalistic standpoint is dominant. *What matters most is the man's duty to the woman, and the woman's duty to the man, by virtue of the fact that they are both persons—and not merely what is beneficial to their health.* The standpoint of clinical sexology gives, then, only a partial view—hence sexology must be subordinated to ethics, and specifically to the demands of the personalistic norm. A man and a woman come to love each other not because they are two sexually differentiated organisms, but because they are two persons. Looking at it from the biological point of view, sexual differentiation exists solely and simply for the purpose of reproduction. The idea that procreation must base itself on love is not derivable from a biological analysis of sex, but only from the metaphysical (i.e. ultra- and super-natural) fact of being a person. Sex as the attribute of a person has a role in the origin and development of love, but does not itself provide an adequate basis for love. Somatic events and physiological processes which belong to the vegetative system affect man's experience of the value 'body and sex' only externally. If this experience can have the sort of importance to love which we indicated in earlier parts of the book (becoming part of the 'raw material' of love between man and woman) this is because sex is an attribute of the human person as a whole.

The Sexual Urge—The existence of somatic differences and the activity of the sexual hormones both release and direct the sexual urge, which however cannot be completely reduced to a combination of anatomical and somatic or physiological factors. The sexual urge is a special force of nature for which those factors are only a basis. The sexual urge is first fully awakened only at puberty (around age 12 or 13 in girls, somewhat later in boys). Physiologically this is identified in girls with the beginning of menstruation and in boys with the ability to produce sperm. Before the age of puberty the sexual instinct exists in a child in the form of a vague and indeed unconscious interest which only gradually becomes conscious. Puberty brings a rapid, indeed one might say explosive, intensification of the urge. Then in the period of physical and psychological maturity the urge becomes stable, passes through a time of heightened activity to middle age (menopause), and gradually declines with age.

The fact that we find different 'thresholds of sexual arousal' in different people means that they react differently to stimuli which cause sexual arousal. The root causes for this are to be found partly in man's somatic and physiological make-up. On this level, sexual arousal occurs as a result of a nervous reflex. It is a state of tension caused by stimulation of the nerve ends of the sensory organs, either directly or else psychologically through associations of the imagination. Sexual stimuli may act upon any of the senses, more particularly touch or sight but also hearing, taste, or even smell, and they produce a peculiar state of tension (tumescence) not only in the genital organs but in the organism as a whole. On the physiological and somatic side, we must take note of the fact that there are places in the human body which conduct sexual stimuli with especial ease—the so-called erogenous zones, which are considerably more numerous in women than in men. The degree of excitement depends immediately on the quality of the stimulus and on the receiving organ. A state of sexual excitement precedes intercourse but may occur independently of it.

Sexology introduces us, in a much more detailed fashion than has been done here, to the complex of somatic and physiological factors conditioning the sensual reactions in which the sexual urge manifests itself in human beings. It is, however, worth remembering that all these things which in themselves must be recognized as manifestations of the sexual urge can be converted in the interior of a person into the real ingredients of love.

Marriage and Marital Intercourse—Can ethics be inimical to health? Can there be any real conflict between the physical health of persons on the one hand and concern for their moral good (i.e. with the objective demands of sexual ethics) on the other? We frequently encounter the view that there is such a conflict. Only a profound conviction of the non-utilitarian value of the person (of the woman for the man, of the man for the woman) enables us to justify fully—fundamentally and irrefutably—the ethical standpoint of personalism as the proper foundation for monogamous and indissoluble marriage (Thus, prohibiting adultery and pre-marital relations). Can sexology give it any support, and so provide additional justification for such personalism?

Though sexual arousal may occur spontaneously, without an express act of the will, sexual intercourse—the sexual act between a man and a woman—is unthinkable without an act of the will, especially on the part of the man. Though she may be comparatively passive, he is always active (and actively aroused) in sexual relations. This raises a problem of great importance. We have defined love as an ambition to ensure the true good of another person, and consequently as the antithesis of egoism. This must also be true in the sexual area. From the point of view of another person, from the altruistic standpoint, it is necessary to insist that intercourse must not serve merely as a means of allowing sexual excitement to reach its climax in one of the partners, i.e. the man alone, but that climax must be reached in harmony—not at the expense of one partner, but with both partners fully involved. Love demands not use or exploitation of the other in sexual relations but that the reactions of the other person, the sexual 'partner', be fully taken into account. Sexologists state that the curve of arousal in woman is different from that in man—it rises more slowly and falls more slowly. The man must take this difference between male and female reactions into account, not for hedonistic but for altruistic reasons—that is, out of love. Both spouses must discover the proper natural rhythm here so that climax may be reached together. The subjective happiness which they then share (flowing from a loving concern for the other) has the clear characteristic which we have called 'frui', of the joy which flows from harmony between one's own actions (and choices) and the objective order of nature. Egoism in this sphere, on the other hand, is inseparable from the 'uti' in which one party seeks only his own pleasure at the expense of the other. Evidently, the elementary teachings of sexology cannot be applied without reference to ethics. Non-observance of these teachings of sexology in the marital relationship is contrary to the good of the other partner and to the durability and cohesion of the marriage itself.

It must be taken into account that with their *difference in natural rhythms of arousal* there is a need for harmonization, which is impossible without *good will*, especially on the part of the man, who must carefully observe the reactions of the woman. If a woman does not obtain natural gratification from the sexual act, there is a danger that her experience of it will be qualitatively inferior, and, thus, *will not involve her fully as a person.* This may provoke nervous reactions and frigidity in the woman. Though this may be due to an inhibition or difficulty in the woman, it is usually the result of egoism in the man seeking his own satisfaction. In the woman, this produces an aversion to intercourse for both psychological (the feeling of being used) and physical (the lack of satisfaction in sexual arousal) reasons. Psychologically, such a situation causes not just indifference but outright hostility. It can lead to such a deep resentment over time that it leads to the collapse of the marriage. It can be prevented by sexual education— not just physiologically but morally, in light of the virtue of love. For it must be emphasized yet again that physical disgust does not exist in marriage as a primary phenomenon but is as a rule a secondary reaction: in women it is the response to egoism and brutality, in men to frigidity and indifference. There is a real need here for sexual education, and it must be a continual process. The main objective of this education is to create the conviction 'the other person is more important than I'. Such conviction will not arise suddenly and from nothing, merely on the basis of physical intercourse. It can only be, must be, the result of an integral education in love. Sexual intercourse itself does not teach love, but love, if it is a genuine virtue, will show itself to be so in sexual relations between married people as elsewhere.

This is where the 'culture of marital relations'—a 'culture of love'—comes in and what it means. Technique alone is not enough; indeed, it is secondary and sometimes even inimical to the purpose which it is supposes to serve. The urge is so strong that it creates in the normal man and the normal woman a sort of instinctive knowledge 'how to make love' whereas artificial analysis and emphasis on technique is more likely to spoil the whole thing, for what is wanted here is a certain spontaneity and naturalness (subordinated of course to morality). This instinctive knowledge must subsequently mature into a 'culture of marital relations'. This involves a deep tenderness, and especially the 'disinterested tenderness' described earlier—such an ability to enter readily into another person's emotions and experiences can play a big part in harmonization of marital intercourse. It has its origin in 'sentiment' (directed primarily towards the 'human being') and so can temper and tone down the violent reactions of sensuality (oriented toward the 'body' and satisfaction). If we take into account the difference in arousal patterns for male and female, we can see the need for tenderness on the part of the man (i.e. sensitive understanding and feeling with the woman, together with self-control on his own part) before, during and after the sexual act in order to maintain its character as a personal act, an act of self-donation. Such tenderness acquires the significance of an act of virtue—specifically the virtue of continence and so indirectly the virtue of love.

What is needed, however, is not shallow sentimentality, nor superficial love. Rather, the genuine *virtue of love* should help one *to understand* and *to feel for* a human being, to learn and be educated about the other. Husband and wife must educate one another. The man must reckon with the fact that the woman is in a sense in another world, unlike himself both physiologically and psychologically. Since he has to play the active role in the marital relationship, he must get to know that other world and indeed as far as possible project himself into it emotionally—this indeed is the positive function of tenderness. Of course, the woman too must try to understand the man, and simultaneously to educate him to understand her. Only then will they relate to one another in love, also in the sexual sphere, rather than in an attitude of 'use' (whether conscious or inadvertent). Neglect of such mutual education and the failure to understand may both be the result of egoism. Sexology itself provides support for this formulation of the principles of morality, and of education for marriage.

Does sexology offer support for the principle of monogamy and indissolubility of marriage? Not directly perhaps, but this might be asking too much of 'sexology'. Nonetheless, indirectly, sexology itself consistently favors natural sexual and marital morality, because it attaches so much importance to the psychological and physical health of man and woman, understood in the most fundamental sense. Thus, harmonious sexual intercourse is possible only where it involves no conflict of conscience, and is not troubled by fears. Conflict of conscience and fear of having a child (even if complete sexual satisfaction is obtained in an extramarital relationship) can play havoc not only with the psyche but with the physical health (the natural biological rhythm) of a woman. Sexology here does not have to directly furnish arguments from which we can deduce these rules—it is enough if it incidentally confirms rules already known from elsewhere and established by other means. A harmonious marriage can deal with these difficulties—and such harmony cannot be the result of 'technique' but only of 'marital culture', or in the last analysis of the virtue of love.

In its very nature, such a marriage is the result not just of sexual 'selection', but of an ethically valid choice. It appears that 'purely' biological attraction does not exist, though on the other hand persons who unite in marriage are certainly interested in each other sexually as well as in other ways—people who from the start feel physical disgust for each other do not enter into marriage. The fact is that sensual and sentimental factors have a powerful effect at the moment of choice, but that rational analysis must nevertheless have the decisive significance.

It must also be stated that the much-recommended 'trial' periods of cohabitation before marriage give no guidance in selecting a spouse, for the specific features in cohabitation *in marriage* are one thing, and those of *pre-marital* cohabitation another. Using the latter to check out 'sexual compatibility' is unreliable as a prediction for the future. Couples who subsequently consider themselves ill-matched very often have a perfect sexual relationship in the initial stage. The collapse of their marriage evidently has some other cause. This view of the matter is in close accord with the ethical principle which rules out pre-marital relations—it does not, to be sure, directly confirm it, but at all events it points toward the rejection of the opposite principle. At no point do the conclusions reached by clinical sexology conflict with the main principles of sexual ethics: monogamy, marital fidelity, the mature choice of the person, etc. Finally, the principle of marital modesty is also confirmed by sexology and psychology, concerning neuroses which may arise over the fear of being taken by surprise during sexual intercourse. Hence the need for a suitable place, one's own home or apartment, in which married life can take its course 'in safety', i.e. in accordance with the demands of modesty and where both man and woman feel that they 'have the right' to live in total intimacy.

The Problem of Birth Control—Any discussion of sexual intercourse from the sexological point of view necessarily confronts us with the problem of birth control. In this context, 'planned motherhood' can be taken to mean the following: 'know how, in the marital relationship, a woman becomes a mother and act so as to become a mother only when that is what you want'. Though this statement sounds as though it is addressed to the woman, it really concerns the man as her 'partner' in the sexual relationship even more. A man and a woman have a responsibility for every conception, not only to themselves but also to the family which they are founding or increasing by conception. But, unfortunately, a programme of 'planned parenthood' may easily ground itself on utilitarian assumptions in conflict with the value of the person. The only way to avoid this conflict in accord with the character of the person, and so the only honorable way, is through the virtue of continence, the pattern of which is more or less indicated by nature itself.

Let us begin, however, by examining the positive side to the question. Sexology speaks of the 'maternal instinct' and the 'paternal instinct'. Whereas the first usually awakens in a woman before the birth of the child, and frequently even before its conception, paternal feelings usually develop more slowly. But it can be seen that the desire to have a child is naturally awakened by marriage and marital intercourse, while resistance to this desire in the mind and the will is unnatural.

However, fear of conception, fear of having a child, is a factor of great importance to the problem of planned motherhood. It is by way of being a paradoxical factor. We know that fatigue, change of climate, stress, and especially fear, can delay or precipitate menstruation. Fear then is a powerful negative stimulus that can destroy the natural regularity of the female cycle. But such fear of conception then makes it that much more difficult to follow the natural rhythm of the cycle. Clinical experience also confirms the thesis that fear of pregnancy also deprives a woman of that 'joy in the spontaneous experience of love' which acting in accordance with nature brings.

All this implicitly shows the decisive importance in this matter of the moral stance analyzed earlier. This can be reduced to two elements: readiness during intercourse to accept parenthood ('I may become a father', 'I may become a mother'), and that readiness to practice continence which derives from virtue, from love for the closest of persons. This context provides the best psychological foundation for the woman to be able to maintain the biological equilibrium without which the natural regulation of conception is unthinkable and unrealizable. On the other hand, egoism is the negation of love; it shows itself in attitudes opposite to those described and is the most dangerous source of that overriding fear which paralyzes the healthy processes of nature. It must be clearly stated that one basic method underlies all natural methods of regulating fertility: the 'method' of virtue (love and continence). Only when this method is accepted in principle and applied in practice will our knowledge of sexual and reproductive processes be effective. For if a human being realizes that fertilization is not a matter of 'chance', of a fortuitous combination of circumstances, but a biological event carefully prepared by nature, and that the preparatory stages can be fully monitored, the possibility of regulating conception rationally and in a natural way will become so much the greater.

Methods of birth control are of two general types, artificial and natural. Artificial methods include biological, chemical, and mechanical means; but such artificial contraceptives are of their very nature harmful to health each in their own way. Perhaps the most frequent method (*circa* 1959) used by married couples is *coitus interruptus* (male withdrawal before ejaculation) which they resort to thoughtlessly, without realizing at the time that it must inevitably have undesirable consequences. Ignoring for the moment the fallibility of this method of preventing fertilization, let us ask ourselves why people resort to it. It may be due to the egoism of the male, or on another level, it may be that he supposes that he is doing so to 'protect' the woman (her basic biological capacity, her fertility, is unaffected). For this reason, women themselves are often convinced that 'it doesn't do any harm'. In this situation, both of them may attain a certain good. But they do so by following an incorrect course. For if a couple have reached the legitimate conclusion that conception must be postponed, instead of interrupting the act once begun the man should refrain from it for the time being, and wait for the period of biological infertility in his wife. But this brings us back to the subject of periodic continence.

The only natural method of regulating conception is that which relies upon periodic continence. It demands precise knowledge of the organism of the woman concerned and of her biological rhythm—and also the peace of mind and the biological equilibrium of which a great deal has already been said. But above all it demands a certain self-denial and self-restraint on the part of both man and woman. A more important task for the man than adapting himself to the biological cycle of the woman is the creation of a favorable psychological climate for their relationship without which the successful application of natural methods is out of the question. Besides continence and the proper moral attitude of the male, the marital relationship demands on his part tenderness, an understanding for the feelings of the woman.

The rhythm adopted is nature's rhythm, so that marital intercourse in accordance with it is also hygienic, healthy, and free from all those neuroses which are caused by artificial methods of preventing pregnancy mentioned above. If a man and a woman use these methods with full understanding of the facts and recognizing the objective purpose of marriage, natural methods leave them with a sense of choice and spontaneity ('naturalness') in their experience, and—most important of all—the possibility of deliberate regulation of procreation. This essentially involves a moral effort and the full virtue of continence in the service of chastity and of love.

There are no grounds for discussing abortion in conjunction with birth control. To do so would be quite improper. Leaving aside its moral aspect (such termination of pregnancy is a very grave offense), it is a highly traumatic interruption of the natural biological rhythm with far-reaching possible consequences— including serious physical effects, enormous feelings of resentment, a grudge against the man who has brought her to it, anxiety neurosis with guilt feelings at its core, possible profound psychotic reaction, and delayed depression and regret.

Sexual Psychopathology and Ethics—There is a widely held view that to go without sexual intercourse is harmful to the life of human beings (and of men in particular), though no one has given the description of any morbid symptoms which might confirm this thesis. Our previous discussion showed that sexual neuroses are mainly the consequences of abuses in sexual life and that they result from failure to adapt to nature and to its processes. So that it is not continence, as such, that produces real diseases, but the lack of it. The lack of a sex life may also be the result of misguided repression of the sexual urge and its manifestations, which is wrongly identified with continence but which in fact has little in common with the real virtue of continence and chastity. The sexual urge in man is a fact which he must recognize and welcome as a source of natural energy—otherwise it may cause psychological disturbances. The instinctive reaction in itself, which is called sexual arousal, is to a large extent a vegetative reaction independent of the will, and failure to understand this simple fact often becomes a cause of serious sexual neuroses. The person involved in such a conflict is torn by two contrary tendencies which he cannot reconcile—hence the neurotic reactions. The indispensable requirement of correct behavior and health is training from childhood upwards in truth and in reverence for sex, which must be seen as intimately connected with the highest values of human life and human love. A sexual urge prematurely awakened, at the wrong time of life, can become the source of neurotic disturbances if it is repressed in the wrong way. Lack of information, and especially lack of training in the correct attitudes, may cause a variety of aberrations (such as infantile and adolescent masturbation).

Therapy—I should like to suggest some ways of preventing such reactions with a few basic points: **(a)** It is often necessary to relieve people of the widespread conviction that the sexual drive is something naturally bad which must be resisted in the name of the good. It is necessary to inculcate a conviction that sexual reactions are on the contrary perfectly natural and proper to man and have no intrinsic moral value or disvalue—morally good or bad uses may be made of them. **(b)** If a man is to acquire the conviction that he is capable of controlling his reactions, he must first be set free from the opinion that sexual reactions are determined by necessity and entirely independent of the will. He must be persuaded that his body can be made to 'obey' him if he trains it to do so. **(c)** People, and particularly young people, must be set free from the belief that sexual matters are an area of incomprehensible, well-nigh calamitous phenomena, in which they find themselves mysteriously implicated and which threaten their equilibrium; instead. we must reduce sex to a set of phenomena which though of great moment and great beauty are totally comprehensible and, so to speak, 'ordinary'. This demands the timely provision of correct biological information. **(d)** The most important thing is to transmit the right hierarchy of values, and to show the position occupied by the sexual urge in that hierarchy. Its use will then be subordinated to the end which it exists to serve. People must be further persuaded of the possibility and necessity of conscious choice. We must, as it were, 'give back' to people their consciousness of the freedom of the will and of the fact that the area of sexual experience is completely subject to the will. **(e)** There are obviously illnesses in which the help of a specialist—sexologist or psychiatrist—is necessary, but the advice given by such specialists must take into account the totality of human aims, and above all the integral, personalistic concept of man. For there are times when the doctor's advice is just what turns the patient into a neurotic, in that it blatantly contradicts the real nature of man. In general, however, the psychotherapy of sexual neuroses is distinct from sex education in that it deals not with people whose sexual inclinations are normal and healthy but with those afflicted by some sexual deviation or illness. Such persons are less capable of 'love and responsibility' and psychotherapy aims at restoring the capacity to them. It aims above all at delivering the patients from the oppressive notion that the sex urge is overwhelmingly strong and inculcating in them the realization that every man is capable of self-determination with regard to the sexual urge and the impulses born of it. Thus, with a proper vision of man, it must try as it were to recapture man's 'interior' and only through its agency to obtain control of his 'outward' behavior. In the formation of that 'inner self' a fundamental part is played by the truth about the sex instinct. But all such approaches must start not just from the 'natural' plane of the sex instinct, but must proceed from the plane of the person, with which the whole subject of 'love and responsibility' is bound up. Knowledge of biological and physiological processes is very important, but it cannot achieve its goal unless it is honestly grounded in an objective view of the person and the natural (and supernatural) vocation of the person, which is love.

—adapted from **Love and Responsibility** by Karol Wojtyla

ORIGINAL UNITY OF MAN AND WOMAN

CATECHESIS ON THE BOOK OF GENESIS

"God created man in his own image, in the image of God he created him; male and female he created them."—Gen. 1:27

"Therefore, a man leaves his father and his mother and cleaves to his wife, and they become one flesh."—Gen. 2:24

"And the Pharisees came up to him and tested him by asking, 'Is it lawful to divorce one's wife for any cause? He answered, 'Have you not read that he who made them from the beginning made them male and female, and said, 'For this reason a man shall leave his father and mother and be joined with his wife, and the two shall become one flesh'? So they are no longer two but one flesh. What therefore God has joined together, let no man put asunder.' They said to him, 'Why then did Moses command one to give a certificate of divorce, and to put her away?' He said to them, 'For the hardness of your heart Moses allowed you to divorce your wives, *but from the beginning it was not so.*'"—Mt. 19:3

Unity and Indissolubility of Marriage—Consideration of the role of the Christian family concentrates our attention on this community of human and Christian life, which has been fundamental *from the beginning*, as Christ stresses in his answer to the question about the indissolubility of marriage. "The beginning" of course refers to the book of Genesis and its account of the creation of man (male and female) in the image of God and for one another: "Therefore, a man leaves his father and mother and cleaves to his wife, and they become one flesh." Christ explicitly means this latter phrase to be *normative* and not merely *descriptive.* This is clear when he adds: "So they are no longer two but one flesh. What therefore God has joined together, let no man put asunder." This sets forth the principle of the unity and indissolubility of marriage as the very content of the word of God, expressed in the most ancient revelation. Moreover, that significant expression: "from the beginning," repeated twice in Christ's response to the questions of the Pharisees, clearly induces his interlocutors to reflect on the way in which man was formed in the mystery of creation, precisely as "male and female." We must investigate the meaning of these words "from the beginning" in light of Christ's interlocutors of today.

Biblical Account of Creation Analyzed—The first (though chronologically later) account of man's creation given in Genesis 1: 1-2 (the Elohist tradition) insert's man's (collective noun: "humanity's") creation as male (masculine) and female (feminine) in the midst of the seven-day account of creation, thus, attributing a special cosmological character to the event: man is created on earth together with the visible world and placed over it by special creative action and word of God. Man alone is described a being *in the image and likeness of God*—affirming the absolute impossibility of reducing man to the "world." Thus, man cannot be either understood or explained completely in terms of categories taken from the "world," that is, from the visible complex of bodies. Nonetheless, an essential truth about man is that he is also corporeal: this is clearly implied in the words *male and female he created them.*

This first account of man's creation presents only the objective facts and presents the reality of creation on a metaphysical plane (man's *existence* is from God and in the image of God) more than just on a physical plane. To this mystery of his creation corresponds the perspective of procreation ("Be fruitful and multiply, fill the earth"). Furthermore, the unassailable point of reference here is that of goodness, of value: "God saw everything that he had made, and behold, it was very good." This again provides a solid basis for metaphysics, anthropology, and ethics (being and good are convertible). This has a special significance for understanding the body as good, for the theology of the body.

The Second Account of Creation: The Subjective Definition of Man—The second (though much more ancient) account of man's creation is given in Genesis 2: 5-25 (the "Yahwist tradition, including Genesis 3 and the first phase of Genesis 4, treating of the conception and birth of man from earthly parents). It is linked to the presentation both of original innocence and happiness and of the first fall; it has by its nature a different character. It has a special profundity in formulating the truth about man in a particularly subjective or psychological way, giving a record of man's self-knowledge and the first testimony of human conscience. Comparing the first (objective) account and the second (subjective) account, we arrive at the conclusion that this subjectivity corresponds to the objective reality of man created "in the image and likeness of God." This fact will also be important for our theology of the body.

When Christ refers to the "beginning," he speaks first of the objective (Elohist) account and then of the subjective (Yahwist) account. Christ words here, referring to the creation and original innocence of man (male and female) also lead us up to the account of the fall, or of original sin. At the beginning of chapter 3 we hear of the fall, linked with the mysterious "tree of the knowledge of good and evil." This tree marks the line of demarcation between the two original situations spoken of in Genesis: original innocence and human sinfulness. This implies two different states of human nature: a state of integral nature and a state of fallen nature. This is also significant for the theology of man and of the body. However, when Christ replies to the Pharisees about divorce, he orders them in a certain sense to go beyond the boundary which runs between the first (innocence) and the second (sinfulness) situation of man. He does not approve what Moses had permitted "for their hardness of heart," and he appeals to the words of the first divine regulation, expressly linked to man's state of original innocence ("no longer two, but one flesh; what God has joined together let no man put asunder"). This means that this regulation has not lost its force, even though man has lost his primitive innocence. Christ's reply is decisive and unequivocal and we must draw normative conclusions from it.

Boundary Between Original Innocence and Redemption—These situations (of original innocence and original sin) have a specific dimension in man, in his inner self, in his knowledge, conscience, choice and decision, and all that in relation to God who is both the Creator and the God of the Covenant—the most ancient covenant of the Creator with his creature, that is, with man. This covenant has been broken in man's heart: this is what delimits the two states of original innocence and original sin, and at the same time of man's hereditary sinfulness which is derived from it. However, *Christ's words,* which refer to the "beginning," *enable us to find in man an essential continuity and a link* between these two different states or dimensions of the human being. The "historical" state of sin plunges its roots—in every man without any exception—in his own theological "prehistory," which is the state of original innocence. That is, the arising of sinfulness as a state is (right from the beginning) *in relation to* this real innocence of man as his original and fundamental state, as a dimension of the being created "in the image of God." It can be said that there is a "co-inheritance" of sin (original sin), but if this sin signifies (in every historical man) a state of lost grace, then it also contains a reference to that grace, which was precisely the grace of original innocence.

Christ however does not merely speak of the state of original innocence as the lost horizon of human existence in history, but rather of the mystery of redemption—already prefigured in the first promise of redemption in the Protogospel of Genesis 3:15. Man, both then and now, participates not only in the history of human sinfulness but also in the history of salvation—as its subject and co-creator. Paul expresses this perspective of redemption when he writes: "...we ourselves, who have the first fruits of the Spirit, groan inwardly as we wait for ... the redemption of our bodies." We cannot lose sight of this perspective as we follow the words of Christ who, in His talk on the indissolubility of marriage, appeals to the "beginning." This "beginning" refers not only to the *original creation* and to *original sin* as a dividing line between the states of innocence and sin, but at the same time opens up the *perspective of redemption*—and indeed "redemption of the body." This perspective guarantees continuity and unity between the hereditary state of man's sin and his original innocence: the perspective of the redemption on which the covenant rests.

In light of these introductory considerations, concerning the "historical" and the theological situations, we must arrive at the conviction that our human experience is, in this case, to some extent a legitimate means for the theological interpretation, and is, in a certain sense, an indispensable point of reference which we must keep in mind in the interpretation of the "beginning." Our understanding of the "beginning" must speak to us with the great richness of light that comes from revelation. It will also be deeply in agreement with our experience if we put ourselves in the position of recognizing that we "groan inwardly as we wait for … the redemption of our bodies."

Meaning of Man's Original Solitude—The starting point for this reflection is the words of God-Yahweh: "It is not good that man (male) should be alone: I will make him a helper fit for him." This original solitude has two meanings: one derived from man's very nature (that is, from his humanity—whether male or female) and the other derived from the male-female relationship (and which is evident, in a certain way, on the basis of the first meaning). The problem of solitude is *manifested* only in the second account of the creation of man. The first account ignores this problem—man is created there in one act as "male and female." The second account, however, which speaks first of the creation of man and only afterwards of the creation of woman from the "rib" of the male, concentrates our attention on the fact that "man is alone." This appears as a fundamental anthropological problem prior (in an existential sense) to the one raised by the fact that this man is male and female—and similarly for the problem of man's solitude from the point of view of the theology of the body. In creating man, giving him the vocation to subdue the earth, putting him in the garden, and establishing the conditions of the first covenant, man's subjectivity—and superiority to the rest of creation—is already emphasized in the Yahwist account. In this way, the first meaning of man's original solitude is defined on the basis of a specific test which man undergoes before God (and before himself): man names every living creature, "but for the man (male) there was not found a helper fit for him" (Gen. 2:20). By means of this test man becomes aware of his own superiority, that is, he cannot be considered on the same footing as any other species of living beings on the earth.

All this is a preparation for the account of the creation of woman, but it has a deep meaning even apart from this creation. Created man finds himself, from the first moment of his existence, before God in search of his own entity, his own definition of himself, his own identity. The fact that he *is not* (negative definition) able to identify himself with the visible world of other living things—he "is alone" in the midst of it—has, at the same time, a positive aspect for this primary search—i.e., though his "definition" is not complete, he discovers something about himself. A further element is present here as well: evidently the original and fundamental manifestation of mankind is through self-definition, through his own self-knowledge. This develops at the same rate as his knowledge of the world, as he discovers his own dissimilarity and superiority to it and the living creatures in it. Consciousness reveals man as the one who possesses the cognitive faculty as regards the visible world: he is revealed to himself as a human person (different from and superior to all other creatures) with the specific subjectivity that characterizes him. He is not only essentially and subjectively alone. Solitude, in fact, also signifies man's subjectivity, which is constituted through self-knowledge. Man is alone because he is "different" from the visible world, from the world of living beings.

Man's Awareness of Being a Person—When God gives the first man the order concerning all the trees that grow in the garden, particularly the tree of the knowledge of good and evil, there is added to the features of man, described above, the moment of choice and self-determination, that is, free will. This completes the first outline of the image of man as a person endowed with a subjectivity of his own: his original solitude includes both self-consciousness and self-determination, as well as true comprehension. This allows us to understand correctly the whole situation of man (created "in the image of God") in the original covenant with God. It also allows us to understand correctly the words constituting the prelude to the creation of woman: "I will make him a helper."

Man as *an image of God* is manifested as *subject of the covenant* and therefore as a "partner of the Absolute" since he must consciously discern and choose between good and evil, life and death. God's first order to man (concerning the trees in the garden) shows directly the submission and dependence of man the creature on his Creator, but at the same time indirectly reveals man as subject of the covenant and partner of the Absolute. To say that man is "alone," then, means that he—through his own humanity, through what he is—is constituted at the same time in a unique, exclusive and unrepeatable relationship with God Himself.

Man, thus, formed, belongs to the visible world: he is a body among bodies—but it is this which makes him at the same time *conscious of being alone.* As he names the animals, he does not conclude that he is simply another one like them, but on the contrary reaches the conviction that he is "alone." This analysis enables us to *link man's original solitude with consciousness of the body,* through which man is distinguished from all the *animalia* and "is separated" from them, and also *through which* he is a *person.* Thus, it can also be affirmed with certainty that man, thus, formed, has at the same time consciousness and awareness of the meaning of his own body.

Man can dominate the earth because he alone—and no other of the living beings—is capable of "tilling it" and transforming it to his own needs (Elohist account). And this first outline of a specifically human activity seems to belong to the definition of man as it emerges from the Yahwist account. Consequently, it can be affirmed that this outline is intrinsic to the meaning of the original solitude and belongs to that dimension of solitude through which man, from the beginning, is in the visible world as a body among bodies and discovers the meaning of his own corporality.

In the Very Definition of Man the Alternative Between Death and Immortality—Consciousness of the body seems to be identified in this case with the discovery of the complexity of one's own structure, i.e. for philosophical anthropology, the relationship between soul ("breathed into his nostrils the breath of life") and body ("formed man of dust from the ground"). And precisely this man ("a living being") distinguishes himself continually from all other living beings in the visible world on the basis of typically human praxis or behavior ("tilling" and "subduing" the earth) revealing man's superiority. But all this awareness would be impossible without a typically human intuition of the meaning of one's own body. Thus, we must speak first of this aspect, as it is revealed in the concrete subjectivity of man. Man is a subject not only because of his self-awareness and self-definition, but also on the basis of his own body. The structure of this body is such as to permit him to be the author of a truly human activity. In this activity, the body expresses the person. It is, therefore, in all its materiality, almost penetrable and transparent, in such a way as to make it clear *who man is (and who he should be)* thanks to the structure of his consciousness and of his self-determination.

And here, with this fundamental understanding of the meaning of his own body, man is placed before the mystery of "the tree of knowledge of good and evil" which "you shall not eat, for in the day that you eat of it you shall die." Man heard for the first time the words "you shall die" without having any familiarity with them in his experience up to then. But on the other hand, he could not but associate the meaning of death with that dimension of life (existence received from the Creator and characterized precisely by subjectivity including also the meaning of the body) which he had enjoyed up to then. The words of God addressed to man confirmed a *dependence in existing,* such as to make man a limited being and, by his very nature, liable to non-existence. And, *it depended on man,* on his decision and free choice of good and evil, if—with solitude—he was to enter also the *circle of the antithesis revealed to him* by the Creator, and thereby make his own the experience of dying and death.

When, therefore, the fundamental meaning of his body had already been established through the distinction from all other creatures (revealing one dimension of man's solitude), when it had thereby become clear that the "invisible" determines man more than the "visible," then there was presented to him the alternative closely and directly connected by God with the tree of the knowledge of good and evil (revealing a further dimension of possible loneliness): *the alternative between death and immortality.* This grasps the eschatological meaning not only of the body, but of humanity itself distinguished from all other living beings (other bodies), while at the same time involving in a quite particular way his own body created from "the dust of the ground." Thus, this alternative between death and immortality enters, right from the outset, the definition of man and belongs "from the beginning" to the meaning of his solitude before God Himself, and also possesses a fundamental meaning for the theology of the body.

Original Unity of Man and Woman—The words, "It is not good that the man should be alone," are as it were a prelude to the narrative of the creation of woman. Together with this narrative, the sense of original solitude becomes part of the meaning of that original unity, which has its roots in the fact of the creation of man as male and female. Corporeality and sexuality are not completely identified here. Although the human body in its normal constitution bears within it the signs of sex and is, by its nature, male or female, the fact, however, that man is a "body" belongs to the structure of the personal subject more deeply than the fact that he is in his somatic constitution also male or female. Therefore, the meaning of original solitude, which can be referred simply to "man," is substantially prior to the meaning of original unity. The latter, in fact, is based on masculinity and femininity, as if on two different "incarnations," that is, on two ways of "being a body" of the same human being, created "in the image of God." Following the Yahwist text, in which the creation of woman was described separately, we must have before our eyes, at the same time, that "image of God" of the first narrative of creation. This second narrative keeps, up to a certain point, the form of a dialogue between man and God-Creator, manifested above all when man (humanity) is definitively created as male and female. The creation takes place almost simultaneously in two dimensions: the action of God who creates occurs in correlation with the process of human consciousness.

In the Yahwist account, we read, "So the Lord God caused a deep sleep to fall upon the man, and while he slept took one of his ribs and closed up its place with flesh: and the rib which the Lord God had taken from the man he made into a woman." This "sleep" implies more than just a dimension of man's subconscious expressed in dreams. We can conclude rather that the man (humanity) falls into that "sleep" in order to wake up "male" and "female." The analogy of sleep here then implies not just a passing from consciousness to subconsciousness, but a specific return to non-being (lack of conscious existence), to a moment preceding the creation, in order that, through God's creative initiative, solitary "man" may emerge from it again in his double identity as male and female. He falls into that "sleep" with the desire of finding a being like himself and discovers a "second self," also personal and equally referred to the situation of original solitude. In this way, the circle of the solitude of the man-person is broken, because the first "man" awakens from sleep as "male" and "female." The fashioning of the woman from the rib of the man symbolizes the *homogeneity of the whole being of both.* This concerns above all the body, the somatic structure, and is confirmed by the man's first words to the woman: "This at last is bone of my bones and flesh of my flesh." The woman, therefore, is created on the basis of the same humanity and has been previously defined as "a helper fit for him."

Somatic homogeneity, in spite of the sexual difference, is so evident that the man (male), on waking up from his genetic sleep, expresses it at once and manifests for the first time joy and even exaltation—for which he had no reason before, due to the *lack of a being like himself.* Joy in the other human being, in the second "self," dominates in the words spoken by the man (male) on seeing the woman (female). All this helps to establish the full meaning of the original unity.

By the Communion of Persons Man Becomes the Image of God—We have seen that the "definitive" creation of man consists in the creation of the unity of two beings. Their unity denotes above all the identity of human nature; the duality, on the other hand, manifests what, on the basis of this identity, constitutes the masculinity and femininity of created man. This ontological dimension of unity and duality has, at the same time, an axiological meaning ("God saw...that it was good"). Man was created as a particular value before God but also as a particular value for himself (the woman for the man, the man for the woman). Moreover, *joy* is revealed as the first circle of the experience lived by man *as value.* One might venture to say that the depth and force of this first and "original" emotion of the male-man in the presence of the *humanity* of the woman, and at the same time in the presence of the *femininity* of the other human being, seems something unique and unrepeatable. Man in his original solitude acquires a personal consciousness in the process of "distinction" from all other living things and at the same time, in this solitude, *opens up* to a being akin to himself, a "helper fit for him." Man's solitude then is presented not only as the first discovery of the characteristic transcendence peculiar to the person, but also as the discovery of an adequate relationship "to" the person, and therefore as an opening and expectation of a "communion of persons." This latter expression indicates precisely the "help" which is derived, in a sense, from the very fact of existing as a person "beside" a person, and this becomes in itself the existence of the person "for" the person. Furthermore, the communion of persons could be formed only on the basis of a "double solitude" of man and woman. That is, they "meet" in their distinction from the world of other living things and this give them the possibility of being and existing in a special reciprocity. The concept of "help" expresses this special reciprocity in existence, which no other living being could have ensured. Indispensable for this reciprocity was *all that constituted the foundation of the solitude* of each of them—and therefore also self-knowledge and self-determination, that is, subjectivity and consciousness of the meaning of one's own body.

If we read this Yahwist text in light of the Elohist text concerning man as an "image of God," we can then deduce that man became the "image and likeness" of God not only through his own humanity, but also through the communion of persons which man and woman form right from the beginning. The image of course reflects the model. Man becomes the image of God not so much in the moment of solitude (reflecting the solitude of a Person who rules the world) but also in the moment of communion (reflecting essentially the inscrutable divine communion of persons). Man here reflects the Trinitarian concept of the "image of God." This is of deep significance for the theology of the body. In the mystery of creation—on the basis of the original and constituent "solitude" of his being—man was endowed with a deep unity between what is (humanly and through the body) male in him and what is (equally humanly and through the body) female in him. On all this, right from the beginning, there descended the blessing of fertility, linked with human procreation.

The male-man utters the words "flesh of my flesh and bone of my bones" only at the *sight of the woman:* he was able to identify and call by name *what makes them visibly similar to one another* and at the same time *what manifests humanity.* Compared to all the other "bodies"—living creatures, *animalia*—the expression "flesh of my flesh" takes on precisely this meaning: the body reveals man. There is contained here a reference to what makes that body truly human, and therefore to what determines man as a person—that is, as a being who, even in all his corporality, is "similar" to God.

The theology of the body, which right from the beginning is bound up with the creation of man in the image of God, becomes in a way also the theology of sex, or rather the theology of masculinity and femininity. This unity through the body ("and the two will become one flesh") possesses a multiform dimension: an ethical dimension and also a strictly theological and sacramental dimension. This is so because that unity which is realized through the body indicates, right from the beginning, not only the "body," but also the "incarnate" communion of persons—*communio personarum*—and calls for this communion right from the beginning. Masculinity and femininity express the dual aspect of man's somatic constitution and indicate, furthermore, the new consciousness of the sense of one's own body: a sense which, it can be said, consists in a mutual enrichment. In the creation narrative, this mutual enrichment (value dimension), through which humanity is formed again as the communion of persons (with a deep consciousness of human corporality and sexuality), establishes an inalienable norm for the understanding of man on the theological plane.

Marriage is One and Indissoluble in the First Chapters of Genesis—The study of the human identity of the one who, at the beginning, is "alone," must always pass through duality, "communion." We understand that knowledge of man passes through masculinity and femininity, which are as it were two complementary "incarnations" of the same metaphysical solitude before God and the world. As Gen 2:23 already shows ("Then the man said, 'This at last is bone of my bone and flesh of my flesh; she shall be called Woman, because she was taken out of Man'"), femininity finds itself, in sense, in the presence of masculinity, while masculinity is confirmed through femininity. Precisely the function of sex (a *constituent part* of the person, not just an *attribute*) proves how deeply man, with all his spiritual solitude—with the uniqueness, never to be repeated, of his person—is constituted by the body as "he" or "she." The presence of the feminine element, alongside the male element and together with it, signifies an enrichment for man in the whole perspective of his history, including the history of salvation. The unity of which Gen 2:24 speaks ("they become one flesh") is undoubtedly what is expressed and realized in the conjugal act. The biblical formulation indicates sex (masculinity and femininity) as that characteristic of man—male and female—which permits them, when they become "one flesh," to submit at the same time *their whole* *humanity to the blessing of fertility.* Here we must not stop at the surface of human sexuality but see it in light of the full dimension of man and of the communion of persons. Sex is something more than the mysterious power of human corporality, which acts by virtue of instinct. At the level of man and in the mutual relation of persons, sex expresses an ever new surpassing of the limit of man's solitude (inherent in the constitution of his body and determining its original meaning). This surpassing always contains within it a certain assumption of the solitude of the body of the second "self" as one's own. Man and woman, uniting with each other (in the conjugal act) so closely as to become "one flesh," rediscover, so to speak, every time and in a special way, the mystery of creation. They return in this way to that union in humanity which allows them to recognize each other and, like the first time, to call each other by name.

This "assumption of the solitude of the body" of the other is bound up with *choice*—"for this reason a man leaves his father and mother" (to whom he belongs 'by nature') "and cleaves unto his wife" (by choice). The body becomes the constituent element of their union when they become husband and wife, but this takes place through a mutual choice. It is the choice that establishes the conjugal pact between persons, who become "one flesh" only on this basis. The first man and the first woman, then, constitute *the beginning and the model* for all men and women intimately united as "one flesh."

Choice here corresponds to the structure of man's solitude, and in actual fact to the "two-fold solitude." Choice, as the expression of self-determination, rests on the foundation of his self-consciousness. Only on the basis of the structure peculiar to man is he a "body" and, through the body, also male and female. When they both unite so closely as to become "one flesh," their conjugal union presupposes a mature consciousness of the body. In fact, it bears within it a *particular consciousness of the meaning of that body in the mutual self-giving of persons.* In every conjugal union there is discovered again the same original consciousness of the unifying significance of the body in its masculinity and femininity. Moreover, in each of these unions there is renewed, in a way, the mystery of creation in all its original depth and vital power. "Taken out of man" as "flesh of his flesh," woman subsequently becomes, as "wife" and through her motherhood, mother of the living (Gen 3:20), since her motherhood also has its origin in him. Procreation is rooted in creation, and every time, in a sense, reproduces its mystery.

Meaning of Original Human Experiences—It can be said that the analysis of the first chapters of Genesis forces us in a way to reconstruct the elements that constitute man's *original* experience (i.e. experiences *of basic significance*). The important thing is not that these experiences belong to man's "theological pre-history," but that they are always at the root of every human experience. That is true even if, in the unfolding of ordinary human existence, not much attention is paid to these essential experiences. They are, in fact, so intermingled with the ordinary things of life that we do not generally notice their extraordinary character. The "revelation of the body" at the beginning helps us somehow to discover the extraordinary side of what is ordinary. Without this introductory reflection, it would be impossible to define the meaning of original nakedness: "And the man and his wife were both naked, and were not ashamed" (Gen 2:25).

This text presents one of the key elements of the original revelation, as decisive as the other texts (2:20 and 2:23), which have already enabled us to define the meaning of man's original solitude and original unity. To these is added, as the third element, the meaning of *original nakedness*, clearly stressed (and not accidental) in the context. This makes a specific contribution to the theology of the body and in such a way that we see that our reflections on the body must be connected to man's subjectivity; it is within the latter, in fact, that consciousness of the meaning of the body develops. They "were naked" and yet "were not ashamed," unquestionably describes their state of consciousness. In fact, it describes their mutual experience of the body—that is, the experience on the part of the man of the femininity that is revealed in the nakedness of the body and, reciprocally, the similar experience of masculinity on the part of the woman. "They were not ashamed" reflects a basic experience of man. In the situation of "historical" man laden with the inheritance of sin, there are now degrees of this experience, yet as we have seen there is some continuity and connection between the states of original innocence and original sin—allowing us to move back from the threshold of man's "historical" sinfulness to his original innocence. Gen 2:25 makes it particularly necessary to cross that threshold.

Moreover, once the first sin is committed (and the first covenant broken) "then the eyes of both were opened, and they knew that they were naked; and they sewed fig leaves and make themselves aprons." The adverb "then" indicates a new moment and a new situation which also implies a new content and a new quality of experience of the body, so that it can no longer be said: "they were naked, and were not ashamed." Here, therefore, shame is an experience that is not only original, but is a "boundary" one. The difference in formulations (before and after sin) testifies about the experience of shame—it takes place at a deeper level than the pure and simple use of the sense of sight, nor is it just a case of "knowing" or "not knowing." It is a radical change of the meaning of the original nakedness. It emerges from their consciences after their sin: "Who told you that you were naked? Have you eaten then of the tree which I commanded you not to eat?" This change directly concerns the experience of the meaning of one's body *before the Creator* ("I was afraid because I was naked, and I hid myself") and in the most direct way possible *in the man-woman, femininity-masculinity relationship.* This is the "border" which crosses the sphere of the "beginning" to which Christ referred. We must now see if we can reconstruct the original meaning of nakedness on the basis of this experience of shame.

Fullness of Interpersonal Communication—With shame, the human being manifests almost "instinctively" the need for affirmation and acceptance of one's true self, according to its rightful value. He experiences it at the same time both within himself, and externally, before the "other." But what does its original absence mean, on the other hand, in Gen 2:25: "They were both naked and were not ashamed"? Note first that this means a real non-presence of shame, not just some under-development or "primitive" form of it. Further, it is not a "lack of shame" in the sense of *immodesty* being present. Rather the words "they were not ashamed" express a particular fullness of consciousness and experience—above all of the true meaning of the body. Thus, the appearance of shame and of sexual modesty is connected with the loss of original fullness.

This fullness of consciousness involves the fact of the "non-identification" of one's own humanity with other livings things (*animalia*), together with the happy discovery of one's own humanity "with the help" of the other human being—and all this directly through the perception of the body. Thus, "nakedness" corresponds to that fullness of consciousness of the meaning of the body, deriving from the typical perception of the senses. This is a direct dimension of human experience—of knowledge concerning the exterior world, and the different things in it, which cannot be disregarded. Nonetheless, it is not possible to determine the meaning of the original nakedness considering only man's participation in exterior perception of the world: it is not possible to establish it without going down into the depths of man. *Human interiority* is necessary to explain and measure that particular fullness of interpersonal communication thanks to which man and woman "were naked and were not ashamed." *Communication* here is directly connected with the subjects, who communicate precisely on the basis of the "common union" that exists between them, both to reach and to express a reality that is peculiar and pertinent only to the sphere of person-subjects. In this context, the "body" then implies not a mere object of external perception of a special type; the body in fact *expresses the person* in his ontological and existential concreteness (which is something more than the "individual") and therefore expresses the personal human "self," which derives its "exterior" perception from within. The body through its own visibility manifests man and, thus, acts as intermediary, that is, enables man and woman, right from the beginning, "to communicate" with each other according to the *communio personarum* willed by the Creator precisely for them. In this connection, the original nakedness cannot be adequately interpreted naturalistically but only personalistically. The words "they were not ashamed" can mean only an original depth in affirming what is inherent in the person, what is "visibly" female and male, through which the "personal intimacy" of mutual communication in all its radical simplicity and purity is constituted. To this fullness of "exterior" perception, there corresponds the "interior" fullness of man's vision *in God*, that is, according to the measure of the "image of God." According to this measure, man "is" really naked, even before realizing it.

***Creation as Fundamental and Original Gift*—** "Nakedness" signifies the original good of God's vision. It signifies all the simplicity and fullness of the vision through which the "pure" value of humanity as male and female, the "pure" value of the body and sex, is manifested. There is no interior rupture or opposition here between the spiritual and the sensible, nor between what constitutes the person humanly and what in man is determined by sex: what is male and female. Seeing each other, as if through the very mystery of creation, man and woman see each other even more fully and distinctly than through the sense of sight itself, that is, through the eyes of the body. They see and know each other, in fact, with all the peace of the interior gaze, which creates precisely the fullness of the intimacy of persons.

If "shame" brings with it a specific limitation in seeing by means of the eyes of the body, this takes place above all because the *personal intimacy* is, as it were, disturbed and almost threatened by this sight. But "in the beginning" they were not ashamed: seeing and knowing each other in all the peace and tranquility of the interior gaze, they "communicate" in the fullness of humanity, which is manifested in them as reciprocal complementariness precisely because they are "male" and "female." At the same time, they "communicate" on the basis of that communion of persons in which, through femininity and masculinity, *they become a gift for each other.* In this way they reach in reciprocity a special understanding of the *meaning* of their own bodies, a meaning which comes about, as it were, at the very heart of their community-communion. We will call it the "nuptial" meaning of the body.

Now, on the way to an adequate anthropology and having looked at solitude, unity, and nakedness in the context of man (male and female) as an "image of God," it is opportune to turn again to those fundamental words of Christ, the word "created" and the subject "Creator," introducing in the considerations made so far a new dimension—a new criterion of understanding and interpretation—which we will call "hermeneutics of the gift." The dimension of the gift decides the essential truth and depth of meaning of the original solitude-unity-nakedness. God reveals himself as Creator: He who "calls to existence from nothingness," and who establishes the world in existence and man in the world, because He is "love." Only love (the divine motive in creation), in fact, gives a beginning to good ("God saw…it was very good") and delights in good. The creation, thus, also signifies *giving*; a fundamental and "radical" giving, that is, a giving in which the gift comes into being precisely from nothingness. Consequently, every creature bears within him the sign of the original and fundamental gift. Furthermore, "giving" indicates the *one who gives* and the *one who receives the gift*, and also the *relationship that is established between them.* Creation is a gift because there appears in it man who, as the "image of God," is capable of understanding the very meaning of gift in the call from nothingness to existence. And he is capable of answering the Creator with the language of this understanding.

Nuptial Meaning of the Body—We must ask ourselves if man, in his original solitude, really "lived" the world as a gift, and with the requisite attitude. The Creator himself, at this point, instead of stressing the aspect of the world as a subjectively beatifying gift for man, points out that man is "alone." There appears here for the first time a certain lack of good: "It is not good that man should be alone." The first "man" says the same thing. None of the other living creatures (*animalia*) are "a helper fit for him," he is still "alone." They do not offer man the basic conditions which make it possible to exist in a relationship of mutual giving. "Alone," man does not completely realize his essence (as a person);

he realizes it only by existing *"with someone"*—and even more deeply and completely, by existing *"for someone."* It is precisely the meaning of the words "alone" and "helper" which indicate as *fundamental and constitutive* for man both the relationship and the communion of persons (existing in a mutual "for," a mutual gift). This relationship is precisely the fulfillment of man's original solitude. This fulfillment is, in its origin, beatifying and belongs to the mystery of creation effected by love. When man (the male) sees man (the female) and says "this at last is bone of my bones and flesh of my flesh," these words express in a way the subjectively beatifying beginning of man's existence in the world. This brings us then to the subject of the "person" and at the same time to the subject of the "body-sex." The simultaneity is essential, for if we deal with sex without the person, the whole adequacy of the anthropology developed here would be destroyed, and the revelation of the body veiled.

There is a deep connection between the mystery of creation, as a gift springing from love, and the beatifying "beginning" of the existence of man as male and female, in the whole truth of their body and their sex, which is the pure and simple truth of communion between persons. When the first man, at the sight of the first woman, exclaims "flesh of my flesh," affirming the human identity of both, he seems to say: here is *a body that expresses the "person"*! This "body" reveals the "living soul" and it expresses *femininity*—which manifests the reciprocity and communion of persons. This is the body: a witness to creation as a fundamental gift, and so a witness to Love as the source from which this same giving springs. Masculinity-femininity—namely, sex—is the original sign of a creative donation and of an awareness on the part of man (male and female) of a gift lived so to speak in an original way. That beatifying "beginning" of man's being and existing, as male and female, is connected with the *revelation* (theological) and *discovery* (anthropological—a reality consciously lived by man) of the meaning of the body, which can be called "nuptial." The creative giving, which springs from Love, has reached the original consciousness of man, becoming an experience of mutual giving, free from shame.

Gen 2:24 speaks of the final purpose of man's masculinity and femininity, in the life of the spouses-parents. Uniting with each other so closely as to become "one flesh," they will subject, in a way, their humanity to the blessing of fertility, namely, "procreation," of which the first narrative (Gen 1:28) speaks. Man at the same time is *free from* any "constraint" of his own body and sex. The original nakedness, mutual and at the same time not weighed down by shame, expresses this interior freedom of man.

The Man-Person Becomes a Gift in the Freedom of Love—This "freedom of the gift" lies precisely at the basis of the nuptial meaning of the body. The human body, with its sex (masculinity and femininity seen in the very mystery of creation), is not only a source of fruitfulness and procreation (as is analogously true in the whole natural order), but includes right "from the beginning" the "nuptial" attribute, that is, the capacity of expressing love: that love precisely in which the man-person becomes a gift and—by means of this gift—fulfills the very meaning of his being and existence. This coincides with the statement of Vatican II that man is the only creature in the visible world that God "willed for its own sake," adding that this man "can fully discover his true self only in a sincere giving of himself." But, to be able to remain in the relationship of the "sincere gift of themselves" and to become such a gift for each other, they must be precisely free with the very freedom of the gift. We mean here freedom particularly as mastery of oneself (self-control): this is indispensable for a man *to be able to give himself*, to become a gift. Thus, the words "they were naked and were not ashamed" can and must be understood as the revelation—and at the same time rediscovery—of *freedom*, which makes possible and qualifies the "nuptial" sense of the body. Moreover, free interiorly from the constraint of his (her) own body and sex, free with the freedom of the gift, man and woman could enjoy the whole truth, the whole self-evidence, of man, just as Yahweh had revealed these things to them in the mystery of creation. As the Council states, this truth about man has two main emphases: that man is the only creature in the world that the Creator has willed "for its own sake," and that this same man can find himself only in the disinterested giving of himself.

If, as we have noted, at the root of their nakedness there is the interior freedom of the gift—the disinterested gift of oneself—precisely that gift enables them both, man and woman, *to find one another,* since the Creator willed each of them "for his (her) own sake." Thus, man, in the first beatifying meeting, finds the woman, and she finds him. In this way he accepts her interiorly; he accepts her as she is willed "for her own sake" by the Creator, as she is constituted in the mystery of the image of God through her femininity; and reciprocally, she accepts him by means of his masculinity. The revelation and the discovery of the nuptial meaning of the body consists in this. The human body, oriented by the "sincere gift" of the person, reveals not only physical masculinity or femininity but also such a value and such a beauty as to go beyond the purely physical dimension of "sexuality." This "completes" the awareness of the nuptial meaning of the body. On the one hand, this meaning indicates a particular capacity of expressing love, in which man becomes a gift; on the other hand, there corresponds to it the capacity and deep availability for the "affirmation of the person"—i.e. the capacity for *living the fact* that the other is, by means of the body, someone willed by the Creator "for his (her) own sake."

This "affirmation of the person" (as someone unique and unrepeatable, chosen by eternal Love) is nothing but acceptance of the gift, which by means of reciprocity creates the communion of persons. This experience is "interior," part of the subjective dimension of man, while at the same time comprising the whole "exterior" of man in the nakedness of the body in its masculinity or femininity. The revelation and discovery of the nuptial meaning of the body explain man's original happiness (in original innocence) and, at the same time, open the perspective of earthly history, in which he can never avoid this indispensable "theme" of his own existence. Though the "historical" perspective will change after original sin, nonetheless in the whole perspective of his own "history," man will not fail to confer a nuptial meaning on his own body. Even if this meaning undergoes and will undergo many distortions, it will always remain the deepest level, which demands to be revealed in all its simplicity and purity (as "in the beginning"), and to be shown in its whole truth (as a sign of the "image of God"). The way that goes from the mystery of creation to the "redemption of the body" also passes here.

The nuptial meaning of the body is a fundamental element of human existence and human happiness in the world and can only be understood in the context of the person—willed for its own sake and only able to discover its true self in a sincere giving of itself. Furthermore, if Christ has also revealed another vocation besides marriage—renunciation of it for the kingdom of heaven—this only highlights the same truth about human nature: that man and woman are capable of making a *gift of themselves* for the kingdom of heaven.

Mystery of Man's Original Innocence—The reality of the gift and the act of giving, outlined in the first chapters of Genesis as the content constituting the mystery of creation, confirms that the radiation of love is an integral part of the same mystery. Happiness is *being rooted in love.* Original happiness speaks to us of the "beginning" of man, who emerged from Love and initiated love. That happened in an irrevocable way, despite the subsequent sin and death. In His time, Christ will be a witness to this irrevocable love of the Creator and Father, which had already been expressed in the mystery of creation and in the grace of original innocence. This "beginning" can also be defined as the original and beatifying *immunity from shame* as the result of love. This immunity directs us towards the mystery of man's original innocence. It is a mystery of his existence, prior to the knowledge of good and evil and almost "outside" it. The fact that man exists in this way, before the breaking of the first covenant with his Creator, belongs to the fullness of the mystery of creation. The interior foundation and source of man's original innocence is grace: the participation in the interior life of God Himself, in His Holiness. This original innocence is highlighted by the statement about nakedness mutually free from shame, a statement unique in its kind in the whole Bible and never repeated—though nakedness will later be connected many times with "shame" and even "ignominy." This innocence belongs to the dimension of grace contained in the mystery of creation, that is, to that mysterious gift made to the inner man—to the human "heart"—which enables both of them, man and woman, to exist from the "beginning" in the mutual relationship of the disinterested gift of oneself. In that is contained the revelation and at the same time the discovery of the "nuptial" meaning of the body (male and female).

"Historical" man tries to understand the mystery of original innocence by means of a contrast, that is, going back also to the experience of his own sin and his own sinfulness. He tries to understand original innocence by starting from his own experience of shame. Original innocence is, however, what radically (at its very roots) excludes shame and eliminates its necessity in man—in his heart, that is, in his conscience. This innocence seems to refer above all to the interior state of the human "heart," of the human will. At least indirectly, there is included in it the revelation and discovery of the human moral conscience, of the whole dimension of conscience, though before the "knowledge of good and evil." In a certain sense, it must be understood as original righteousness. Since happiness and innocence are part of the framework of the communion of persons, the beatifying awareness of the meaning of the body is conditioned by original innocence. It seems that there is no impediment to understanding that original innocence as a particular "purity of heart," which preserves an interior faithfulness to the gift according to the nuptial meaning of the body. Consequently, original innocence is manifested as a tranquil testimony of conscience which (in this case) precedes any experience of good and evil; and yet this serene testimony of conscience is something all the more beatifying—indeed, awareness of the nuptial meaning of the body becomes "humanly" beatifying only by means of this testimony.

Man and Woman: A Mutual Gift for Each Other—The human will is originally innocent and in this way, the reciprocity and the exchange of the gift of the body (male and female) *as a gift of the person* is facilitated. Thus, original innocence can be defined as innocence of the mutual experience of the body. To understand this innocence, we must try to clarify in what consists the interior innocence in the exchange of the gift of the person. We can say that interior innocence (righteousness of intention) in the exchange of the gift consists in reciprocal "acceptance" of the other, such as to correspond to the very essence of the gift; in this way, mutual donation creates the communion of persons. It is a question, therefore, of a receiving, accepting, or welcoming of the other person, of such a kind that it expresses and sustains (in mutual nakedness) the meaning of the gift and therefore deepens the mutual dignity of it. This dignity corresponds to the fact that the Creator wills man (male and female) "for his own sake." The innocence "of the heart," and consequently the innocence of experience means *a moral participation in the eternal and permanent act of God's will.* The opposite of this "welcoming" would be a *privation of the gift* itself and, therefore, a changing and even a reduction of the other to an "object for myself" (object of lust, of misappropriation, etc.). This *extorting of the gift* from the other and reducing him (her) interiorly to a mere *object for me,* should mark precisely the beginning of shame. The latter, in fact, corresponds to a threat inflicted on the gift in its personal intimacy and bears witness to the mutual collapse of innocence in the mutual experience.

The exchange of the gift, in which the whole of their humanity (body and soul, femininity and masculinity) participates, is actualized by preserving the interior characteristic (that is, precisely, innocence) of the donation of oneself and of the acceptance of the other as a gift. These two functions of mutual exchange are deeply connected in the whole process of "gift of oneself." The giving and the accepting of the gift interpenetrate, so that the giving itself becomes accepting, and the acceptance is transformed into giving. Gen 2:23-25 enables us to deduce that woman who, in the mystery of creation, "is given" to man by the Creator, is (thanks to original innocence) "received," that is, accepted by him as a gift. At the same time, the acceptance of the woman by the man and the very way of accepting her become, as it were, a first donation, so that the woman in giving herself (from the first moment in which she was given to man by the Creator), "rediscovers" at the same time "herself"—thanks to the fact that she has been accepted and welcomed, and thanks to the way in which she has been received by the man. So she finds herself again in the very fact of giving herself, when she is accepted *in the way in which the Creator wished her to be, that is, "for her own sake,"* through her humanity and femininity. Only then does she reach the inner depth of her person and full possession of herself. Let us add that this finding of oneself becomes the source of a new giving of oneself, which grows *by virtue of* the interior disposition to the exchange of the gift and *to the extent* to which it meets with the same and even deeper acceptance and welcome, as the fruit of a more and more intense awareness of the gift itself.

Man "from the beginning" seems to have the function of the one who, above all, receives the gift: the woman is entrusted to his eyes, to his consciousness, to his sensitivity, to his "heart." But he also must ensure the exchange of the gift, the mutual interpenetration of giving and receiving as a gift, which, precisely through its reciprocity, creates a real communion of persons. If the woman, in the mystery of creation, is the one who is "given" to the man, the latter, on his part, in receiving her as a gift in the full truth of her person and her femininity, thereby enriches her and at the same time he, too, in this mutual relationship, is enriched. The man is enriched not only through her, who gives him her own person and femininity, but also through the gift of himself. The man's giving of himself, in response to that of the woman, is an enrichment of himself. In fact, there is manifested in it, as it were, the specific essence of his masculinity which, through the reality of the body and sex, reaches the deep recesses of the "possession of self," thanks to which he is capable both of giving himself and of receiving the other's gift. The man, therefore, not only accepts the gift, but at the same time is received as a gift by the woman, in the revelation of the interior spiritual essence of his masculinity, together with the whole truth of his body and sex. Accepted in this way, he is enriched through this acceptance and welcoming of the gift of his own masculinity. Subsequently, this acceptance, in which the man finds himself again through the "sincere gift of himself," becomes in him the source of a new and deeper enrichment of the woman. The exchange is mutual, and in it the reciprocal effects of the "sincere gift" and of the "finding oneself again" are revealed and grow.

Original Innocence and Man's Historical State—It seems quite clear that the "experience of the body" in Gen 2:23&25 indicates a degree of "spiritualization" of man different from that after original sin (Gen 3) and which we know from the experience of "historical" man. It is a different measure of "spiritualization," which involves another composition of the interior forces of man himself, almost another body-soul relationship, other inner proportions between sensitivity, spirituality, and affectivity (i.e., another degree of interior sensitiveness to the gifts of the Holy Spirit). All this conditions man's original innocence and at the same time determines it. We have tried to arrive at the original meaning of the body through the category of the "historical *a posteriori,*" that is, by going back through man's historical state after original sin to try to discern the meaning of his original innocence, the body, and the mutual gift of male and female to one another. It is important and essential to define this connection, not only with regard to man's "theological prehistory," in which the life of the couple was almost completely permeated by the grace of original innocence, but also in relation to its possibility of revealing to us the permanent roots of the *human* and particularly the theological aspect of the *ethos of the body.* The fundamental fact of man's existence at every stage of his existence is that God "created them male and female;" in fact, He always creates them in this way and they are always such. Understanding of the fundamental meanings, contained in the very mystery of creation, such as the nuptial meaning of the body (and the fundamental conditionings of this meaning), is important and indispensable *in order to know who man is and who he should be,* and therefore how he should mold his own activity. It is an essential and important thing for the future of the human *ethos.*

Gen 2:24 notes that the two, man and woman, were created for marriage: "Therefore, a man leaves his father and his mother and cleaves to his wife, and they become one flesh." In this way a great creative perspective is opened:

precisely the perspective of man's existence, which is continually renewed by means of "procreation" (we could say "self-reproduction"). This perspective is deeply rooted in the consciousness of humanity (Gen 2:23) and also in the particular consciousness of the nuptial meaning of the body (Gen 2:25). The man and the woman, before becoming husband and wife (later Gen 4:1 speaks of this in the concrete), emerge from the mystery of creation as brother and sister in the same humanity. Understanding of the nuptial meaning of the body in its masculinity and femininity reveals the depths of their freedom, which is freedom of giving. From here there begins that communion of persons, in which both meet and give themselves to each other in the fullness of their subjectivity. Thus, both grow as person-subjects, and they grow mutually for the other also through their body and through that "nakedness" free from shame. In this communion of persons the whole depth of the original solitude of man (of the first one and of all) is perfectly ensured and, at the same time, this solitude becomes in a marvelous way permeated and broadened by the gift of the "other." If the man and the woman cease to be a disinterested gift for each other, as they were in the mystery of creation, then they recognize that "they are naked" (Gen 3). And then the shame of that nakedness, which they had not felt in the state of original innocence, will spring up in their hearts. Original innocence manifests and at the same time constitutes the perfect *ethos* of the gift.

Man Enters the World a Subject of Truth and Love—Through the ethos of the gift the problem of the "subjectivity" of man, who is a subject made in the image and likeness of God, is partly outlined. In the narrative of creation "the woman" is certainly not merely "an object" for the man, though they both remain in front of each other in all the fullness of their objectivity as creatures, as male and female, both naked. *Only the nakedness that makes woman an "object" for man, or vice versa, is a source of shame.* The fact that "they were not ashamed" means that the woman was not an "object" for the man nor he for her, due to their interior innocence as "purity of heart." This means that they were united by awareness of the gift; they were mutually conscious of the nuptial meaning of their bodies, in which the freedom of the gift is expressed and all the interior riches of the person as subject are manifested. This mutual interpenetration of the "self" of the human persons, man and woman, seems to exclude subjectively any "reduction to an object." In this is revealed the subjective profile of that love of which it can be said, on the other hand, that "it is objective" to the depths, since it is nourished by the mutual "objectivity" of the gift. After original sin, this nuptial meaning of the body will cease to be a simple reality of revelation and grace for man and woman, but it will continue as a *commitment* given to man by the ethos of the gift, inscribed in the depths of the human heart, as a distant echo of original innocence. From that nuptial meaning, human love in its interior truth and its subjective authenticity will be formed. And man—also through the veil of shame—will continually rediscover himself as the *guardian* of the mystery of the subject (the freedom of the gift) so as to defend it from any reduction to the position of mere object. But man originally appears in the world as the highest expression of divine gift, and with this gift-character he brings into the world his particular likeness to God—with which he transcends and dominates also his "visibility" in the world (his corporality, his masculinity or femininity, his nakedness). A reflection of this likeness is the primordial awareness of the nuptial meaning of the body pervaded by the mystery of original innocence.

Thus, we have here a primordial *sacrament*—a sign that transmits in the visible world the invisible mystery hidden in God from time immemorial. The sacrament, as a visible sign, is constituted with man, as a "body," by means of his "visible" masculinity and femininity. The body, in fact, and it alone, is capable of making visible what is invisible: the spiritual and the divine (the mystery of truth and love, of divine life, in which man participates). Thus, man (male and female) as an image of God reveals the very sacramentality of creation, of the world. Against this vast background, we understand fully the words of Gen 2:24 ("A man leaves his father and his mother and cleaves to his wife, and they become one flesh") that constitute the sacrament of marriage, as well as Gen 2:25 ("they were both naked and were not ashamed") which express the fact that *together with man, holiness entered the visible world*, created for him. The sacrament of the world, and the sacrament of man in the world, comes from the divine source of holiness, and at the same time is instituted for holiness. Awareness of the gift *conditions*, in this case, "the sacrament of the body:" in his body, as male or female, man feels he is a subject of holiness. With this consciousness of the meaning of his own body, man, as male and female, enters the world as a subject of truth and love. Gen 2:23-25 narrates, as it were, the first feast of humanity in all the original fullness of the experience of the nuptial meaning of the body. This original meaning and sacrament is a continuing sign of hope, despite the fact that very soon the horizon of sin and death is extended over that original feast.

Analysis of Knowledge and of Procreation—Sin and death entered man's history, in a way, through the very heart of that unity which, from "the beginning," was formed by man and woman, created and called to become "one flesh." Thus, we must pass, after the earlier analyses concerning the state of original innocence, to the last of them, to the analysis of "knowledge and of procreation." Thematically, it is closely bound up with the blessing of fertility (Gen 1: 27-28) but historically it is already inserted in that horizon of sin and death (Gen 3) which has weighed on the consciousness of the meaning of the human body, together with the breaking of the first covenant with the Creator.

In Gen 4 we read: "Adam knew Eve his wife, and she conceived and bore Cain, saying, 'I have gotten a man with the help of the Lord.' And again, she bore his brother Abel." It is significant that the situation, in which husband and wife unite so closely as to become "one flesh," has been defined as "knowledge." This term "knowledge" here is important as regards the "archetype" of our way of conceiving of corporeal man (male and female): the conjugal relationship whereby they become "one flesh" was raised, by the use of this term, into the specific dimension of persons. Gen 4:1-2 speaks only of "knowledge" of the woman by the man, stressing his activity. It is possible, however, to speak of the reciprocity of the "knowledge," in which man and woman participate by means of their body and their sex. Thus, with the biblical "knew" we find ourselves in the presence of, on one hand, the direct expression of human intentionality (characteristic of knowledge) and, on the other, of the whole reality of conjugal life and union, in which man and woman become "one flesh." This indicates the deepest essence of the reality of married life and authorizes the statement that "the husband knows his wife" or that they both "know" each other. Then they reveal themselves to each other with that specific depth of their own human "self" which, precisely, is revealed by means of their sex, their masculinity and femininity. And then, in a unique way, the woman "is given" to the man to be known, and he to her. But it is not enough here just to speak of "sexual life together." Each of them, man and woman, is not just a passive object, defined by his or her own body and sex, and in this way determined "by nature." On the contrary, precisely because they are a man and a woman, each is given to the other as a unique and unrepeatable subject, as "self," as a person. Sex decides not only the somatic individuality of man, but defines at the same time his personal identity and concreteness. Precisely in this personal identity and concreteness, as an unrepeatable female-male "self," man is deeply "known" in the conjugal act.

Mystery of Woman Revealed in Motherhood—Knowledge, which was at the basis of man's original solitude (naming the animals, "knowing" and differentiating himself from them), is now at the basis of this unity of man and woman—and this is active personal "knowledge" not a mere passive determination by the body and sex. In this "knowledge," man confirms the meaning of the name "Eve," given to his wife, "because she was mother of all the living" (Gen 3:20). Thus, in this "knowledge," the mystery of femininity is manifested and revealed completely by means of motherhood. The woman stands before the man as a mother, the subject of the new human life that is conceived and develops in her, and from her is born into the world. Likewise, the mystery of man's masculinity, that is, the generative and "fatherly" meaning of his body, is also thoroughly revealed. "Knowledge" conditions begetting—and begetting is a perspective, which man and woman insert in their mutual "knowledge." The latter, therefore, goes beyond the limits of subject-object (such as man and woman seem to be mutually), since "knowledge" indicates on the one side him who "knows" and on the other side her who "is known" (or vice versa). In this "knowledge" is enclosed also the specific consummation of marriage.

Procreation brings it about that "the man and the woman (his wife)" know each other reciprocally in the "third," sprung from them both. This "knowledge" becomes a discovery and a revelation of the new man, in whom both of them again recognize themselves, their humanity, their living image. "Knowledge" means here not just a passive "biological" determination of man by his body and sex; rather, "knowledge" reaches the specific level and content of self-conscious and self-determinant persons. Therefore, it involves a particular consciousness of the meaning of the human body, bound up with fatherhood and motherhood.

The whole exterior constitution of the woman's body—its particular aspect, the qualities which, with the power of perennial attractiveness, are at the beginning of the "knowledge"—are in close union with motherhood. The Bible (and the liturgy) with its characteristic simplicity, speaking of the second Eve (Mary, the mother of Christ), honors and praises throughout the centuries "the womb that bore you and the breasts that you sucked." These words constitute a eulogy of motherhood, of femininity, of the female body in its typical expression of creative love. The first woman, at the moment when the maternal maturity of her body was revealed for the first time, said, "I have gotten a man with the help of the Lord" (Gen 4:1). These words express the whole theological depth of the function of begetting-procreating. The woman's body becomes the place of conception of the new man. The somatic homogeneousness of man and woman ("This is bone of my bones, flesh of my flesh") is confirmed by the words of the first woman-mother: "I have gotten a man!" The first woman, giving birth, is fully aware of the mystery of creation (renewed in human generation) and of the creative participation therein of God (His work and that of her husband) since she says: "I have gotten a man with the help of the Lord." There cannot be any confusion of action of the causes. The first parents—even after sin—transmit to all human parents the fundamental truth about the birth of man in the image of God, according to natural laws. In this man—born of the woman-parent thanks to the man-parent—there is reproduced every time the very "image of God," of that God who constituted the humanity of the first man. Although there are deep differences between man's state of original innocence and his state of hereditary sinfulness, that "image of God" constitutes a basis of continuity and unity. The "knowledge," of which Gen 4:1 speaks, is the *act which originates being*, or rather, which in union with the Creator, establishes a new man in his existence. Thus, the words of the Book of Genesis, which are a testimony of the first birth of man on earth, enclose within them at the same time everything that can and must be said of the dignity of human generation.

Knowledge-Generation Cycle and Perspective of Death—With biblical "knowledge," man (male-female) not only gives his own name, as he did when he gave names to other living creatures (thus, taking possession of them), but "knows" in the sense of Gen 4:1, that is, *realizes* what the name "man" expresses—realizes humanity in the new man generated. In a sense, therefore, he realizes himself, that is, the man-person. The man and the woman, in this "knowledge," in which they give rise to a being similar to them, are almost "carried off" together, are both taken possession of by the humanity which they, in union and in mutual "knowledge," wish to express again in the conjugal and creative act. In this sense, biblical "knowledge" can be explained as "possession." Is there a parallel here with the Platonic *eros?* Perhaps, although these are two different conceptual spheres, only with great caution can they be used to interpret each other. It seems, however, that in the original revelation the idea of man's possession of the woman, or vice versa, *as of an object*, is not present. On the other hand, due to sinfulness, man and woman must now reconstruct, with great effort, the meaning of the disinterested gift. The revelation of the body in the Book of Genesis, particularly in chapter 3, shows with impressive clearness that the cycle of "knowledge-generation," so deeply rooted in the potentiality of the human body, was subjected—after sin—to the law of suffering ("in pain you shall bring forth children") and death ("you are dust, and to dust you shall return"). The horizon of death extends over the whole perspective of human life on earth, life that was inserted in that original biblical cycle of "knowledge-generation." Man, who has broken the covenant with his Creator, is detached by God-Yahweh from the tree of life. In this way, the life given to man has not been taken away, but restricted (by the limit of conceptions, births, and death) and further aggravated by hereditary sinfulness; but nonetheless his life is given to him again, in a way, as a task in the same ever-recurring cycle. Thus, each man bears within him the mystery of his "beginning" closely bound up with awareness of the generative meaning of the body: "Adam knew his wife Eve, and she conceived and bore...." This is precisely the threshold of man's history. It is his "beginning" on earth. On this threshold man, as male and female, stands with an awareness of the generative meaning of his own body: masculinity conceals within it the meaning of fatherhood, and femininity that of motherhood. In the name of this meaning, Christ will one day give the categorical answer (proscription against divorce) to the question that the Pharisees has asked him.

Awareness of the *meaning of the body* and awareness of its *generative meaning* come into contact, in man, in the awareness of death—the inevitable horizon they bear within them. Yet there always returns in the history of man the "knowledge-generation" cycle, in which life struggles, ever anew, with the inexorable perspective of death, and always overcomes it. It is as if the reason for this refusal of life to surrender, which is manifested in "generation," were always the same "knowledge," with which man goes beyond the solitude of his own being and, in fact, decides again to affirm this being in another. Both of them, man and woman, affirm it in the new man generated. In this affirmation, biblical "knowledge" seems to acquire an even greater dimension. Man, in spite of all the experiences of his life, in spite of suffering, disappointment with himself, his sinfulness, and finally in spite of the inevitable prospect of death, always continues to put "knowledge" at the "beginning" of "generation." In this way, he seems to participate in that first "vision" of God Himself: God the Creator "saw…and behold it was very good." And, ever anew, He confirms the truth of these words.

Marriage in the Integral Vision of Man—Questions about marriage, of course, are asked not only by the Pharisees in Christ's day, but by many today: single persons, married couples, fiancés, young people, but also by writers, journalists, politicians, economists, demographers, in a word, by contemporary culture and civilization. However,

Christ would not be "surprised" by any of these situations, and I suppose that in answering them he would again refer above all to the "beginning"—and all the more resolutely as our culture seems to be moving more and more away from that "beginning." It can be said that, in the answer to the Pharisees, Christ put forward a "total vision of man" (called for in Pope Paul VI's encyclical *Humanae Vitae*), without which no adequate answer can be given to questions connected with marriage and procreation. Precisely this total vision of man must be constructed from the "beginning." This applies also to the modern mentality. We are, in fact, children of an age in which, owing to the development of various disciplines, this total vision of man may easily be rejected and replaced by multiple partial conceptions which, dwelling on one or other aspect of the *compositum humanum,* do not reach man's *integrum,* or leave it outside their own field of vision. Man then becomes more an object of determined techniques than the responsible subject of his own actions. Christ, in his answer given to the Pharisees, wishes man (male and female) to be this subject, that is, a subject who decides his own actions in the light of the complete truth about himself, since it is the original truth, or the foundation of genuinely human experiences.

Though lacking in naturalistic or scientific knowledge about the human body, the Book of Genesis reveals the truth that is important for the total vision of man in the most simple and full way. This truth concerns the meaning of the human body in the structure of the personal subject, and in the whole sphere of intersubjectivity, especially in the perennial man-woman relationship. Thanks to that, we acquire with regard to this relationship a perspective which we must necessarily place at the basis of all modern science on human sexuality in the bio-physiological sense. This is the context in which to interpret the findings of science. It is necessary—through all the single elements of contemporary science—to arrive always at what is fundamental and essentially personal, both in every individual, man or woman, and in their mutual relations. Thus, we start at the "beginning," with the theology of the body. This should not astonish or surprise anyone who is aware of the mystery and reality of the Incarnation. Through the fact that the Word of God became flesh, the body entered theology—through the main door. The Incarnation—and the Redemption that springs from it—became also the definitive source of the sacramentality of marriage.

Questions raised by modern man about marriage, of course, are not only questions of science, but, even more, questions of human life—and are also questions for Christians. The answer given by Christ to the Pharisees, zealots of the Old Testament, is particularly important to them. Those who seek the accomplishment of their own human and Christian vocation in marriage, are called, first of all, to make this "theology of the body," the "beginning" of which we find in the first chapters of Genesis, the *content of their life and behavior.* In fact, how indispensable is thorough knowledge of the meaning of the body, in its masculinity and femininity, along the way of this vocation! How necessary is a precise awareness of the nuptial meaning of the body, of its generating meaning—since all that which forms the content of the life of married couples must constantly find its full and personal dimension in life together, in behavior, in feelings! And all the more so against the background of a civilization which remains under the pressure of a materialistic and utilitarian way of thinking and evaluating. Modern bio-physiology can supply a great deal of precise information about human sexuality. However, knowledge of the personal dignity of the human body and sex must still be drawn from other sources. A special source is the Word of God Himself, which contains the revelation of the body, going back to the "beginning."

When Christ orders man to go back to this "beginning," does He not mean to tell him, perhaps, in this way, that the path along which He leads man (male-female) in the sacrament of marriage—that is, the path of the "redemption of the body"—must consist in regaining this dignity in which there is accomplished, simultaneously, the real meaning of the human body, its personal meaning and its meaning "of communion"?

—adapted from **Original Unity of Man and Woman by Pope John Paul II**

From *Person and Community*

"Thomistic Personalism"

1. Introductory Remarks—St. Thomas was familiar with the concept of the person and defined it very clearly. This is not to say, however, that he was equally familiar with the problem of *personalism* or that he presented it as clearly as the problem of the person. *Personalism* is not primarily a theory of the person or a theoretical science of the person—its meaning is largely practical and ethical: it is concerned with the person as a subject and an object of activity, as a subject of rights, etc. But, since St. Thomas presented the problem of the person so clearly, he also provided at least a point of departure for personalism in general. Moreover, we find in his system not just a point of departure, but also a whole series of additional constitutive elements that allow us to examine the problem of personalism (a problem formulated much later and now part of contemporary thought and life) in the categories of St. Thomas' philosophy and theology. Thus, we can speak of Thomistic personalism.

2. The Theological History of the Question—The concept of person that we find in the philosophy and above all in the theology of St. Thomas has a history of its own going back many centuries, beginning with the patristic period.

Here the mystery of the Trinity (three persons in one divine nature) and the Incarnation (one person in a hypostatic union of two natures, divine and human) had to be clarified by the Church in order to exclude faulty ways of understanding them. In order to present these mysteries, and particularly in order to give them greater speculative clarity and depth, what was especially needed was a concept of person and an understanding of the relation that occurs between person and nature. Thus, the theologians of the patristic period very thoroughly examined the concept of person. St. Thomas had here, then, a prepared ground. But this is also why in St. Thomas' system the person performs more of a theological function. In Christian thought, theological personalism is prior to humanistic personalism—this is also true of St. Thomas' thought. We encounter the word *persona* mainly in his treatises on the Trinity and the Incarnation, *whereas it is all but absent from his treatise on the human being.*

Nonetheless, besides this foundation coming from theology, there is also a philosophical basis in St. Thomas for his approach to God as a personal being. St. Thomas presents the matter in the following way: whatever is a true perfection in the created world must be found in the highest degree in God, and so the person, too, which signifies the highest perfection in the world of creatures, must be realized in an incomparably more perfect degree in God. Thus, he discovers a philosophical access to the concept of a personal God, based upon an analysis of created reality. Creatures provide the basis for our knowledge of the divine essence, since whatever is a true perfection in the created world must in some incomparably more perfect way be found in God. St. Thomas asserts, however, that in the created world the person is indeed the highest perfection: the person is *perfectissimum ens.* And this forms the philosophical basis (i.e., founded on an analysis of reality accessible to human reason itself) for St. Thomas' conception of a personal God.

3. The Definition of Person and the General Characteristics of St. Thomas' View of the Person—St. Thomas, even in treating of the Trinity and the Incarnation, continually has recourse to a philosophical definition of the person, that of Boethius: *persona est rationalis naturae individua substantia*—the human being is an individual substance (*individua substantia*) of a rational nature. A rational nature subsists only as a personal being. The person is a subsistent subject of existence and action—which can in no way be said of a "rational nature." That is why God must be a personal being. St. Thomas says that in the visible world the human being is objectively the most perfect being due to its rational, and, thus, spiritual, nature, which finds its natural complement in freedom. Both of these spiritual properties of the nature—reason and freedom—are concretized in the person, where they become properties of a concrete being, which exists and acts on the level of a nature that has such properties.

St. Thomas uses the term *persona* mainly in his purely theological treatises on the Trinity and the hypostatic union. In his treatise on the human being, he adopts a hylomorphic view: the human being as a composition of matter and form. In his analysis of this *compositum humanum,* St. Thomas presents an especially profound analysis of the human soul, which in the *compositum* performs the role of substantial form. This is the rational soul (*anima rationalis*), the principle and source of the whole spirituality of the human being, and, therefore, also that by virtue of which the human being may properly be ascribed the character of a person. The human person is, like every other person (e.g., a Divine Person or an angelic person, both of whom are purely spiritual), an individual of a rational nature. This definition is verified in every person. What is peculiar to the human person, however, is that this person has a rational nature only because of a spiritual soul, which is itself the substantial form of the body. This fact is of basic importance for understanding the whole uniqueness of the human person, as well as for explaining the structure of the human person.

The human soul is a spiritual substance (the principle of the life and activity of the human being) whose natural properties are reason and freedom (the faculties that express and actualize the soul's—and, thus, the human being's— spirituality). Based on their activity, the whole psychological and moral personality takes shape. But these are not the only faculties of the human soul. As the substantial form of the body, the soul also has faculties intrinsically dependent on matter—primarily sensory faculties, both cognitive and appetitive. These contribute in their own way to the shaping of the psychological and moral personality. St. Thomas is well aware of this reality and formulates his characterization of the spirituality of the human being accordingly. This spiritual aspect, he says, is eminently suited to unite into a substantial whole with the corporeal, and, thus, also with the sensory. This union must, therefore, also play a special role in shaping the human personality. This position differs fundamentally from the Platonic and from the Cartesian positions.

4. The Relation of the Objective Element (Being) to the Subjective Element (Consciousness)—A hallmark of Descartes' view is his splitting of the human being into an extended substance (the body) and a thinking substance (the soul), which are related to one another in a parallel way and do not form an undivided whole, one substantial *compositum humanum.* Eventually in philosophy this led to a kind of hypostatization of consciousness—it becomes an independent subject of activity (reachable by introspection), and indirectly of existence, occurring somehow alongside the body, which is a material structure subject to the laws of nature, to natural determinism (reachable by external observation). Under this schema, the tendency naturally arises to identify the person with consciousness. This view lacks a sufficient basis for including the body, the organism, within the structural whole of the person's life and activity; it lacks the notion of the spiritual soul as the substantial form of that body and as the principle of the whole life and activity of the human being. The modern view proceeds by way of an analysis of consciousness (particularly self-consciousness), along with an emphasis on freedom—but this freedom, conceived in an indeterministic way as total independence, is more of a postulate than a property. Freedom as a property of the person (an attribute of the will) disappears completely from this subjectivistic view of the person in modern philosophy. Rather there is an absolutizing of the subjective element. The person is not a substance, an objective being with its own proper subsistence (in a rational nature). Rather the person becomes merely a property of lived experiences, conscious and self-conscious, and these latter constitute the essence of the person. This is completely different from the treatment we find in St. Thomas, where consciousness and self-consciousness are something derivative, a kind of fruit of the rational nature that subsists in the person, a nature crystallized in a unitary rational and free being, and not something subsistent in themselves. The person acts consciously because the person is rational. Self-consciousness, in turn, is connected with freedom, which is actualized in the activity of the will.

Through the will, the human being is the master of his or her actions, and self-consciousness in a special way reflects this mastery over actions.

We can see here how very objective St. Thomas' view of the person is. It almost seems as though there is no place in it for an analysis of consciousness and self-consciousness as totally unique manifestations of the person as subject. For St. Thomas the person is, of course, a subject, capable of and with a disposition toward consciousness and self-consciousness. But, when it comes to analyzing consciousness and self-consciousness—the chief interest of modern philosophy and psychology—there seems to be no place for it in St. Thomas' objectivistic view of reality. In any case, that in which the person's subjectivity is most apparent is presented by St. Thomas in an exclusively—or almost exclusively—objective way. He shows us the particular faculties, both spiritual and sensory, thanks to which the whole of human consciousness and self-consciousness—the human personality in the psychological and moral sense—takes shape, but that is also where he stops. Thus, St. Thomas gives us an excellent view of the objective existence and activity of the person, but it would be difficult to speak in his view of the lived experiences of the person.

5. The Activity of the Person—*Thought as the Basis of Creativity.* The person in St. Thomas view is always a concrete being, one in which the potentiality proper to the rational nature is realized. This potentiality is realized, first of all, by means of thought. Human thought has a creative character—it is the basis of creativity and the source of culture—yet it has a very realistic and objective character. It is also the basis for deriving new truths from reality and for controlling reality. The better we know the world, the more we are able to subordinate it to ourselves and make use of it. Similarly with our self-knowledge, the better we know ourselves—our possibilities, capabilities, talents—the more we are able to derive from ourselves and the more we are able to create, making use of the raw material we find in ourselves. Because we think, we are by nature creators, not just consumers. And because our thought (our rational nature) is also the basis of our personalities, one could say that we are creators because we are persons. Creativity is realized in action: when we act as persons, we always create something either in the world or in ourselves our both. Creating (as derived from thinking) is in fact an infallible sign of a person, a proof of a person's existence or presence. In creating, we also fill the external world around us with our thought and being. There is a certain similarity here between ourselves and God, for the whole of creation is an expression of God's own thought and being.

Free Will as the Basis of Morality. Although thought is the basis of our creativity as persons, this creativity neither ends nor culminates in thought. That which is most characteristic of a person, that in which a person (at least in the natural order) is most fully and properly realized, is morality. Thought is merely a condition of morality, which is directly connected with freedom, and therefore with the will. The point is to will a true good (such an act of will makes us good human beings), and also to will it in a good way (if we will it in a bad way, we ourselves become morally bad). Morality, therefore, presupposes knowledge, the truth concerning the good, but it is realized by willing, by choice, by decision. In this way, not only does our will become good or evil, but our whole person also becomes good or evil. Thanks to our will, we are masters of ourselves and of our actions, but because of this the value of these actions of our will qualifies our whole person positively or negatively. Clearly, then, freedom of will is not just an exceptional property but a difficult one. According to St. Thomas, freedom is not given to us as an end in itself, but as a means to a greater end. Freedom for freedom's sake has no justification in the Thomistic view of the cosmos; freedom exists for the sake of morality and, together with morality, for the sake of a higher spiritual law and order of existence—the kind of order that most strictly corresponds to rational beings, to persons.

6. The Person as a Subject and Object of Love— Although human beings are intellectual-sensory, spiritual-material composites, as a result of which energies of sensory love also operate in them, the love proper to human beings is spiritual love. Such love is directed in a special way toward other persons, for in them we find an object commensurate with ourselves. True love, the kind of love of others worthy of a human person, is that in which our sensory energies and desires are subordinated to a basic understanding of the true worth of the object of our love. Love in St. Thomas' view is, on the one hand, a kind of need of nature, and, on the other, a demand and even an ideal of morality. Love brings about the union of persons and makes it possible for people to mutually enjoy the good that each person is, as well as the good of their union, which love engenders. In this atmosphere of spiritual harmony and peace, a mutual sharing of self becomes possible.

The whole of human coexistence should be based on love. The evangelical counsel to love one's neighbor is a thoroughly personalistic principle, affecting every community—especially the most intimate. Personalism is very much at the basis of all conjugal and familial morality and of the importance of education and self-education—based on a deep understanding of the value of the person as well as on an understanding of love, whose proper object and subject is the person. This relation between human persons goes in a horizontal direction. But there is also a vertical direction in St. Thomas' reflections: between God and human beings. God is a subject of love, whose object includes human beings—and human beings, in turn, are subjects of love, whose objects include God. Christianity involves an extremely personalistic understanding of religion, and St.

Thomas presents a profound interpretation of this understanding.

7. The Person and Society: The Principle of the Correlation Between the Good of the Person and the Common Good—The relation of the person to society and of society to the person forms a separate chapter in Thomistic personalism. The human being is always an individual within the human species. But this individual is a person, and the species is a collection of persons—though not a chaotic collection, but one formed naturally into various societies and communities. This is an effect of an elementary law of nature, but in the case of human beings not a law of blind necessity but allowing for the full involvement of consciousness and freedom. Consequently, the relation of the human being to society and of society to the human being is subordinate to morality, just as individual life and interpersonal relationships are. One must seek a relationship between the individual and society that results in the fullest possible correlation between the person's true good and the common good that society naturally seeks. If persons attempt to place their own good above the common good and subordinate the latter to themselves and use it for their individual good, we have the error of individualism—which gave rise to liberalism in modern history and to capitalism in economics. On the other hand, society (in aiming at the alleged good of the whole) may attempt to subordinate persons to itself in such a way that true good of persons is excluded and they themselves fall prey to the collectivity. This is the error of totalitarianism, which in modern times has borne the worst possible fruit. Thomistic personalism maintains that the individual good of persons should be by nature subordinate to the common good at which the society aims—but this subordination may under no circumstances exclude and devalue the persons themselves. There are certain rights that every society must guarantee to persons, for without these rights the life and development proper to persons is impossible. One of these rights is freedom of conscience—violated by totalitarianism, which would make the person completely subordinate to society in all things. In contrast, Thomistic personalism maintains that the person should be subordinate to society in all that is indispensable for the realization of the common good, but that the true common good never threatens the good of the person, even though it may demand considerable sacrifice of the person.

8. The Person and Eternity—In connection with the above, we should note that society as such is always a temporal product, whereas the person is destined to live on forever. The eternity of the person is strictly connected with the spirituality of the rational nature in which the person subsists. That which is spiritual cannot undergo disintegration, destruction or death. The truth of the immortality of the soul is simultaneously the truth of the indestructibility of the person. Eternity belongs to the person in the sense that whatever is spiritual is indestructible, that is, by nature capable of lasting without end. This is one aspect of the eternity of the person, and it is connected with another aspect. The values by which the person as such lives are by nature transtemporal, and even atemporal. Such values include truth, goodness, and beauty, as well as justice and love, and, in general, all the values by which the person as such continually lives. One can say, therefore, that the very content of the person's life points to the eternity of the person. These values demand a more complete realization than they find in temporal life within the confines of bodily existence. In fact, since these values are themselves absolute, they demand some sort of more complete and definitive realization in the dimensions of the Absolute. The person is not the Absolute; the human being is a creature, a contingent being. God alone is the Absolute. Thus, for the full attainment of the spiritual life, the person must exist beyond the bodily conditions of human existence—in the dimensions of God.

This particular need of the person is addressed by the Gospel in the revealed doctrine of the beatific vision. While it is true that Thomistic personalism is a philosophical view, it would be hard to deny that this supernatural perspective not only corresponds to it extremely well, but also even ultimately explains everything that—when viewed in the light of reason alone—must remain a deep and impenetrable mystery of human existence.

—adapted from **Person and Community: Selected Essays (Catholic Thought from Lublin)** by Karol Wojtyla, ed. by Theresa H. Sandok

"Subjectivity and the Irreducible in the Human Being"

1. The State of the Question—The problem of the subjectivity of the human being seems today to be the focal point of a variety of concerns. *Today more than ever before we feel the need—and also see a greater possibility—of objectifying the problem of the subjectivity of the human being.* In this regard, contemporary thought seems to have more or less set aside the old antinomies (subjectivism-objectivism, idealism-realism) in epistemology which formed as though an inviolable line of demarcation between the basic orientations of philosophy and which created conditions that discouraged dealing with human subjectivity—for fear that this would lead inevitably to subjectivism. This latter fear was in some sense warranted by the subjectivistic and idealistic character—or at least overtones—of analyses conducted within the realm of "pure consciousness."

This only served to strengthen the line of demarcation between the "objective" view (the ontological view, the human being as a *being*) and the "subjective" view, which seemed inevitably to sever the human being from this reality. Today we are seeing the breakdown of that line of demarcation—and for some of the same reasons that gave rise to it in the first place, i.e. as a result of phenomenological analyses conducted in the realm of "pure consciousness" using Husserl's *epoche*: bracketing the existence, or reality, of the conscious subject. I am convinced that *the line of demarcation between the subjectivistic (idealistic) and objectivistic (realistic) views in anthropology and ethics must break down and is in fact breaking down on the basis of the experience of the human being.* This experience automatically frees us from the pure consciousness (as the subject conceived and assumed *a priori*) and leads us to the full concrete existence of the human being (to the reality of the conscious subject). With all the phenomenological analyses now at our disposal, we can no longer go on treating the human being exclusively as an objective being, but must now treat the human being as a subject in the dimension in which the *specifically human subjectivity* of the human being is determined by consciousness—this is none other than *personal* subjectivity.

2. The History of the Question—This matter requires a fuller examination, in the course of which we must consider the question of the irreducible in the human being—that which is original and essentially human, that which accounts for the human being's complete uniqueness in the world. Traditional Aristotelian epistemology defines man as a *rational animal* under the genus (living being), species (human being), specific difference (endowed with reason) format. But this definition excludes—when taken simply and directly—the possibility of accentuating the irreducible in the human being. It implies—at least at first glance—a belief in the reducibility of the human being to the world. Such reducibility is maintained in an attempt to understand the human being—to categorize him in relation to other things in the world—in a cosmological way. Such a definition has been unquestionably useful and has become dominant in metaphysical anthropology. It has been the basis of a whole philosophical and scientific tradition which has yielded great results and spawned a variety of particular sciences. But there is also another tradition in philosophy. *A belief in the primordial uniqueness of the human being, and, thus, in the basic irreducibility of the human being to the natural world,* seems just as old as the need for reduction expressed in Aristotle's definition. This belief stands at the basis of understanding the human being as a *person,* which has an equally long tenure in the history of philosophy.

In the *man is a rational animal* tradition, the human being was mainly an *object,* one of the objects in the world to which the human being visibly and physically belongs. Objectivity in this sense was connected with the general assumption of the reducibility of the human being. Subjectivity, on the other hand, is, as it were, a term proclaiming that the human being's proper essence cannot be totally reduced to and explained by the proximate genus and specific difference. *Subjectivity is, then, a kind of synonym for the irreducible in the human being.* If there is an opposition here, it is not between objectivism and subjectivism, but only between two philosophical (as well as everyday and practical) methods of treating the human being: as an object and as a subject. At the same time, we must not forget that the subjectivity of the human person is also something objective.

Aristotle's definition does not itself justify treating the human being as a mere object in the world. The traditional definition of the human being as a *being* required the postulate that the human being is 1) a separate *suppositum* (a subject of existence and action) and 2) a person (*persona*). Still, the traditional view of the human being as a person (Boethius: *rationalis naturae individua substantia)* expressed the individuality of the human being as a substantial being with a rational (spiritual) nature, rather than the uniqueness of the subjectivity essential to the human being as a person. Thus, the Boethian definition mainly marked out the "metaphysical terrain"—the dimension of being—in which personal human subjectivity is realized—thus, creating, in a sense, a condition for "building upon" this terrain on the basis of experience.

3. Lived Experience as an Element in Interpretation— The category to which we must go in order to do this "building" seems to be that of lived experience. This category is foreign to Aristotle's metaphysics and cannot be fully captured even under his categories of *agere* and *pati.* Though these categories are useful in distinguishing what *happens* in man from what man *does,* the dynamic reality of the human being is not fully captured here. In each case, there is an aspect not directly apprehended by such a metaphysical interpretation or reduction, namely, the aspect of lived experience as the irreducible, as the element that defies reduction. Now this may seem unnecessary. Even without the category of lived experience, we obtain an adequate understanding of the human being and of the fact that the human being *acts* and that things *happen* in the human being. Such an understanding formed the basis of the entire edifice of anthropology and ethics for many centuries.

But as the need increases to understand the human being as a unique and unrepeatable person, especially in terms of the whole dynamism of action and inner happenings proper to the human being—in other words, as the need increases to understand the personal subjectivity of the human being—the category of lived experience takes on greater significance, and, in fact, key significance. For then the issue is not just the metaphysical objectification of the human being as an acting subject, as the agent of acts, but the revelation of the person as a subject *experiencing* its acts and inner happenings, and with them its own subjectivity.

One might immediately ask whether, by giving lived experience such a key function in the interpretation of the human being as a personal subject, we are not inevitably condemned to *subjectivism.* I would reply that so long as in this interpretation we maintain a firm enough connection with the *integral experience* of the human being, not only are we not doomed to subjectivism, but we will also safeguard the authentic personal subjectivity of the human being in the realistic interpretation of human existence.

4. The Necessity of Pausing at the Irreducible—In order to interpret the human being in the context of lived experience, the aspect of *consciousness* must be introduced into the analysis of human existence. The human being is then given to us not merely as a being defined according to species, but as a concrete self, a self-experiencing subject. Our own subjective being and the existence proper to it (that of a *suppositum*) appear to us in experience precisely as a self-experiencing subject. If we pause here, this being discloses the structures that determine it as a concrete self—and this in no way signifies a break with reduction and the species definition of the human being. Rather, it signifies the *pausing at the irreducible.* We should pause in the process of reduction (a *cosmological* understanding of man in the world) in order to understand the human being inwardly (this type of understanding may be called *personalistic*). The personalistic understanding of man is not the antinomy of the cosmological type but its complement. The definition of Boethius only marks out the "metaphysical terrain" for interpreting the personal subjectivity of the human being. The experience of the human being cannot be derived by way of cosmological reduction; we must pause at the irreducible, at that which is unique and unrepeatable in each human being, by virtue of which he or she is not just *a particular human being*—an individual of a certain species—but a personal subject. Only then do we get a true and complete picture of the human being. We cannot complete this picture through the reduction alone; we also cannot remain within the framework of the irreducible alone (for then we would be unable to get beyond the pure self). The one must be cognitively supplemented by the other. Nevertheless, we must always leave the greater space in this cognitive effort for the irreducible—it must have the upper hand when thinking about the human being, both in theory and in practice. For the irreducible includes everything that is invisible and wholly internal, whereby each human being, myself included, is an "eyewitness" of his or her own self—of his or her own humanity and person.

My lived experience discloses not only my *actions* but also my inner *happenings* in their profoundest dependence on my own self. It also discloses my whole personal structure of *self-determination*, in which I discover my self as that through which I possess myself and govern myself—or, at any rate, *should* possess myself and govern myself. The dynamic structure of self-determination reveals to me that I am given to myself and assigned to myself. This is precisely how I appear to myself in my acts and in my inner decisions of conscience: as permanently assigned to myself, as having continually to affirm and monitor myself, and, thus, in a sense, as having continually to "achieve" this dynamic structure of my self, a structure that is given to me as self-possession and self-governance. This is a completely internal and totally immanent structure, a real endowment of the personal structure; in a sense, it *is* this structure. *In my lived experience of self-possession and self-governance, I experience that I am a person and that I am a subject.* These structures of self-possession and self-governance, essential to every personal self, are experienced by each of us in the lived experience of moral value—good and evil. Experience teaches that *morale* is very deeply rooted in the *humanum*, or, more precisely, in what should be defined as the *personale.* Morality defines the personalistic dimension of the human being in a fundamental way; it is subjectified in this dimension and can also by properly understood only in it. At the same time, *morale* is a basic expression of the transcendence proper to the personal self. Our decisions of conscience at each step reveal us as persons who fulfill ourselves by going beyond ourselves toward values accepted in truth and realized, therefore, with a deep sense of responsibility.

5. A Challenging Perspective—When it comes to understanding the human being, the whole rich and complex reality of lived experience is not so much an element as a dimension in its own right, at which we must necessarily pause if the subjective personal structure of the human being is to be fully delineated. What does it mean to *pause cognitively at lived experience*? This pausing should be understood *in relation to the irreducible.* The philosophical tradition would have us believe that we can, so to speak, pass right over this dimension, that we can cognitively limit it by means of an abstraction that provides us with a definition of the human being as a being, i.e. with a cosmological type of reduction (*homo=animale rationale*). But in so defining the essence of the human being do we not in a sense leave out what is most human, since the *humanum* expresses and realizes itself as the *personale*? If so, then the irreducible would suggest that we cannot come to know and understand the human being in a reductive way alone. This is what the contemporary philosophy of the subject seems to be telling the traditional philosophy of the object. But that is not all. The irreducible signifies that which is essentially incapable of reduction, that which cannot be reduced but can only be *disclosed or revealed. Lived experience essentially defies reduction.* This does not mean, however, that it eludes our knowledge; it only means that *we must arrive at the knowledge of it differently,* namely, *by a method or means of analysis that merely reveals and discloses its essence.* The method of phenomenological analysis allows us to pause at lived experience as the irreducible. This method is not just a descriptive cataloging of individual phenomena (in the Kantian sense, i.e., phenomena as sense-perceptible contents). When we pause at the lived experience of the irreducible, we attempt to permeate cognitively the whole essence of this experience. We, thus, apprehend both the essentially subjective structure of lived experience and its structural relation to the subjectivity of the human being. Phenomenological analysis, thus, contributes to transphenomenal understanding; it also contributes to a disclosure of the richness proper to human existence in the whole complex *compositum humanum.*

Such a disclosure—the deepest possible disclosure—would seem to be an indispensable means for coming to know the human being as a personal subject. At the same time, this personal human subjectivity is a determinate *reality*: it is a reality when we strive to understand it within the *objective totality* that goes by the name *human being.* The same applies to the whole character of this method of understanding: lived experience is also—and above all—a reality. A legitimate method of disclosing this reality can only enrich and deepen the whole realism of the conception of the human being. The thinker seeking the ultimate truth about man no longer moves in a "purely metaphysical terrain." Rather, the personal profile of the human being enters the sphere of cognitive vision; thus, the composition of human nature, far from being blurred, is even more distinctly accentuated—elements are found in abundance testifying to both the materiality and the spirituality of the human being, elements that bring both aspects into sharper relief and form building blocks for further philosophical construction.

Certain questions always remain: Are the cosmological and the personalistic understandings of man ultimately mutually exclusive? Where, if at all, do *reduction* and the *disclosure of the irreducible* in the human being converge? How is the philosophy of the subject to disclose the *objectivity* of the human being in the personal *subjectivity* of this being? These seem to be *the questions that today determine the perspective* for thinking about the human being, the perspective for contemporary anthropology and ethics.

—adapted from **Person and Community: Selected Essays (Catholic Thought from Lublin)** by Karol Wojtyla, ed. by Theresa H. Sandok

Made in the USA
Coppell, TX
11 February 2022